# HAPPILY EVER AFTER?

Ros Ballaster

Women's Worlds.

# Happily Ever After?

*Women's Fiction in Postwar Britain
1945–60*

## Niamh Baker

St. Martin's Press
New York

First published in the United States of America in 1989

Printed in Hong Kong

Library of Congress Cataloging-in-Publication Data
Baker, Niamh.
    Happily ever after? : women's fiction in postwar Britain, 1945–60
/ Niamh Baker.
      p.   cm.
    Bibliography: p.
    Includes index.
    ISBN 0–312–03232–3.—ISBN 0–312–03233–1 (pbk).
    1. English fiction—Women authors—History and criticism.
2. English fiction—20th century—History and criticism.   3. Women
and literature—Great Britain—History—20th century.   4. Women—
Great Britain—Books and reading—History—20th century.   5. Women
in literature.   I. Title.
PR888.W6B35   1989
823'.91409'9287—dc20                                    89–6165
                                                          CIP

*To my daughter Siobhan Breslin*

'She has made the change from governess to mistress of the house very charmingly,' said Tinty. 'It is like one of the fairy tales.'

'But not a fairy tale in which I should want to be the heroine,' said Margaret. 'One begins to see what is meant by "they lived happily ever after".'

(Elizabeth Taylor, Palladian)

# Contents

*Preface*                                                                    viii

*Acknowledgements*                                                              x

**Introduction: a myth of happiness**                                          1

1.   **Something to love: heroines and their heroes**          25

2.   **Happily ever after? The consequences of acceptance**    44

3.   **Odd women**                                             66

4.   **'Remember Madame Bovary': infidelity**                  86

5.   **Ugly sisters**                                         109

6.   **Children: 'strange unexpected flowerings'**            125

7.   **Women and work**                                       141

8.   **Fictions: subverting the stereotypes**                 163

9.   **Conclusions**                                          174

*Notes and References*                                                       177

*Bibliography*                                                               192

*Index of Women Novelists*                                                   197

# Preface

I am aware that by arbitrarily selecting a group of women writers who produced novels during the fifteen years following the Second World War, I am offending against literary practice. What is worse, these writers have little in common: their backgrounds, class, political opinions and attitudes to feminism are too varied to include them in anything that could remotely be called a 'movement'. However, such categories are not always as homogenous as they appear. John Wain's preface to the 1978 reissue of his novel *Hurry On Down* points out the anomaly of his novel supposedly belonging to 'The Movement' when, in fact, not only did it pre-date it, but Wain did not see himself as part of it (although he suggests he may have originated it). To explain the reasons for my choices, I have first to explain why I set out to look at women writing novels in this period.

What first drew me to the period was my irritation at the assumption by the feminist movement that feminism had somehow died during the period and had had to be reinvented in the 1970s. The second assumption – by feminists and social historians – that the Wife/Mother image of women during the 1940s and 1950s was widely and uncritically accepted also seemed to me quite wrong, for how was it possible for a movement, many of whose members were still alive, to die out completely?

Because of the lack of a strong and coherent feminist movement at the time (although there were many separate feminist organisations), it is difficult to find out what women's real aspirations were during this period. I have tried to find some evidence of these submerged feelings in a few of the novels written by women at the time. The texts I use were chosen haphazardly, sometimes on the basis of what I could actually get hold of, and my criteria for selection is described at the end of the Introduction, in the section headed 'Women Novelists'. Throughout the book the views I discuss are those that surface in these novels. Because they are only a small sample of women writing at the time, they do not necessarily represent views held by all women, or even by a majority of their readers. They are, however, evidence that the orthodoxies of the time were not universally supported: that there was a certain amount of female rebellion.

These are not 'feminist' novels, as defined by Rosalind Coward,[1] but novels which represent individual women novelists' views of what life was about for women. Perhaps they more clearly match Andrea Zeman's definition of serious women novelists: those engaged in 'telling women accurately where they stood at a given moment'.[2] Where they differ from her definition is that in a period that was highly prescriptive for women, the fiction stands back from clear moral statements, preferring to explore the dilemmas rather than suggest solutions.

In the Introduction, 'A Myth of Happiness', I have given a very brief summary of the situation of women during the period. For a fuller and more detailed background, I recommend Elizabeth Wilson's *Only Halfway to Paradise. Women in Postwar Britain: 1945–1968*.[3] The rest of the book looks in detail at some novels written by women during the period.

NIAMH BAKER

# Acknowledgements

I would never have considered writing this book if it had not been for Pat Spallone, who not only suggested I do so, but pushed me into the first tentative steps. My thanks to her and to Bryan Baker, who provided meals and encouragement during the writing. I am grateful to Plymouth Central Library, whose staff uncomplainingly made trips to the 'stack' to find novels no longer on the shelves. I must also acknowledge my debt to Elizabeth Wilson's *Only Halfway to Paradise*, which was invaluable in providing the social background to the postwar period.

NIAMH BAKER

# Introduction

# A myth of happiness

Women were wanting to escape the net just as men were climbing back into it.[1]

## The myth

The period immediately following the Second World War, especially the decade of the 1950s, produced an image of Woman almost as enduring – and in my opinion as mistaken – as that powerful image of the Victorian lady palely reclining on her couch, smelling-salts held delicately to her nostrils. The postwar British woman was more robust than her Victorian grandmother, but she was still the Angel in the House. A slightly battered angel it is true, one that during the war years had been seen in sensible overalls and unglamourous headscarf at the factory and on the land doing men's jobs, but now that 'normality' was restored, an angel who wished to return to her proper sphere, the home. Whether this image reflected the reality or not is another matter. The war, which had taken women out of their homes, was over, and as the postwar reconstruction began, there was an intensification of official and media debate over the place women should occupy in the brave new world that was envisaged. During the war, government agencies, backed by newspapers, magazines, propaganda films and radio, had explored the way that the traditional sexual divisions of labour could be altered by using a combination of exhortation and the presentation of images of women doing jobs normally done by men. The need to draw on women's labour to keep the war effort going had overcome the usual prejudices and assumptions about what

1

women were capable of doing. Periodicals and newspapers had printed photographs of women at work, and newsreels had shown them operating heavy machinery, piloting planes, working on the land – a remarkable departure from the usual way of portraying women. These women did not look invitingly at the photographer but bent purposefully over their work, glamour and sex appeal sacrificed to practicality. The government's most difficult job may have been to convince men that this was the proper role for women, and it is significant that concessions were made to male egos by ensuring that, despite the long working hours, women were still responsible for the home and family. The image of women as home-makers and child-carers was not significantly challenged, and there-fore, when the war ended, the assumption was that women would happily return to the home, which was, after all, their natural place.

Even so, it was not possible to return to pre-war conditions. The election of a Labour government, the creation of a welfare state[2] and, when the postwar years of austerity ended, the importance of the housewife as consumer, meant that what women did with their lives, what choices they made, came to be seen as central to the proper working of society. Consequently a spate of books, docu-ments, articles and government papers examined the female part of its society from schooldays onwards. Underlying the whole debate was the assumption that girlhood and young womanhood was a preparation for marriage and, once married, a woman's main preoccupation was the successful maintenance of married life and the raising of children. It was widely accepted at the time that that was what women themselves wanted and what, on the whole, they were getting. It is noticeable when reading commentaries written during the period that no one seriously challenged this assumption. Difficulties were admitted, and there was disagreement about how women were to go about their homemaking, but the consensus about woman's role was virtually unanimous. Even when the need to attract women back into the workforce became so pressing that the government found itself promoting two contradictory images of women, this was smoothly explained away by the term 'dual role'. Myrdal and Klein's studies of the phenomenon of women combin-ing marriage and work delineated many of the problems such a dual role entailed, but their assumption was still that home and family came first and that work for women was subsidiary to their commitment to married life.[3] In fact, the very term 'dual role' creates an over-simplified image of a working wife's problems. If it were simply a question of two roles, how uncomplicated life would be!

The myth that women were universally happy in the role ascribed to them in the postwar period, that they passively accepted, or were deceived into accepting, this narrow view of their potential, is still held as a truth about the 1950s, even by the critical intelligence of the present women's movement. The widespread success of Betty Friedan's *The Feminine Mystique*[4] did nothing to help dispel this myth. Friedan cannot be blamed; she was writing truthfully and painfully about a particular aspect of American society, but her study has been universalised. Certainly there were aspects of the study that ring an uncomfortable bell as far as Britain is concerned, but conditions for women were in many ways very different from the American scene, not least for economic reasons. Books such as *The Women's Room*[5] have, like the hackneyed picture of the swooning Victorian lady, tended to strengthen the image of the postwar woman actively embracing, or at least uncritically accepting, her destiny as wife and mother. Certainly the most outstanding characteristic of postwar discussion of woman's role is the centrality given to marriage. To be 'womanly' was to be a wife and mother.

Women's magazines reflected this view in the fiction they published, the problems they discussed and the advice they gave.[6] Stories and articles in these magazines portrayed women conforming to their role. When there was rebellion it was either swiftly abandoned when the woman came to realise where her 'best interests' lay, or it was punished. Once wed and shut into her 'dream home', a woman was expected to run it efficiently so that when her children came home from school she could be totally at their disposal until the arrival of her husband – generally by commuter train – when the efficient cleaner/child/psychologist metamorphosed into a combination of wife/hostess/mistress. The 'wife' would serve the effortlessly produced meal in the comfortable surroundings of the home she cleaned; the 'hostess' would feed the man questions which, while not too demanding, were designed to elicit stories of success or setbacks, which would receive support and encouragement (never criticism or advice); while the 'mistress' would present him with the picture of a beautifully dressed and made-up woman who was permanently available sexually, but never demanding. Her problems, it was assumed, were trivial and secondary and He should not be burdened with them. Any doubts the man may have had about whether this was really what he wanted were probably dissipated by his wife's failure to fulfil the dream, and his irritation would have been compounded by his belief that other men did have satisfactory wives. The wife who failed to create this perfect woman would blame herself for the failure, and in this she was seconded by the women's magazines, whose main content was devoted to teaching her first how to get a man and then how to keep him happy. The break-up of a marriage *had* to be her fault; it was the result of her poor job performance, since keeping the marriage going was her job and not her husband's. No matter what his behaviour, from complaining about her cooking to beating her up, according to the magazines, she must have done something or neglected something to provoke him to such actions. If the problem was 'Another Woman', then she was not giving her husband what he deserved from a wife. Doubts about this simplistic view were often expressed in the problem pages that most women's magazines carried, but even the often repeated, almost stereotyped letter which began, 'I have a lovely husband and two beautiful children but . . .', did not lead to a genuine exploration of the problems such a woman might be suppressing. The writer was generally fobbed off with suggestions to make her conform even more to the ideal she was already having difficulty with, and often she was briskly admonished for her lack of gratitude at having all the things that women were supposed to need. Nor was it ever suggested that this image did not reflect reality.

The persistence of the image of the happy housewife–mother during the 1950s led to a belief that it represented a general truth about women at this time and obscured the fact that many women did not lead this sort of life, that conformism to this narrow ideal of womanhood was not as widespread as had been imagined. If the present women's movement has done nothing else, it has ensured that the public debate about women has widened to take in all the categories ignored by professional commentators on the social scene. At last we are aware that women do choose, or have thrust upon them, other lifestyles; that as well as single women, single mothers and lesbians, there are widows, divorcees, deserted and deserting wives, and that even the apparently uniform model of the Average Marriage promulgated by advertisers and social commentators is a false one, undermined by a variety of strains and accommodations. Why then cannot the insights of the 1970s and 1980s into the complexities of women's lives be used to throw light on postwar women's problems?

The present women's movement sees itself as beginning in the 1970s, after the 'death' of feminism in the fifties. The convention is that the tradition of feminism is constantly broken and its gains have to be fought for over and over again. The most recent break in this tradition is believed to be the twenty or so years following the end of the war and what is seen as women's eager grasping at an easier life and their betrayal of feminist ideals, which had to be rediscovered by a later generation of women, keen to blame their mothers for not handing the tradition on to them. The least attractive element of this view is the way one generation of women denigrates another. Postwar women are accused of colluding with men and wilfully rejecting the gains an earlier feminist generation achieved. The fifties, it is agreed, is dead as far as feminism is concerned.

I disagree with this verdict. As Elizabeth Wilson says, it seems:

> improbable that a powerful social movement and political crusade, an expression of the aspirations of (potentially) half the population, should suddenly have withered away, only to reappear as suddenly, and – as it seemed – as if out of nowhere, around 1970. Yet so pervasive was this myth that it has become the 'facts' for the women's liberation movement too.[7]

In fact, the more closely one looks at the postwar period, the more deceptive its bland surface appears.

## Work

I began this chapter by describing the myth. It is more difficult to find the reality, given that the social history of women during this period has been very neglected.[8] There does, however, seem to be a gap between what women were believed to be doing and what they were actually doing. This was particularly the case in relation to work.

The assumption was that married women were only too glad to relinquish work outside the home and return happily to being wives and mothers. It may well have been the case that many women were initially relieved to be able to give up the long hours of war work they had had to undergo in addition to their domestic duties. Shifts of ten to twelve hours had not been unusual, and the need to queue for food and everyday necessities had certainly placed an immense burden on working women responsible for running their homes. Rationing of food and queuing for scarce commodities was part and parcel of life in the years immediately following the war,[9] and despite newspaper and magazine articles claiming that women's work was now lighter because of the invention of domestic appliances, the reality was that few homes had these labour-saving machines. The boiler and hand-wringer remained features of washday, not to mention 'blueing' and starching; kitchens often had wooden drainers and working surfaces, which had to be scrubbed and bleached; floors in these pre-vinyl days were covered with linoleum that had to be washed and polished; carpets were still often cleaned by the use of a manually operated type of carpet-sweeper and by being beaten on a clothesline in the backyard. Tinned foods were limited, frozen foods largely unavailable and modern convenience foods had not yet appeared. With their men back at home, the shortcuts that most women on their own use to limit housework and cooking had to be abandoned. Housework was now a full-time activity, even for the middle class, who found it too difficult or too expensive to employ domestic servants. In addition, the war nurseries and work canteens were being closed, despite pressure by women's groups, making it very difficult for the mothers of young children to work, whatever they may have wished. Add to this the moral pressure exerted on women to vacate jobs in favour of men returning from the fighting, and the effort to continue working may have seemed to be too much.

Despite all these factors, though, the proportion of married women in the workforce was higher than before the war (21 per cent in 1951 compared with only 10 per cent in 1931), and by 1961 had risen to 32 per cent of the workforce.[10]

What those who ceased to work thought and felt is more difficult to ascertain. Again the problem pages of women's magazines published letters from women who seemed to have been far from satisfied with their return to the confinement and isolation of their own homes. It was not so much the quality of the work itself they missed; much of the work women did during the war was repetitive and boring. There had, however, been two compensations: companionship and money. Working outside the home had meant spending a lot of time with other women, and social life had often been based on work friendships. The sharing of problems and joys had cut into the solitariness of a home-based life. It is a common-place that men often look back on the war years with pleasure because of the companionship they enjoyed, but it is less appre-ciated that women too found this side of war work the most rewarding. Money was also an important factor. No longer depend-ent on being given housekeeping money, women had earned their own and had had control over how it was spent. Also, as factory work had expanded during the war there had been a flight from domestic labour. Not only were the wages in factories considerably better, but there was no attempt to control women's lives; once outside the factory they were independent of their employers' whims. To give up the power and independence that earning your own money confers was not welcomed by many women. There were also letters to women's magazines from women who had been employed in the armed forces and who dreaded the return to boring and repetitive work or constricted lifestyles.

In spite of all the discussion about women and work during the postwar period, little was done to find out what women themselves really wanted. Viola Klein and Alva Myrdal had great difficulty in writing *Women's Two Roles* because of the lack of systematic research into women's problems during this period. As they said, it became:

> a constant source of surprise and regret that at practically each point in the discussion we have had to look in vain for evidence that had been scientifically collected and examined.[11]

They specifically mentioned the lack of surveys on women's desire to work and how women between the ages of 50 and 65 spent their lives.[12] The letter page in women's magazines seems to have become one of the few outlets of expression for women, but inevitably the writers of the letters are a tiny proportion of the readers and the number who felt they could openly challenge existing assumptions would be small. In addition, editors of magazines, which were becoming increasingly identified with the currently acceptable images of women, would not necessarily select and publish letters which contradicted these images. Cynthia White describes the general attitude of women's magazines during this period:

> in one important area of counselling, namely women's employment, the women's magazines acquiesced in a regressive tendency and later used their influence positively to discourage women from trying to combine work and marriage. In this they were doing no more than reinforce the traditional view of a woman's role, but as a result of the war, and women's part in it, the time was propitious for a radical redefinition of that role to encompass fuller citizenship and wider social participation. Many women were willing for their new social position to become permanent; others, with a little encouragement, might have come to share their views. But the traditionalist camp was strong, and it found a sympathetic mouthpiece in the women's press, particularly the popular weeklies. *My Weekly* reflected the conflict in its fiction and came down firmly on the side of domesticity. In the words of one of its fictional heroines, 'I've spent a week discovering I'd rather be Mrs Peter Grant, housewife, than Rosamund Fuller, dress designer.'[13]

My own reading of women's magazines of the period confirms this view. Although many did carry articles about careers for women, the careers outlined remained, depressingly, the traditional 'service' ones: secretary, nurse, teacher, social worker. Women were certainly not encouraged to envisage themselves taking over managerial careers and there were no indications that they might find outlets in the higher ranks of the professions or even in the creative field. There was, therefore, no platform for women who wanted to work but found themselves prevented from doing so. The only indication of their real wishes is that they voted with their feet, for the proportion of married women in the workforce continued to rise each decade.

Unfortunately, the nature of the work available to most women remained fundamentally unchanged. Although there was a huge reduction of women in domestic service, the increase in clerical, distributive and professional services still left women largely in the lower ranks: as secretaries rather than directors; shop assistants rather than managers; nurses rather than doctors; and classroom teachers rather than heads of schools or school inspectors. In the civil service it was the clerical ranks women filled; less became career civil servants. The removal of the marriage bar did mean women were not automatically dismissed when they married, but the ghosts of marriage and children continued to haunt their working lives, leading to the assumption that women were not

interested in a 'career'. Such concepts as the 'family wage', the idea
that women could be used as a reserve labour force, and the
blinkered belief that only men had to support others (the National
Association of Schoolmasters arguing that '*all* men had greater
responsibilities in terms of dependents than *any* woman'[14]), had led
to the supposition that work was, in all cases, marginal to women's
lives. Women who did demonstrate a serious attitude to their jobs
were labelled 'career girls', a subtly pejorative term that suggests
such a person to be somehow abnormal. (Who ever refers to a
'career man'?) The combination of a 'career woman' and 'mother'
was a monstrosity, and working mothers were attacked for leaving
their children to fend for themselves when they came home from
school. Such children were labelled 'latchkey children' and it was
popularly believed that it was among their ranks that virtually all
juvenile delinquents could be found. The hysteria about latchkey
children was one symptom of the entrenched belief in the incompatibility of true femininity (proved by becoming a wife and
mother) and the pursuance of career objectives, which was considered aggressive and therefore masculine.

The contradictions inherent in the need to recruit women into the
workforce, while still upholding marriage and the care of children as
their true role, were rationalised by the use of the term 'dual role'.
According to Myrdal and Klein, there were different stages in a
woman's life: full-time work before marriage and then perhaps until
there were children; total devotion to being a wife and mother while
the children were young; part-time work when the children went to
school; then resumption of full-time work once the children were
adult.[15] The fact that this pattern condemned women to low-skill,
low-status and low-paid jobs was not thought significant, as work
was considered to be of only secondary importance to a woman,
whose main commitment would remain to her home and family.
Also, because the way a career is built up is based on the male
pattern of uninterrupted work from young adulthood to retirement,
the breaks in women's working lives were construed as instability
and lack of commitment, and this led to women being passed over
when promotion was considered. Thus the attitudes of management
and fellow workers, coupled with the ambivalence shown by trade
unions to women workers, meant that even if a woman was not
married, or was married but without children, she was still viewed in
the same light. Marriage, or the possibility of marriage, not only

blighted married women's working lives, but cast its shadow backwards to embrace *all* women, regardless of status and circumstances. Therefore, although during the postwar period virtually all single women and a third of all married women worked outside the home (the figures for home work might well swell this number), the picture of work as an inessential frill on the fabric of a women's life persisted.

## Education

Nor was it just women's working lives that were influenced by what was considered to be their biological destiny; the education of girls was also affected. Feminist triumphs in securing women's access to education at all levels up to university had certainly resulted in a huge improvement in women's ability to compete with men in the workforce. But the insistence that earlier feminist teachers had placed on the need to give girls the same education as boys began to be undermined by the 'Equal but Different' lobby, which saw education in terms of preparing girls for their roles as wives and mothers.

It is instructive to skim through the various education reports produced from the end of the war up to the Newsom Report in 1963. During this period the state was taking over the responsibility for educating all its citizens; from the 1944 Education Act onwards, all children, male and female, had the statutory right to education up to a specified age (initially 14, then increased to 15 and later to 16). The last barriers to further education were demolished and, in theory, every child should have been able to achieve her or his full potential. Reality was less rosy. Various reports looked into the failures of this ideal and speculated on the reasons, but these were seen largely in terms of the 'two nations' theory, social background or inadequate funding of schools, and so on. No thought was given to sexual differences and how these might affect attainment. The composition of the committees producing these reports is perhaps indicative of some unquestioned assumptions. Predictably, women formed a low proportion of the members of such committees, from the McNair Report in 1944 onwards – this despite the overwhelming amount of women engaged in education. Two, significantly, had no women representatives: the Percy Report, set up in 1945 to examine the needs of higher technical education,[16] and the Barlow Report, which in 1946 considered what policies should govern the use and development of scientific manpower and resources in the following ten years.[17] Science and technology were still seen as essentially masculine areas. As late as 1959 the Crowther Report (less than one-fifth of whose committee were women) still discussed technical education as being a *boy's* education.[18] The Newsom Report in 1963 slightly improved matters by having one-third of its committee female; on the other hand, Newsom is notorious for his strict adherence to a conventional view of women as future wives and mothers. A slightly fusty air rises from these reports. The idealism is there and they represent the government's genuine wish to get its decisions right, but the statements made and the language in which the reports are sometimes couched, have an aura of middle-class complacency. The Albemarle Report, for example, with its quotations from Burns and Auden, is redolent of cigars, and I almost hear the clink of the port decanter being handed round.[19]

Against this background the debate about the right sort of education for girls was bedevilled by a lack of any hard facts about what was really happening to girls in the education system. It was known that university and higher education generally showed a lower take-up by girl school-leavers. A survey of the number of 17-year-olds continuing at school showed that the percentage of boys had risen from 6.2 per cent in 1947 to 11.1 per cent in 1958, while for girls in the same period it had risen from 4.8 per cent to 8.8 per cent, showing that the proportion of girls to boys had not improved over these eleven years.[20] Nor were things to get any better, according to several analyses:

The proportion of girls with two or more A-levels who went on to university in 1967 was 44 per cent; in the case of boys the figure was 67 per cent. In full-time and part-time further education the percentage of boys far out-stripped that of girls, and only in the colleges of education was the percentage of women higher than that of men. The fact that only a quarter of students in British universities were women was a factor in the Robbins Committee's assessment of the likely future expansion of higher education; the rising professional standards of some occupations taken up by girls was likely, the committee believed, to lead to more girls entering them via full-time courses of higher education. By the beginning of the 1970s, however, these differentials in higher education were still marked.[21]

If this is contrasted with the fact that more girls than boys passed the 11+ entrance examination to grammar schools (a phenomenon that led to the nefarious practice of results being separated by sex so as to ensure the same number of boys as girls actually went to grammar school),[22] the continued failure of many women to enter higher education is significant.

Discussion of the education of girls during this period was hampered by the assumption that all girls would marry and devote their lives primarily to domestic duties. It was thought that this was particularly the case with working-class girls. Both the Crowther Report and Newsom held firmly to these beliefs. The Crowther Report, which was published in 1959, enshrined much of the thinking about girls' education during this period. It still saw motherhood as inevitable and stated that 'the prospect of courtship and marriage should rightly influence the education of the adolescent girl'. The report disguised the sexism in such a remark (do not boys also have 'the prospect of courtship and marriage'?) by claiming that it was only asking for girls to be treated as adults in view of their 'greater social and psychological maturity'.[23] The members of the Advisory Council for Education who drew up the report had responded to the change that was taking place in attitudes to working married women by accepting that motherhood took up less of women's lives than in the past, and that there was therefore a need to educate women who might be taking up careers later in life. However, it had a limited view about what these 'careers' were to be, citing teaching, social work, the health services, the clothing trade and commerce as the most suitable to be combined with marriage.[24] It did not appear to envisage careers other than these traditional ones, and continued to ignore the actual working lives of many women, married or not. The Council, it seemed, still saw girls and women *only* in relation to men. The Newsom Report did not challenge these views. In fact, Newsom's views were already known, as he had clearly stated them in 1948 in *The Education of Girls*, and his opinion had not appreciably changed by the time he chaired the 1963 Committee.[25] Yet those who opposed him still accepted his basic premise – that girls were destined to be wives and mothers – so although the article he wrote in September 1964 in *The Observer*[26] reiterated his view that girls should stick to 'feminine' skills, most of the consequent refutals of his opinions did not question his basic assumption that all but a few exceptional women were destined for a domestic role.

**Femininity and achievement**

It was not just intellectual debate about woman's role and educational thinking and policy which limited girls' aspirations. A more insidious influence was the belief that 'braininess' and 'femininity' were mutually hostile. The old Victorian biological argument that women's reproductive ability would be damaged by too much intellectual endeavour was refurbished and modernised. Being clever, the 1950s' version suggested, could seriously affect a girl's chance of a 'normal' life with a husband and family. 'Braininess' became suspect because it could lead women to become too interested in intellectual things and to compete with men, thus ruining their chances of capturing a husband, for the received wisdom was that men were repelled by brainy women. Women who excelled in any field were constantly advised to hide their superiority from men. Eventually braininess became equated with plainness in a woman; physical beauty was the important factor in attracting a man and intellectuality made a woman ugly. This idea was so much part of the folk wisdom that surrounded girls that it led to what Judith Bardwick called 'the fear of success'.[27] Bardwick also mentions Margaret Mead's description of girls' 'quest for failure' in work. She suggested that the anxiety women feel about being categorised as unfeminine at a period in their lives before they have fully established their sexual identity – their femininity – will make them especially vulnerable to any suggestion that certain activities or types of behaviour will result in them becoming de-sexed.[28]

Concepts of femininity vary from one period to another. To be 'feminine' in the Victorian age meant something quite different from being 'feminine' in the postwar period, particularly during the 1950s. Being female does not confer femininity. A female can be unfeminine, and the term 'masculine woman' has been used to express contempt for a woman who breaks the current role stereotype and asserts her individuality too strongly. The concept of femininity is largely defined by men, but it is strongly upheld – and enforced – by women who have conformed to it. The essence of femininity is difference; it is the opposite, or negative of masculinity. As Susan Brownmiller says, 'biological femaleness is not enough':

> Femaleness always demands more. It must constantly reassure its audience by a willing demonstration of difference, even when one does

not exist in nature, or it must seize and embrace the natural variation and compose a rhapsodic symphony upon the notes . . . To fail at the feminine difference is to appear not to care about men, and to risk the loss of their attention and approval. To be insufficiently feminine is viewed as a failure in core sexual identity.[29]

Femininity is not confined to physical appearance or biological difference. It is supposed to be intellectual and emotional as well. The 'rhapsodic symphony' has to weave together all three strands, and the composition and content of the symphony will change and develop as time passes.

In the postwar period ideas about femininity were complex and often contradictory. Traces of the Victorian image of womanhood persisted and the Freudian view of 'normal femininity' began to gain wide and generally uncritical acceptance. It was as if two ideologies co-existed, one which believed in the separate spheres of women and men, and one that stressed woman's new image as worker and citizen. As Viola Klein pointed out in *The Feminine Character*, the traits necessary for these two roles were mutually incompatible. True femininity required a woman to be 'pretty, sensitive, adaptable, unassertive, good-humoured, domesticated, yielding and soft and, if possible, not too intelligent'. However, if she worked she would be expected to possess 'efficiency, courage, determination, intelligence, a sense of reality, responsibility, independence'.[30] Perhaps if women had been allowed to keep these characteristics separate, displaying the first group at home, the second at work, things would have been relatively simple. The problem arose because they were expected to display both simultaneously. The good secretary was not just expected to be competent at her job: she had also to provide 'wifely' services for her boss. The good wife had to be able to run her home, make decisions about her children, choose wisely in the market-place and balance her accounts, while appearing to remain gently dependent on her male partner. Governments did not help matters by first exhorting women to remain in their feminine sphere at home, and then encouraging them to go out to work for the good of the country. Increasingly during the 1950s they demanded both at the same time. The only thing women could be certain of was that if they married, and above all if they had children, they could be sure they were really feminine. The wearing of a wedding ring became the only rock-bottom proof of true femininity, making it very difficult, and painful, for women to question the institution of marriage. If they did, they opened themselves to the accusation of not being feminine – of suffering from a 'masculinity complex'.

## Women and marriage

Discussion of marriage itself was confined to debating what satisfaction it held for the husband and children, and it was assumed that the achievement of their happiness was the woman's task. Anything that suggested that marriage should be discussed in terms of the woman's satisfaction or happiness was either ignored as irrelevant, or attacked as selfishness on the woman's part. Sexuality itself could only be expressed in the context of marriage, as the 'double standard' was still accepted as the norm. Even contraception – freely available to men in the form of condoms over the counter – was supposed to be only available to married women. A single woman applying to the Family Planning Association for contraceptive advice had to produce cast-iron evidence that she was engaged to be married in the very near future, and even then was often treated as if she should only be considering contraception after having had at least one child. Even its name, the Family Planning Association, lays the emphasis on planning the number of children to have, rather than avoiding having them at all. The FPA did not change its policy about giving advice on contraception outside marriage until 1966, and even then for perhaps dubious reasons.[31] The lack of contraceptive advice in women's magazines of the 1940s and early 1950s is noticeable. Married women writing to problem pages with worries about becoming pregnant were cryptically answered, though the magazine *Woman's Own*, for example, did offer to send 'advice' directly to the correspondent. Inevitably, back-street abortion flourished and homes for un-married mothers had to be set up. However, even those who had earlier pressed for birth control advice to be given outside marriage (for example, Leah Manning) justified it on the grounds that sex before marriage was good for marriage itself.

The tendency at this time was to justify any reform to do with marriage or sexuality on the grounds that it benefited the institution of marriage. Both those for and those against divorce law reform argued on the basis that what they suggested was for the good of the family. Because of the high divorce rate immediately after the war,[32] there was fear that making divorce easy would lead to the break-up of the institution of marriage itself. Those who demanded the reforms argued that easier divorce would strengthen the commitment to marriage by allowing a second chance. The debate was therefore carried on without questioning whether marriage itself was a good or a bad thing.

Marriage was the sounding-board for many reforms and changes. The question 'Would it be good or bad for marriage?' became the sole criterion for a whole range of legal reforms, policy decisions and welfare provisions. Elizabeth Wilson has pointed out that the postwar debate was notable for *absences*, for the exclusion of many of the most serious problems confronting women. 'The most significant things about women,' she says, 'were not said at all, but were represented by a silence.'[33] But she too, like most later commentators on the postwar period, also fails to correct the most outstanding absence of all: the women who were not wives and mothers. She mentions widows in passing, but, like the contemporary postwar commentators, chooses to discuss women in postwar Britain as though the only sort of woman around was a composite Wife/Mother figure. The invisibility of women who were not attached to a husband is remarkable.

## Feminism

This invisibility was partly linked with a reaction against the feminist movement, which, contrary to popular belief, did not cease to exist, but continued to campaign for legal and economic equality. However, though certainly not dead, the movement lacked a coherent philosophy and was fractured into sometimes-warring factions. It failed to question the fundamental assumptions underlying the concept of femininity at this time, and generally went along with the idea that equality could be achieved even while accepting that woman's role was different to man's. 'Equal but different' was the slogan, and some feminists strongly supported the view of women as primarily wives and mothers, to the exclusion of all else: equal access to education, but a difference in that education because of women's future role in marriage; equal access to work, but acceptance of the 'dual role' and the constraints of family and domestic responsibilities. A few warning voices were raised from time to time, pointing out the trap this sort of thinking could lead to, but on the whole the feminists who were making public pronouncements failed to identify the source of the continuing failure by women to make fundamental changes to their status in society. Legislation in favour of women continued throughout the period, but there was an assumption that all the major battles had been fought and it was now just a matter of clearing up some odds and ends so that women could achieve true equality. The title of an article in *The Economist*, 'The Feminists Mop Up', epitomises this attitude, and its paternal pat on the head for the feminist movement – 'A sensible and moderate programme which deserves to command general support' – is modified by its ascription of the hostility engendered by feminist demands to the tendency of feminists to see everything in terms of the sex war. The ordinary woman, it claimed:

persists in the belief that in marriage an ounce of perfume is worth a peck of legal rights, and her dreams of power still feature the *femme fatale* rather than the administrative grade of the civil service.[34]

Feminism, the article suggested, is all right as long as it knows its place.

There was at this time wholesale rejection – even hostility – to militancy. It is not necessary to scratch very deeply before coming across male rejection of equality as defined by earlier feminists. Ashley Montagu, in his book, *The Natural Superiority of Women*, supposedly set out to prove women's superiority to men, but in fact did the opposite. Women's superiority, he claimed, lay in being different, in the supremacy of their biological role to bear children, their emotional role as the carers and nurturers, and their spiritual role to act as the upholders of moral values. Any woman who tried to claim real equality with men was a 'pseudo male' who was trying to cover her failure as a true woman by aping the manners of her 'superior', man. He launched a savage attack on what he called the 'phony feminists':

who behave as if they believe that by beating men at their own jobs they thereby demonstrate their own equality with men. The sexes should not compete . . . women should not try to be like men . . .

Can there be anything more egregious or pathetic than the woman with close-cut hair and tailored suit parotting the manner of the male? . . . When we encounter a feminine male we suspect – generally correctly – a somewhat abnormal psychological history. The 'inferior' models himself upon his 'superior'; rarely does the 'superior' pattern himself after the model of the 'inferior'. 'Phony feminists' are rarely mistaken for anything other than what they are: persons with inferior feelings who are attempting to compensate for their feelings of inferiority as women.[35]

Philip Wylie was even more virulent in his book, *Generation of Vipers*, using the techniques of a hellfire sermon to attack what he saw as the ills of the modern generation in the United States – all due to 'mom', particularly since she got the vote.[36] Both these men's attitudes to feminist demands for genuine equality underlay much male discussion of women at this time. Also, by suggesting that feminism was hostile to true femininity they helped to ensure that many women wished to distance themselves from the movement. This was coupled to a mistaken belief that the early feminists had ignored the desire of many women to marry and have children, and in so doing had created a dichotomy between marriage and a career. Consequently there had arisen a feeling among women that feminism was unable to fulfil their aspirations during this period. The goals of feminism came to be associated with being unmarried, childless and probably middle-class.

### Images of women

It wasn't just the 'experts' who purveyed these ideas about women. Women's magazines tacitly upheld the view of them as wives and mothers and portrayed single women largely in terms of their pursuit of a suitable mate. Where there was conflict between career and marriage, it was almost invariably resolved in favour of marriage. Weekly visits to the 'pictures' further reinforced this philosophy as the cinema, on the whole, reflected the beliefs of the period. As one commentator said:

> The Women Alone figure in fifties' movies is a creature so negative and pitiful that one can interpret the vogue as little other than a reinforcement of the decade's belief in marriage-as-salvation.[37]

Why was this image so sedulously cultivated at the time, so that even debate among feminists was affected? The classic question 'Cui bono?' may shed some light. Who did benefit from the emphasis on the home and women's place in it? Obviously men, individually and collectively. I don't believe this was a male conspiracy to keep women down, but it certainly helped men to live the sort of lives they wanted. The pleasures of home life, of living once again in a family, particularly as the head of that family, must have come as a welcome relief to men returning from war. A woman safely at home, keeping that home ready for the man's return from daily work, is an appealing arrangement. It also gave men a greater sense of security: the upsets of war could be forgotten, and life would go on, as far as family relationships were concerned, as it always had done. I think they genuinely enjoyed the resumption of family life, particularly now that their homes were becoming more comfortable and their wages and leisure better. It must have been confusing and distressing for them to find that the women they returned to felt differently; and the best ways of shutting out a disturbing fact are to deny its existence, strenuously to state the opposite, or to vilify those who attempt to discuss the fact openly.

Men seemed to have accepted the images of women current in their time. But were these images accepted uncritically by women, or is there evidence of alienation? In the past, the creation, through religion, art, literature and folk tale, of such images as virgin, whore, witch, monster, has been almost wholly in the power of men. What women were, or should be, was a male creation. With the invention of the cinema and the development of the popular press and advertising, these images became more pervasive. By the 1950s the representations of women that appeared on the screen, and in advertising, seemed even more alien. The sultry temptress, frequently blonde, still luring men to their doom and coming to a bad end herself, was juxtaposed with the girl-next-door, only waiting for Mr Right so that she could become the happy housewife heroine. If she was Doris Day,[38] she not only kept herself and her house bright and shiny, but could sing and dance as well. Houses gleamed and smelled of baking and no dark shadows of dirt or despair were allowed to intrude. The short trajectory between becoming ready for marriage and actually achieving it was never so emphasised before as being woman's sole story, her unique quest. Occasionally films hinted at something darker – the sloven in *Woman in a Dressing Gown*, for example – but these women were aberrations and their fate could be viewed from a comforting distance. Men still controlled the depiction of women, not only painted and sculpted them, but now decided what roles they would play on the screen, what they would look like in advertisements, what they would say and do on stage. An army of experts, largely male, had risen to dissect the nature of women and femininity; psychologists, sociologists and anthropologists united with educationalists and child experts to define who a woman was and what she should be. Even though increasing access to education ensured that these experts now included some women, the structure of the disciplines studied was created by men and reflected the male viewpoint. Women as wives, women as mothers, women as men's sexual outlet, were seen in relation to others rather than as autonomous beings.

For women themselves these images must have become increasingly alienating. No matter what they did to themselves in the way of dress and make-up, regardless of how hard they worked to make their homes and their children conform with what was presented as a norm, their internal reality could not match these external images. In addition, the fifties' demand for women workers, including married women workers, co-existed uneasily alongside a general condemnation of the working wife and mother, and this only strained the credulity of women who could see little correspondence between the values current in society and the reality of their lives.

## Women novelists

During other periods when there has been an apparently overwhelming acceptance of a specific image of women, criticism and rejection of the current image, though overtly silenced, seeps through whatever cracks it can find. Feminist literary criticism, by close textual analysis and highlighting of the gaps in women's texts, has revealed how such unacceptable views can be expressed through the fiction written by women. The contention of this book is that one place to look for divergence from the apparently seamless garment of orthodoxy during the postwar period, is in the fiction written by some of its women writers. The gaps and tears in the seemingly smooth representation of women appeared in one art form in which women had managed to gain more than a foothold – the novel. Women not only wrote stories, they also probably comprised considerably more than half the readership. Fiction had become more accessible than ever through private and public lending libraries, through cheap reprints by book clubs, by being serialised in popular women's magazines and made increasingly available in paperback, and even read on the radio.

There were still constraints on how women novelists could represent women in their fiction and the confinement of a romantic tradition of storytelling that insisted that a woman's 'story' was courtship, and the end of her story, marriage. What happens afterwards, whether the prince remains a prince or becomes a toad, or whether the heroine does indeed 'live happily ever after', is not at issue. But women writers now had a tradition behind them of their foremothers who had found ways of expressing subversive ideas and of depicting a true reality, either consciously or semi-consciously, while appearing to write with circumspection and decorum. In addition, the gains of feminists in terms of the legal and economic emancipation during two world wars of working in men's jobs, had opened doors to possibilities which could not now be ignored. However, the questioning of traditional roles assigned to women had, to a certain extent, to go underground in the face of the overwhelming push back to the home that occurred in the immediate postwar period, together with the elevation of the happy housewife heroine.

One of the curious factors in the postwar period was how many of the writers popular during this period wrote about women in ways that questioned the images current in their time. In the pages of these novels we can find women who do not fulfil the stereotypes, who strive towards self-realisation and who find marriage and children less fulfilling than the dream would have them. Sometimes these women are created deliberately and openly, at other times they creep behind the fabric of the story and we have partial glimpses of them as they struggle to free themselves. For one of the effects of the two wars and the need for women to leave home and go out to work was that women now met other women in places outside the restrictions of home; this was especially important during the wars, when their husbands were away and men in general were either absent or marginal to their lives. They could begin to feel and understand some of the universals of women's experience and articulate some of the questionings that arose. Marriage, above all, was no longer accepted as the sole goal of a woman's life, or even as necessarily a major source of satisfaction. The novels of the postwar period questioned the relationship between women and men, especially in the unequal partnership of marriage, reflecting doubts that many women held. What is interesting about the period is not just that so much of its fiction does represent marriage ambiguously, but that this ambiguity is not confined to the intellectual novel but permeates more popular fiction. Its presence suggests that it fulfilled a need, that it was here alone that ordinary women could find the reassurance that they were not monsters for finding marriage and motherhood problematical, and that many women who did not live married lives – single women, widows, divorced and separated wives, unmarried mothers – could find women like themselves. Here also were heroines – and villains – who experienced life directly, not refracted through the prism of a man's mind. Female identity, these novels suggest, was more complex and varied than men ever suspected.

I have concentrated on women writers who fall into that imprecise area between 'literature' and 'popular' fiction, sitting uneasily on the borderlines. I have also chosen to look specifically at novelists who write mainly about women, and from the woman's point of view. I wanted to see how women novelists wrote, not just about love, but about marriage itself, at a time when marriage was considered woman's true role, the only one that would bring her happiness; whether, in effect, they saw it as a true-life happily-ever-after. Iris Murdoch, Muriel Spark and Doris Lessing are generally conceded to belong in the category 'literature' and have received a great deal of critical examination, so I have not included them. In addition, the first two do not fit my second criterion. Others I have included are regarded by some as literature and by others as popular, and the difficulty in placing these writers makes them particularly interesting. I am at a loss, for example, to explain why Elaine Showalter, in her book on British women novelists,[39] includes Penelope Mortimer and Enid Bagnold, but excludes Elizabeth Taylor and Olivia Manning. Some of the novelists are generally thought of as definitely in the popular category (for example, Elizabeth Goudge and Susan Ertz), but cannot be dismissed as merely writers of escapist romantic novels since they confront issues that face women. A few of the writers, originally dismissed as merely popular, are now being republished and reassessed (Barbara Pym and Kate O'Brien, for example). Most of the writers are from what can loosely be called the middle class, though bearing in mind that nearly all of them were born in the first two decades of the twentieth century, there are differences peculiar to women of that period, particularly in the education they received.

Before the 1944 Education Act the education a middle-class girl got was very dependent on what her parents saw as necessary. The debate about whether it was worthwhile educating girls at all, particularly at university level, lingered into the postwar period, so their education could have ranged from the sort of schooling Elizabeth Goudge received at a small private boarding school, where the teaching was so sketchy that none of the pupils sat any examinations. . .

> from an academic point of view we learned almost nothing and were not in any way prepared for any future profession. Such an anachronism was this school, blooming there among the rhododendrons and pines of its high garden, that working for a living was hardly considered. In spite of the war raging on the other side of the English Channel it was assumed that we should all go home and help our mothers do the flowers, be presented at court and get married.[40]

. . . to the type of schooling that led to Oxford, as in Barbara Pym's case. For some, the opportunity to take their education as far as possible was limited by money. Pamela Hansford Johnson, who received an excellent education at Clapham County Secondary School, could not go on to university because she needed to help support her widowed mother. Kate O'Brien got to Dublin University by means of winning scholarships. She has vividly described, in *The Land of Spices*,[41] the difficulties faced by a girl in a large family where there are boys who automatically have prior claims to the dwindling funds available.

These authors also differed from present-day women writers in that most had lived through two world wars and major social upheavals. They grew up during the flourishing period of feminism at the beginning of the century and saw many of the battles for equality won. They also saw how little changed women's position in society was. Some claimed to be socialist; several were, or became, right wing. Their attitudes to the feminist movement varied and were sometimes contradictory, with only one being overtly feminist.

The novels themselves were all widely read and popular, reprinted by book clubs and available in public libraries. At least two writers had films made of their novels. Paradoxically, the fact that their novels were not considered 'literature' may have given them more freedom to create women who are not stereotypes and to question contemporary beliefs about the nature of women. Also, by not being subject to 'literary' criticism, they could escape the male-centred criteria for judging fiction, and more particularly, heroines. Their readers were probably mainly women who could find in their novels women characters who did not conform to contemporary stereotypes and who reflected the dilemmas they themselves confronted.

# 1

# Something to love: heroines and their heroes

> She thought she must have grown up with a picture in her mind of the man she would like to marry and that Jervis did not at all resemble this picture. Our lovers, she thought, should be most of all jealous of the men we have hoped and expected to love. Those are their most dangerous, most fatal rivals.[1]

> She had fallen in love at first sight, so she loved an image which she had invented and which might easily be rubbed away in daily wear and tear.[2]

Women writers have often tried to answer that petulant question 'What *do* women want?' by using the freedom of fiction to explore how a woman awakens to love and how that love first fastens on one person rather than another. In the two decades following the Second World War, women novelists continued to portray their heroines falling in love, with the happy or unhappy consequences of that love. Their disquiet about men as lovers – and potential husbands – runs counter to the ideas of the period, which emphasised the desirability of attracting men and turning them into husbands. Love and marriage went together, as the words of a contemporary song said, 'like a horse and carriage'. The same song ended by stating categorically, 'You can't have one without the other'. Postwar women writers appear to have disagreed: love is one thing, they suggest, marriage another.

## Love

About love itself, they were in agreement: the need to love, to experience love, overrides other considerations in the lives of these postwar fictional heroines. Love is important to them, not so much because its object is a man, but because of what it does for the woman herself. It is the realisation of her full potential, and her tragedy is that it can be the source of her downfall. But this does not mean that it is not an ecstatically transforming experience. The writers may be critical of men as lovers, but the emotion of love itself is treated as one of the highlights in a woman's life. The first quickening of sensual love, the power that sexual attractiveness confers, and the heightened sensitivity that accompanies falling in love, are such heady attractions that few women who have experienced them once can resist the temptation of trying again. They persuade themselves that *this* time it went wrong because the man was wrong. Next time their choice of lover will be wiser, luckier. The experience of love itself is too pleasurable for a woman to forgo and she reaches out again to another and, she hopes, better lover.

Overwhelmingly during the period, fictional love is heterosexual, and although affection, and even love, may exist between women, it is very rarely depicted as sexual love. The lover is therefore virtually always a man, and the dilemma for the woman is that this seems to be the flaw, since the incompatibility of men and women means that the chance of happiness is threatened from the beginning, isolation and loneliness being the more likely outcome. The unsatisfactory nature of so many of the suitors in their fiction seems to reflect a disillusionment with the nature of men, but not necessarily with the nature of love. The writers explore why women persist in falling in love, not once, but over and over again. Nancy Mitford suggests one explanation in a remark by one of the most optimistic of 'fallers in love' in fiction, the Bolter. Fanny, the narrator in *The Pursuit of Love*,[3] has been brought up by her aunt because her mother, soon after her marriage and Fanny's birth, 'bolted'. This was the first of many such flights, and by the time Fanny herself is married, her mother, known in the family as 'the Bolter', has had eight or nine marriages (no one is absolutely sure of the number) and countless affairs. Fanny, worried that her cousin Linda also appears to have become a Bolter, justifies Linda's final passionate affair by claiming, ' "He was the great love of her life, you know" ', but the Bolter points out how universal that feeling is: ' "One always thinks that," ' she says, ' "Every, every time." '[4]

The Bolter in *The Pursuit of Love* is perhaps more fortunate than most heroines because she refuses to allow disillusion to take root. Her daughter, Fanny, has always assumed, along with everyone else in the family, that the Bolter must be an unhappy woman and is surprised when her strait-laced and rather unimaginative husband challenges this assumption and rebukes her for her blindness:

> 'Deeply as I disapprove of your mother and her activities, I don't think she could be described as unhappy . . . You should try to see things as they are, Fanny. Whether her behaviour has been desirable or not is a different proposition from whether it has made her unhappy. I don't think it has; I think she is perfectly happy and always was.'[5]

The Bolter's happiness arises from the fact that she continues to repeat the joy of falling in love, and as soon as the fading of that first rapture begins, she takes off in search of another love. She can never be disillusioned, because at the first hint of disappointment in the lover's character, she abandons him. The Bolter, like many other characters in women's fiction, is in love with love; the object of that love tends to get in the way of the pleasure of feeling love itself.

Barbara Pym is another novelist who writes about women's longing for love. Most of her novels were published in the 1950s, and she writes about a generation of women whose chances of marriage had been considerably lessened by the effects of two world wars. The young men they should have married or fallen in love with, died in those wars and left them with little possibility of finding a permanent mate. Through her heroines, Barbara Pym expresses her own longing for happiness with a man, but because she herself never married she is aware of the pleasures and rewards of the single state as well as its defects. Her ambivalence is expressed through her heroines, who fall in love with men out of reach, at the same time remaining uncomfortably aware that, given the opportunity to marry, they might not be as pleased to give up their spinsterhood as they imagine. Like Nancy Mitford, she too has a 'Bolter' among her fictional characters. Prudence, in *Jane and Prudence*,[6] appears, superficially, to be searching for a husband, and her married friend, Jane, is anxious to bring her together with potential mates, but in fact Prudence, like the Bolter, is easily disillusioned. Love itself is eternally attractive to her, but lovers, sooner or later, lose their romantic appeal. Prudence is a romantic, and whoever she is in love with at the time is given the attributes of an ideal lover. Unfortunately she is not a complete romantic; sooner or later reality obtrudes and dissatisfaction creeps in. Prudence solves this dilemma by moving lightly from one lover to another, never allowing disappointment to sour or blight her expectation that the next time will be better. Her disappointment over the loss of one lover resembles more the symptoms of flu than those of heart-break, and she is soon distracted by finding another:

> It appeared that Prudence had forgotten Fabian to the same extent as she had forgotten Philip, Henry, Laurence and the others. That is to say, he had been given a place in the shrine of her past loves – the urn containing his ashes had been ceremoniously deposited in the niche where it would always remain. Philip, Henry, Laurence, Peter, Fabian and who could tell how many others there might be?[7]

It seems that the problem lies not with love, but with the lover. For love, sadly, does need an object:

> Some tame gazelle, or some gentle dove:
> Something to love, oh, something to love![8]

The heroines try to match their expectations of love and their picture of the lover with a reality which threatens painful disillusion-ment. The novels of this period explore the strategies women use to wrench happiness from the most unsatisfactory situations, handling the theme humorously, ironically or tragically, but even the most humorous treatment carries a hint of sadness, a breath of 'Ah, if only . . .' Very often this 'if only' suggests that if men were different, more like women's idea of the perfect lover, there would be no problem.

## The lover

Many of the lovers in women's fiction during the postwar period seem the opposite of the dynamic male that is generally thought to be the type of man a woman is supposed to long for. On the contrary, they are often weak and vacillating, sometimes need to be dragged into marriage, at times seem somewhat feminine.

Manliness in itself is not enough. Because they are writing from the woman's point of view and portray their male characters through women's eyes, what the women writers see and how they judge these male characters as lovers is influenced by the characteristics women search for in lovers, what they think will bring them happiness and the chance to experience all the joys of loving (rather than being loved) without the danger of this love being rejected or misunderstood. This difference in perception and viewpoint is one that is often not taken into account when literary critics, particularly male literary critics, evaluate characters created by women novelists.[9] These critics often express their displeasure at the way women portray men in their fiction by claiming that they can't draw male characters realistically, the underlying suggestion being that whereas men can penetrate the complexities of female character, so simple compared to the male, women, cursed by the inadequacies of their sex, cannot create believable men in their fiction. Their irritation is increased when women portray men as lovers – they seem a poor lot, not the sort that real women are attracted to, not like *them*. The irritation is understandable: lovers very frequently do cut a poor figure in women's fiction; they can even appear ridiculous. Men have for too long believed that the reason women remain attracted to them, and continue to pursue them, is entirely because of their overwhelmingly manly qualities. When, therefore, women novelists suggest that it is not the characteristics prized by men that women look for in lovers or in marriage partners, but other qualities, ones that men may despise or consider womanly or effeminate, the men may feel threatened and take refuge in a refusal to believe that male characters who display these facets are anything like 'real' men.

Women novelists writing in the postwar decades were no exception. Not only do their successful suitors seem more feminine, but even the 'Don Juans' are sometimes made more acceptable by being involved in the feminine world and knowledgeable about women's things. Conrad in *The Long View*[10] knows about clothes, food and interior decoration, and he 'educates' Antonia in these matters, seeing himself as the expert rather than her. Both Fabrice in *The Pursuit of Love*[11] and Charles-Edouard in *The Blessing*[12] are completely at home in a feminine world and as knowledgeable about it as the women themselves, but it is perhaps significant that both are French (the masculine men in Nancy Mitford's novels are often English). One of the most attractive of these feminine men is Davey, in Nancy Mitford's Radlett novels,[13] probably the most appealing male character she created: a perfect husband, a charming and amusing step-uncle to Fanny and a humorous but compassionate friend. In fact, generally, Nancy Mitford's feminine men are the guardians of logic and balance, while the manly men are illogical and swayed by emotions. The masculine men in her fiction do not appear to be as successful as the feminine men in making women happy – or even in being able to hold them. Nancy Mitford herself always had a soft spot for both homosexuals and what used to be called 'aesthetes', and one of her most successful comic creations is the homosexual, Cedric Hampton, in *Love in a Cold Climate*,[14] who, like some Nancy Mitford herself knew, brought happiness and a renewed interest in life to an ageing woman.

Strongly masculine men often repel the heroines in fiction of the period, and this attraction to the feminine man suggests an ambiguity in women's sexuality. Many of these 'suitors' have little in common with the stereotyped dynamic lover of romantic fiction: they fail to rush heroines off their feet and frequently need to be wooed or pushed into wooing. Vacillating, childishly egocentric, they are still what women choose to love. I can only speculate about the reasons for this feminisation of fictional lovers. There appears to be an implicit rejection of masculine values and a desire to stay in the feminine world, which suggests fear and rejection of the male principle and of entry into the wider world: the world of men. The writers seem to be hinting that this masculine world is hostile to women; that their emotional and sexual needs will best be served by finding more sensitive men who can share their feminine world and provide a background against which they can fulfil themselves as women, not in the narrow 1950s' sense of wife and mother, but in their own right. The problem for the heroine is to find a lover who will fulfil her dreams. She has little to go on: a limited experience and a gallery of fictional lovers, many created by male storytellers. The few signposts that do exist may prove to be untrustworthy, yet the ability to distinguish between the true and the false lover is crucial, for a mistake can bring death, literal as well as figurative.

## The lover as death

Elizabeth Taylor's novels explore this dilemma, portraying women turning towards men who seem to bring a promise of life, of awakening, but who really represent death. In *A Wreath of Roses*,[15] the lover is a man who has already murdered one woman and may kill again. Camilla meets him on a train journey, and the catalyst that brings them together is the violent suicide they witness on a quiet branch-line station, a death made even more shocking by the peaceful scene it shatters. As Camilla, bored with her spinster life, dreading her return to the school where she teaches and the drab predictability of her days, is drawn into a sinister relationship which seems to resemble love, Elizabeth Taylor uses images of violence to suggest that this country idyll is no 'romance'. The opening paragraph of the novel, set against a quintessentially quiet English country scene, suggests that below this tranquil surface, violence threatens: 'The spiked shelter prints an unmoving shadow on the platform, geraniums blaze, whitewashed stones assault the eye.'[16] The railway bridge from which the suicide leaps, rupturing the calm of the summer day, is mirrored by the Abingford railway bridge, whose shadow falls like a guillotine between the apparently innocent life Camilla leads and her secret liaison with a killer. Its threatening presence serves as a metaphor for the split in Camilla's life and prefigures the violent death at the end of the novel.

Elizabeth Taylor wrote the novel just after the end of the Second World War, and although she did not write directly about the war, many of the novels she wrote during the period indirectly suggest the violence and horror of war and its effects on people. In the case of Richard Elton, Camilla's lover, the effect has been extreme, and he represents the damage that immersion in violence does to men. Elizabeth Taylor turns upside-down the concept of the returned soldier as a noble figure of romance and, through Camilla, suggests the dangers such concepts hold for women. Camilla's initial revulsion from Richard is ambiguous; he is conventionally good-looking, the type of man that Camilla 'believed' she despised, but her belief that his life could never touch hers is based on Camilla's own failure to know certain things about herself, delicately suggested by Elizabeth Taylor's use of the word 'believed'. Something draws her to him, something she thinks might be love, or at least excitement. When she finally penetrates his mystery, she recoils in horror: 'Parting the leaves to look for treasure, love, adventure, she inadvertently disclosed evil.'[17] Violence, male violence, is seen as essentially hostile to women's happiness.

Richard is literally death to women; others of Elizabeth Taylor's lovers carry an aura of death. Throughout her fiction she counter-poises the awakening into life that the lover promises, with the death, literal and figurative, that he really represents. Richard Elton has murdered a woman and may kill again, but the death others bring is less obvious. In *The Sleeping Beauty*,[18] middle-aged Vinny falls in love with Emily, the Sleeping Beauty of the title. A terrible accident, which changed Emily's face and scarred her body, has left her in an almost deathlike trance from which Vinny awakens her. Vinny as a lover, though, is ambiguous. Again, Elizabeth Taylor opens the novel with an image of death linked to the lover-hero. '"There's Vinny going in with the wreaths"', Isabella remarks, seeing him arrive to condole with her over the death of her husband. Isabella has known Vinny for many years and associates him with death and disaster. His skill at consoling the bereaved, although appreciated, reminds her of the trappings of funerals and death: closed blinds, wreaths, undertakers. All these associations with death give a chilling and slightly sinister colouring to Vinny's character. For passion has not been Vinny's strongest emotion up to now – it has been pity; and although Vinny denies that his love for Emily is merely pity, Emily herself seems to have become addicted. At the end of the novel there is a suggestion that Emily's awakening is not a true awakening into life and independence, but a change of dream perhaps, or another sleep.

What many of Elizabeth Taylor's heroines seem to be awaiting is a liberation from the narrow world they inhabit. Finding themselves in a vacuum, they grasp at whatever they think might release them and, mistakenly, assume that the liberator will be a lover. In *Palladian*,[19] Cassandra draws her ideas about love from fiction, seeing herself as a modern Jane Eyre. The similarities in their respective positions are too striking not to promise a Mr Rochester. Orphaned, setting out to take a position as a governess in a country house where a widower needs someone to look after his daughter, Cassandra is prepared to find herself falling in love with the owner of Copthorne Manor (the name of the house echoing, so satis-factorily for Cassandra, the name of Mr Rochester's house, Thornfield, in *Jane Eyre*). Marion does not disappoint her. Melancholy, reclusive and, above all, feminine – 'He will do to fall in love with', she thinks.[20] So she falls in love and ends by marrying him. However, the fundamental defects in Marion's character remain and do not promise happiness. Marion is obsessed with thoughts of death and loss, and Cassandra, observing that he cannot forget his dead wife, senses that the dead Violet will always be a barrier, preventing him from fully partaking in life.

Vinny, Richard and Marion are all 'twilight' suitors, casting shadows on what should be a dawn in the women's lives. Vinny is described as loving 'twilight rather than midday, the echo more than the voice, the moon more than the sun, and women better than men',[21] and the same could be said to be true of Richard and Marion. All three novels begin with a death, all have heroines floating in a world that has changed too much for them to be able to grasp at love as a solution to their problems. They first meet their lovers through a death – the suicide in *A Wreath of Roses*, Isabella's husband's death in *The Sleeping Beauty*, and Violet's death in *Palladian* – and this suggests that whatever love may be, it is not an entry into life.

**The dream lover**

In many of her novels, Elizabeth Taylor portrays women whose longing for love is seen as an attempt to give meaning to their lives. They blind themselves to reality, preferring to believe that the chosen lover is what romantic fiction has promised them. The gap between the imagined lover and the real man seems unbridgeable. What women seek in their lovers may not be there. How many of us have at one time sighed for Mr Rochester, but has there ever been a man like that? The very qualities that allow a woman's love to expand and flourish may be unattainable, and the gap has to be filled somehow, a lover chosen who will not shatter the image of the ideal lover. The need to love ensures a blindness towards the loved object – as long as he 'will do to fall in love with'. There are two strategies open to the heroines of these novels if they wish to retain their illusions: they can ignore the true nature of the real man they love, or they can pin their love to an absent, lost or even dead lover.

The dream lover is, of course, ubiquitous in romantic fiction, but the more perceptive women novelists of this period are too realistic to believe in such mythical creatures. Instead they portray their heroines triumphantly imposing an ideal mask on a flawed lover. A striking instance of this ability to turn unsatisfactory material into the ideal lover is described in Elizabeth Taylor's *Angel*,[22] whose heroine, Angelica Deverell, is, revealingly, a romantic novelist. Angel has pursued her very successful career as a writer of romantic fiction with a ferocious singlemindedness, her main object being to escape from the sordid and petty life she has been born into. Having achieved her aim of fame and fortune, she gradually finds herself hungering for love. At the peak of her success she suddenly feels a lack in her life. Angel had often written about romantic love in her novels, but she had never experienced it. Suddenly feeling the need to experience it herself, she casts around for an object and vents all her romantic yearnings on the weak and vicious Esmé. Angel has never had any problem ignoring reality. At the beginning of her writing career she found she was 'learning to triumph over reality, and the truth was beginning to leave her in peace',[23] so she has no difficulty in ignoring Esmé's indifference to her and turns his sordid sexual affairs into Byronic romance. Angel, successful romantic novelist that she is, has created the perfect lover and husband. The fact that the reality does not match it is no barrier to her happiness; she had found in her writing that experience was merely a 'baffling obstacle' to the free play of her imagination and she is therefore blissfully happy in the imagined world she has created. Significantly, it is Esmé's entrance into Angel's life that starts her decline as a successful romantic novelist. It is as if all her inventive powers are absorbed into the task of turning Esmé into the ideal lover, leaving none for the creation of her fiction.

**The unattainable lover**

Esmé's eventual death is fortuitious, because Angel is left with her illusions intact – for a time anyway. She can mourn the loss of her love and build a monument to an ideal that never existed. For it is not love which is flawed, but the lover, and love without the presence of a real lover might be preferable. 'Better to have loved and lost than never to have loved at all', the old saying goes; some women writers suggest it is better to have loved and lost than to have loved and won. In Elizabeth Jane Howard's *The Beautiful Visit*,[24] for example, the heroine's one brief experience of love, an intense but unconsummated affair, is cut short by the lover's death. The perfection of the few days she spends with Rupert is uncontaminated by what happens later. Rupert has epitomised all that a woman might long for in a lover and his speech about love remains as a suggestion of what might have been. However, the heroine's experience of true love later enables her to reject a false suitor, one who is too damaged to be able to give her what she apprehended in Rupert.

Less tragically and more humorously, Barbara Pym also suggests that a lost love is preferable to one that results in marriage. Belinda, in *Some Tame Gazelle*,[25] was the first of Barbara Pym's unmarried heroines and she epitomises their contradictory feelings about men and love. Middle-aged, the object of her long, unrequited devotion living in the same village, Belinda examines what her feelings might be if the man she loves became a widower and perhaps available to her. Ruefully she faces up to what has happened to her passion: 'For she was now a contented spinster and her love was like a warm, comfortable garment, bedsocks, perhaps, or even woollen combinations – certainly something without glamour or romance.'[26] Belinda is, perhaps, another version of Prudence in *Jane and Prudence*; in Belinda's case she can remain faithful to one man because he is reassuringly out of reach. New love may be ecstasy and heightened awareness, but lost love is eventually comforting and painless, since it has encompassed no disillusionment.

Through her heroines, Barbara Pym expresses the dilemma that faces women: if they wish to find satisfaction in love or marriage, they will have to be less clear-sighted and idealistic, more prepared to compromise. This is basically the message that women were receiving in the advice columns of women's magazines during the period. But though Barbara Pym appears to go along with this view, her novels, with their malicious wit and their portraits of self-satisfied, inadequate men, constantly undermine the certainties current in her time. Even to suggest that any woman would, like Belinda and her sister, actually decide that of two evils – marriage to an unsatisfactory man, or spinsterhood – the lesser was spinsterhood, was something that would never have been admitted in any of the romantic novels or magazines her women characters would have been reading at this time. Nor would a woman reader have found such questioning in much contemporary male fiction, which continued to support the conventional beliefs of the time.

## Lovers in contemporary male fiction

The novels generally identified with the 1950s are those written by the so-called 'Angry Young Men', such as Wain, MacInnes and Amis.[27] These 'Angry Decade' writers are often considered to have challenged the social and cultural assumptions of their time; in fact they were far less radical than was supposed, particularly in their treatment of women characters in their novels. At least one social and cultural assumption they did not question was the function of women in men's lives. Nor did they deviate from the traditional fictional treatment of heroines – who have to wait to be rescued. Immured in castles, chained to dragons' caves, surrounded by briars, the traditional heroine has always known she had only to wait patiently for a knight to come trotting up to rescue her and marry her. Male novelists of the period followed this tradition in their portrayal of women, emphasising their passivity. In the fiction of writers such as Wain, MacInnes and Amis, women characters are two-dimensional, their function merely to provide a prize at the end of the male hero's quest, or to be blocks to the hero's progress. One curious aspect of some of these male novels is the way the hero climbs socially by marrying or pursuing a woman outside his own class, so that the radical declaimings become falsified by his evident satisfaction at rising to a higher social stratum. Women perform a symbolic role, and failure or success with them is equated with failure or success in life goals. The heroes' personal feelings about the women they pursue are ambiguous, often veering from hatred and contempt to obsessive lust. The women are frequently portrayed as out of reach of the hero for economic or social reasons, and very often already attached to other, more powerful men, these men invariably being presented as in some way unworthy.

A classic example of the pattern occurs in John Wain's *Hurry on Down*.[28] Though the novel is set in postwar Britain, the plot follows the lines of a traditional folk story. Charles Lumley, the hero, sets out on a quest like a chivalric knight, without a specific aim in view. He meets and falls in love with an unattainable lady, Veronica, who is held by the 'enchanter/wicked magician/ogre', Roderick. Charles is at first defeated in his struggle against Roderick, and even suffers physical injury. While recovering from his wounds, he has a brief romance with a working-class girl, whom he abandons (hints of the fair maid of Avalon administering to the wounded Lancelot).

Finally he triumphs and wins Veronica because he has acquired 'magic' power – money. Similarly in Colin MacInnes's *Absolute Beginners*,[29] the hero is at first unsuccessful in his pursuit of Suze, who rejects him for the moneyed, but effeminate, Henley. However, at the end, Suze comes to offer herself to the hero, who has vanquished the powers of evil, represented in the novel as the racialists of the Notting Hill Gate riots, but Charles, ambiguously, leaves her and sets out for America. Again, Suze herself is particularly badly characterised and her motivation left unclear.

The desire these 1950s heroes feel for women out of their reach, and the reasons for their rejection of the women more easily available to them, are succinctly stated in Kingsley Amis's *Lucky Jim*.[30] Dixon, in the midst of a desultory and inconclusive affair with the unattractive Margaret, first sets eyes on Christine and, noting her physical features and the 'tasteful' way she dresses, begins to lust after her:

> The sight of her seemed an irresistible attack on his own habits, standards and ambitions: something designed to put him in his place for good. The notion that women like this were never on view except as the property of men like Bertrand was so familiar to him that it had long since ceased to appear an injustice. The huge class that contained Margaret was destined to provide his own womenfolk; those in whom the intention of being attractive could sometimes be made to get itself confused with performance; those with whom a too-tight skirt, a wrong-coloured, or no, lipstick, even an ill-executed smile could instantly discredit that illusion beyond apparent hope of renewal.[31]

Here Amis reflects a widespread view of woman as product: money or status buying the better-quality, more 'tasteful' model. Amis is particularly interesting when he explores his heroes' ambivalent feelings for the women they desire and the peculiar contempt many men feel for plain, sexually unattractive women. Prettiness is enough: 'Beauty without *real* sweetness or *real* mind was as beautiful as beauty with.'[32] It can even be confused with being 'nice'. Christine is nice because she is pretty – Amis tells us she is nice – but the evidence for this quality is singularly lacking in her behaviour. The main objective of the hero is to acquire, no matter how, the desirable woman: 'the possession of the signs of sexual privilege is the important thing, not the quality nor the enjoyment of them'.[33] Bertrand, in *Lucky Jim*, states, ' "I am having Christine because it's my right" ',[34] and Jim Dixon only objects because *he* is being told what to do, not because Christine is being spoken of as an object, without volition of her own. For the women in these novels are seen merely as reflections of men, as prizes or marks of social class. The women themselves are opaque – their words and actions noted, their outward appearance described, but their inner selves, their motives and feelings are ignored. Again, Amis has the best formulation of this view of women: 'It was queer how much colour women seemed to absorb from their men-friends, or even from the man they were with for the time being. That was bad when the man in question was bad; it was good when the man in question was good'.[35] The chameleon quality of women is noticed and described; the reasons for its existence are not even hinted at.

Perhaps the worst example of this superficial view of women is in the character of Jenny Bunn in *Take a Girl Like You*.[36] Amis gives us what he supposes are the inner workings of the mind of a girl of Jenny's class and background. It is apparent he has drawn his inspiration for Jenny's thoughts from a close perusal of the women's magazines of the period (his frequent references to the contents of his fictional magazine, *Women's Domain*, show how familiar he was with this type of publication), but he fails to perceive that the representation of women in such magazines, whether in their romantic stories or their advice pages, is itself a fiction.

Generally these novels of the so-called 'Angry Decade' are really old wine in new bottles. The backgrounds – lower-working-class life, Notting Hill Gate riots, the cavortings at the 'new' universities with their grammar school intake – cannot disguise the fact that the novels follow very traditional storytelling patterns, ranging from the knightly chivalric quest, through the *Bildungsroman* to the picaresque. In them, as in those traditional forms, women do not act, they are acted upon, and despite superficial modernity, heroines in postwar male fiction still perform the same passive role as in the past.

**The woman as pursuer**

In contrast, many women novelists during the same period placed women at the centre of their novels, exploring their characters and motives in a complex and realistic way. But though most of them had lived through major changes in the lives of women, they knew that the stereotypes presented as real women in male fiction were still accepted as true. In the past, women had been discouraged from taking an active role in the pursuit of lovers, and had had to choose from amongst those bold enough to approach them. This was still, to a certain extent, the case in the postwar period. Greater economic freedom for young women and the possibility of leaving their families and living on their own, or with other single women, stretched the convention of the passively waiting heroine and the bold adventurous young lover overcoming obstacles to get to her, but the convention that the woman did not overtly take the initiative still held. Living openly with a lover remained a daring thing to do; illegitimacy in those pre-pill days brought social disgrace, which could result in being cast out of your family and left to the hard charity of unmarried mothers' homes. A girl had to tread carefully, creating her own hedge of briars, thick enough to deter the seducer but not so thick as to frighten off the desired lover. The freedom of the young unattached woman had its dangers, for she herself had now to decide between the true and the false lover, without having the worldly experience her parents possessed. Even when young women continued to live at home before marriage, most now had jobs and expected to be able to mix freely with both sexes. Despite this wider field of action, ideas of passivity, or deferring to the male, of retaining 'femininity' while independent, meant that women could not obviously make the first approaches, nor take the initiative in lovemaking. It also meant that women could not make their desires clear, partly because they were discouraged from understanding themselves and partly because convention still decreed that femininity meant mystery: the woman who revealed all her secrets probably had none worth keeping. Given the traditional view of men as pursuers and women as the pursued, the problem for such women was how to pursue actively, while appearing to be passively waiting.

Both Elizabeth Jenkins and Barbara Pym have women characters who actively pursue the men of their choice. In *The Tortoise and the Hare*,[37] Elizabeth Jenkins draws the portrait of a plain, middle-aged and rather masculine woman who lures the husband of the delicately beautiful Imogen to her bed and eventually marries him. Elizabeth Jenkins analyses the subtle and careful moves Blanche makes to attract, against all odds, a handsome and eligible man.

Barbara Pym's heroines are also plain women, and they too actively pursue the men they desire, while at the same time taking care to cover their tracks. If they don't, they run the risk of becoming figures of fun. In *Jane and Prudence* and *A Glass of Blessings*,[38] Jessie Morrow and Mary Beamish are dim mousy creatures, the sort of women who are never really seen. But they too search for 'something to love', and when they find a man to love they pursue their ends singlemindedly.

Jessie Morrow's problem, in *Jane and Prudence*, is that she is a 'little brown woman' whom we first see, through the eyes of a more attractive woman, carrying a vase of dead flowers which seems to suggest that love's flowering is not for her. But Jessie's 'brownness' masks a shrewd intelligence and a sharp eye, and she uses these attributes to capture the handsome and eligible Fabian, stealing him from under the nose of the attractive Prudence. Realising that up to now Fabian has barely noticed her, she knows she has to shock him into seeing her as a woman. She starts by behaving out of character, then uses the skills of make-up to draw attention to herself, preparing her appearance in much the same way as a warrior prepares for battle. Her strategy works, Fabian is caught, and the neighbours have to come to terms with this surprising and unforeseen marriage – unforeseen because Jessie's bold manœuvres have taken place when she was alone with Fabian. In public she continues to play her usual role of self-effacing companion, thus cleverly avoiding the possibility of public ridicule should she fail.

In *A Glass of Blessings* a similar situation arises, described rather dismissively by the attractive Wilmet as that 'hopeless and hackneyed situation – dowdy parish worker in love with handsome celibate priest'.[39] Wilmet is blind to the reasons for Mary's sudden interest in dress, and is deeply shocked when Mary's brother suggests that Mary has been plotting to hook the handsome Marius Ransome. Wilmet prefers to believe that Mary had had no inkling of Marius's interest until he proposed to her and she rejects the cynical interpretation offered by Mary's approving brother.

Barbara Pym mildly satirises men's expectations of women, their seduction by what is superficial or false: a new dress, a thickly made-up face. Neither Jessica nor Mary sees anything useful in depending on intelligence or goodness; in fact the first quality can be a major deterrent. Barbara Pym does not portray these manœuvres negatively, though, and there is a suggestion throughout her fiction that women who are more realistic about the men they pursue will not suffer the disillusionment felt by more attractive and romantic heroines. What is more interesting is that her predatory heroines manage to appear passive in the mating game, while manœuvring with delicacy and skill to hook their fish.

## Passive, waiting heroines

Contrasted with this celebration of actively pursuing women, is the portrayal of women who follow the conventional guidelines. In *The Long View*,[40] Elizabeth Jane Howard suggests that the passive, waiting role can be dangerous; the isolated heroine, like an imprisoned princess, may become the victim of an unscrupulous adventurer. Antonia is a modern version of such a fairy-tale princess. Isolated from her contemporaries, she has no one to turn to or to confide in. Her mother is her rival and her enemy, and her father turns his hatred of women against his daughter. Antonia's passivity is stressed throughout the novel; as a young woman she sleeps during the day as well as at night, waiting to be awakened. She has no control over her own life and makes no effort to take charge. She is never self-defined, always other-defined, even though she is perceptive enough to know that these other-definitions are false. Purely defensive in her reactions to injury, she retires deeper and deeper into her shell. Her very innocence and purity ensure her destruction. Because of her beauty she becomes a 'prize', her beauty always attracting the wrong man. Yet outwardly she fulfils the conventional expectations of women: marriage to a well-to-do man, motherhood. Her story ends in desertion and isolation. Superficially it may seem that the character of Antonia is that of the conventional passive heroine, like those portrayed by Elizabeth Jane Howard's male contemporaries. But because her viewpoint is totally different, the reader begins to apprehend exactly what has turned an intelligent and responsive young girl into a withdrawn matron.

Elizabeth Jane Howard's portrayal of Antonia is more sympathetic than her portrayal of another passive heroine in her first novel, *The Beautiful Visit*. In this novel she contrasted the attitudes of two young women: her heroine, who is determined to take control of her own life, and the sister, who has accepted the traditional passive role of women, who states that 'things don't matter', who 'could sew and read and go to church, and for walks, and stay the same size, and complete herself within that tiny sphere'.[41] The heroine (unnamed in the novel)[42] rejects her sister's philosophy, and though this rejection leads to hardship, in the end she is freed, while the sister who had accepted her passive role goes mad.

## Women-centred and male-centred love stories

Essentially, then, women writers during these two decades after the Second World War express a viewpoint that is fundamentally different from that current in their time. While accepting that love itself can be rapturous, they are less enthusiastic about the lover. At a time when the debate about women concentrated on their function rather than their nature – when the question 'What *can* a woman do?' was ignored in favour of 'What *should* a woman do?' – these writers seemed little concerned with morality and rules, emphasising instead women's needs in terms of love and lovers. They challenge the critical assumption that, because the male supposedly represents the universal, an inability to depict male characters satisfactorily excludes women writers from 'great' literature. According to this view, inability to draw rounded, credible women characters is not a flaw, since women are marginal to the male quest, and it is therefore acceptable for male storytellers to use stereotypes of women to represent a limited range of options for the hero as lover: madonna, whore, temptress, witch, and so on. I think that when critics devalue women's novels because of their authors' so-called inability to create credible men, they are applying male-centred rules, without understanding the *function* of heroes and lovers in women's fiction. Not all women writers centre their fiction on the women's viewpoint, but when they do, and when they are exploring women's dreams and wishes about love and lovers, the male heroes they create represent facets of men which make them, *from the woman's point of view*, true or false lovers. This fundamental difference between woman-centred and male-centred fiction needs to be accepted more widely, so that the premises on which narrow critical judgements, such as that made in *The Observer* by Godfrey Smith, on Margaret Drabble's male characters,[43] will be seen as false.

In effect, then, what women novelists of this period appear to be saying is that, regardless of the real difficulties heterosexual love involves, it is still an experience worth having. They are realistic about the strategies women use in their pursuit of love and aware of the self-deception needed to be happy with their choice of lover. Even so, it *is* still 'better to have loved and lost than never to have loved at all'. When they come to write about marriage, though, the picture is less clear.

# 2

# Happily ever after? The consequences of acceptance

'I married you,' he said slowly and clearly, 'because you are going to be extremely beautiful, which means for me that you will be a pleasure to see, a delight to be with, and because, possessing you, I shall be envied by others.'[1]

. . . the tragedy of marriage is not that it fails to assure woman the promised happiness . . . but that it mutilates her; it dooms her to repetition and routine.[2]

During the postwar period marriage was considered woman's prime, if not only, career choice. While this view was reinforced by the romantic fiction of the period, other fiction written by women chose to question the bland assumptions behind the 'happily ever after' ending. Their ambivalence about such happy endings was centred on the woman's choice of husband rather than on marriage itself.

## Women and marriage

There is a fundamental difference between a love story written by a man, from a man's point of view, and a love story written from a woman's standpoint. The male love story's happy resolution is partly the satisfaction of the hero's lust, but more importantly the setting of a seal on his life. What he does, where he lives, his status, power and financial standing are not usually dependent on whom he marries. They may be affected by a spendthrift or faithless wife, or his way forward can be aided by a wealthy and supportive wife, but essentially his life follows the lines he sets down. A male love story is more about the hero's pursuit of the life he wants to live than about his pursuit of the loved one.

The female love story is about the choice of a future. A sensible woman must not only balance passion and practicality, but assess a man's character well enough to predict his future as breadwinner, for despite all the freedom women now have to enter the world of work and earn money, few can achieve anything near economic parity with men. Postwar Britain, with its emphasis on marriage as the major career choice for women and its insistence on working women as a reserve labour force, only underlined how crucial it was for women to make the right choice of marriage partner. Yet if women wanted advice on this important matter they really had nowhere to turn. Romantic fiction, whether in the form of novels or women's magazine stories, was escapist. Advice columns seemed to be more concerned about attracting *any* male, and said little about how to judge the male attracted. Marriage itself was the goal, rather than the achievement of happiness or financial security. Women were encouraged to view themselves as product, something the successful male would acquire to add lustre to his life. By choosing marriage, women fulfilled the role society expected, their femininity was attested and they proved they were true women. At the same time, traditional 'happily ever after' endings in fiction reinforced the view that marriage marks the end of a woman's growth; that once she gets her man her 'story' is told.

Some women writers of this period questioned this assumption, portraying the narrowing of horizons that it led to. They did this in several ways: by portraying marriage realistically from the woman's point of view; by setting out the dangers that lay in passive acceptance of a role; and by describing happy marriages that broke contemporary stereotypes.

### 'Clouded' happy endings

Women writers sometimes cast doubts on conventional love stories by using 'clouded' happy endings to suggest that reliance on finding happiness and fulfilment solely through marriage was self-deluding. An example is Olivia Manning's *The Doves of Venus*,[3] which ends with Ellie's marriage, bringing to a conclusion Ellie's search for a more challenging life and reuniting her with her mother, whose only ambition for her daughters has been marriage. Unemployed, hungry, Ellie has found Simon and marriage, and she returns triumphantly to visit her mother, whose disapproval of Ellie's bid for independence turns into glowing approbation of her daughter's fulfilment of the 'true' end for a woman: '"Both my girls married before they're twenty. I never dared hope for such happiness"', she gloats.[4] Earlier, at the age of fourteen, Ellie had envisaged a different future, full of vague but exciting possibilities: '"What am I?"' she had written in her diary then, '"What will *I* become?"'[5] The breadth of these questions has narrowed to the answer, 'Another wife'. For these questions do not belong to the heroine; the only question she is supposed to ask herself is, 'Who will I marry?'. The apparently happy ending to *The Doves of Venus* is undermined by the cynicism of the older married men around Ellie, who remind her she will grow old and that husbands rarely remain faithful.

Throughout the novel Ellie's dependence on men has been emphasised, so the reader is left uncertain about what really awaits her in the future. Another shadow is cast over her marriage by the ironical juxtaposition of the start of Ellie's marriage and the end of Petta's life as a successful 'femme fatale'. Petta has depended all her life on her beauty and her ability to attract men, on being a 'pet' as her name suggests, but by the time Ellie becomes engaged to Simon, the ageing Petta has sunk to grasping at whatever man she can find. Petta's end as a rejected wife and mistress adds weight to the married men's warnings to Ellie about her new marriage and suggests that Ellie's dependence on men may eventually bring her to the same end as Petta.

Elizabeth Taylor, too, brings ambivalence to her 'happy endings'. *Palladian*[6] echoes *Jane Eyre* in its plot – penniless governess falls in love and marries her employer – and its heroine, Cassandra, is fully aware of the Jane Eyre overtones of her situation. Here it is not so much the social pressures towards conformity, as Cassandra's predilection for romantic love stories, which causes her blindness. Like a female Quixote, her expectations of life and love are based on what she has read and she interprets events in the light of what this has taught her. Knowing what is due to the heroine of a novel, she feels sure she will marry

Marion and live happily ever after. But Marion is no reformed Rochester, Copthorne Manor is crumbling away and drunken Tom and fearsome Nanny remain. Cassandra has failed to gain her independence, as Jane Eyre did, and her flight from Copthorne Manor does not lead to growth but is a return to her beginning and to the enclosing comforts of Mrs Turner's sitting room. Like Ellie in *The Doves of Venus*, she has chosen marriage as a way out of the only other fate that seems to await her, that of a lonely school-mistress. Faced with so meagre a choice, Cassandra flees from one dead-end only to embrace another. It is not surprising that when Tinty, Marion's aunt, suggests that Cassandra's marriage is 'like one of the fairy tales', Marion's cousin, Margaret, remarks drily, '"But not a fairy tale in which I should want to be the heroine . . . One begins to see what is meant by 'They lived happily ever after'."[7]

Similarly *The Sleeping Beauty*[8] ends with Emily's marriage to Vinny, but shadows fall across that 'happy ending'. Not only is the marriage bigamous – and known to be so by others – but Vinny's curious sexual distaste for the female body may awaken if Emily should reassume her old identity, that of a sexually adventurous woman. Like Ellie and Cassandra, Emily has not grown, merely exchanged an unhappy passivity for a happier one. Her new identity is not her own, merely one that Vinny has created for her. The awakened Emily is no more real than the almost catatonic Emily that Vinny has found. He has 'invented' her and she has become a fiction in his mind.

*A View of the Harbour*[9] also ends with a marriage between the elderly Bertram, who has never been married before, and Tory, a divorcee who is deeply in love with her best friend's husband and needs to avoid betraying her friend by distancing herself. Bertram has married for home comforts; Tory to suppress her illicit passion. It is impossible to imagine this marriage will be a happy one.

**Marriage as dead end**

Another way that writers questioned ideas about marriage was by dissecting marriage itself, looking critically at that period of life which starts with the 'happily ever after'. Their novels focus on women's discontent, rather than men's, assuming that whereas men have an outer, public life from which they can gain satisfaction, no such mitigation of discontent is available to the wife, who is expected to derive all her satisfaction from her private function as wife and mother.

In Elizabeth Jane Howard's *The Beautiful Visit*,[10] Deb's apparently successful marriage has become a desert for her, totally lacking in meaning. She wants to exchange the dull certainties of marriage for 'excitement, uncertainty and love', and attempts to explain her feelings to an uncomprehending husband. She expresses the disillusion many women feel about the narrowing, rather than the widening they had hoped for: '"I thought marriage meant *more* freedom, not less. I didn't know it meant years of plans, and having children, and sitting by myself all day."'[11] Feeling that even her sexuality is taken for granted – a bit of home comfort that can be turned on or off at the end of the day, depending on Aubrey's needs, not hers – she complains of the passionless predictability of marital sex:

> 'Whatever we do I know that at the end of every day you will empty your money out of your pockets and spill it over the dressing-table and undress. You will open the window, draw back the curtain, and make some remark about the night. Then you will climb into bed with me and we shall lie side by side in the dark. Then either you will say that you have had a frightful day and kiss my forehead, or you will make love to me. It all happens like that.'[12]

Deb wants a lover, but the lover in Aubrey has vanished, replaced by a man who only demands the small physical satisfactions of a comfortable married life. His excitement can come from the rest of his life, with his home as a 'haven'; Deb, representing that haven, must not have requirements that do not match his.

Barbara Pym, too, wrote about the differences between the needs and expectations of women and men in marriage. Like Deb, Jane, in *Jane and Prudence*, craves romance, love – but all she gets are 'mild, kindly looks and spectacles'.[13] The days when she quoted poetry to her husband have faded and gone. Barbara Pym's treatment of marriage is critical and ironic, but not tragic. She celebrates women's ability to extract satisfaction from their unsatisfactory lives, and even in her later, darker novels, this capacity for 'coping' can save some, if not all. She shows her women having to accept that though they are expected to put marriage and the family at the centre of their lives, they cannot assume that men will do likewise. They must resign themselves to being marginal in men's lives, a comforting background which men can almost forget, like Fabian, whose wife's death 'came as a great shock to him – he had almost forgotten her existence'.[14] Fabian – like many other married men in Barbara Pym's fiction – does not want excitement in his marriage; he can go elsewhere for that. The romantic Jane, contemplating Fabian's choice of dull, plain Jessie for his wife, instead of glamorous Prudence, reflects, 'Perhaps this was after all what men like to come home to, someone restful and neutral, who had no thought of changing the curtains or wallpapers?'[15] The 'background' role of women in marriage is one that not all women resent and, even when they do, they often resign themselves to jogging along in marriages which are unsatisfactory but not too destructive. But where there is deeper disillusion, there are two paths open: rebellion or passive acceptance.

## Passive acceptance

Elizabeth Jane Howard's *The Long View*[16] is a bleak description of what happens to a woman who resigns herself to a half-life. Antonia's passivity is not even rewarded by success: in middle age she is cast aside by her husband and left totally alone. The character of Antonia could very easily have infuriated the reader but for Elizabeth Jane Howard's subtle understanding of how she came to choose such a self-defeating path. The novel itself moves backwards through Antonia's life, from the moment of her husband's final desertion to her first love affair, picking significant moments which gradually reveal what has led to Conrad's desertion and her loneliness. The structure of the novel not only makes cause and effect clearer, but because the reader knows the end of Antonia's story, her ineffective struggles to retain happiness become tinged with irony. But it is not until the reader comes to the last section, which is, in fact, the beginning of Antonia's life as an adult woman, that she fully understands the reasons for the almost infuriating passivity that Antonia has shown in her marriage. This last part ends with Conrad entering Antonia's life. Without the knowledge we already have, it might seem a new dawn for her. But the reader has not had to wait until the end of the novel to learn of Conrad's bad faith. By the time she reaches Conrad's promise to Antonia – ' "You will not be by yourself. I shall see to it that you are never alone. I love you, you see." [17] – she already knows that the promise will be broken, and the earlier description of an older Conrad, heartless in his egoism, remains to haunt the young Conrad in his guise of the 'true' lover. The 'happy ending' comes so long after we know what that happy ending truly means, that it is impossible not to feel that all such happy endings are suspect.

The description of Antonia's marriage carries many of the features other women writers use: the mutual incompatibility between women and men in marriage; the need for self-abnegation by the women to avoid conflict, which in turn leads to a passive acceptance; and the terrifying isolation that awaits a woman who has invested all in her marriage. Conrad's insistence that Antonia's only role is to be his wife, and his refusal to see Antonia except in relation to himself, at first causes Antonia to rebel against this alteration of herself, but she fails to assert her separateness and individuality, and the more she bends herself to Conrad's will, the less she prepares herself for at last being on her own.

Of all the writers I mention, Elizabeth Jane Howard is the most effectively chilling in her descriptions of isolation and loneliness. Her heroines seem cut off from all other human comforts: no family on whom they can rely, no close women friends whom they can trust and reach out to for comfort. Antonia has been rejected by family and lovers and is no closer to her two children than she was to her parents. She has nothing and no one to fall back on. The heroine of *The Beautiful Visit* [18] is the same: distanced from her family, her lover dead, and even her friend, Elspeth, a shadowy, symbolic figure, not a flesh and blood woman friend.

Barbara Comyns's view of marriage is more difficult to ascertain. Sophia's and Charles's marriage in *Our Spoons Came from Woolworths* [19] is a modern version of the Clerk of Oxford's story in Chaucer's *The Canterbury Tales*. Sophia too appears to be a 'patient Griselde', a naïve and unworldly young girl who accepts the selfishness and neglect of her artist husband without complaint. There are significant differences though: Sophia resents her fate, has an affair and, at one point, even attacks her infuriating husband with a chair. But she claims she is ashamed of her unfaithfulness and even of her quite justified attack on Charles. I say 'claims', because my own view of Sophia's motive appears to differ from other critics and may also differ from the author's. The blurb on the Virago edition talks of the 'endearing, ebullient Sophia' and it mentions her 'child-like eyes'. But Sophia is twenty-one years old at the beginning of the novel, and by the end, when she is supposedly narrating her own story, she is well into her thirties. She is no innocent child, yet the writing suggests a naïve and inexperienced, almost simple-minded young girl.

*Our Spoons Came from Woolworths* is interesting because, unlike the other novels I mention, it contains descriptions of poverty and the life of a couple without money. It is not working-class poverty, which develops its own survival skills, but middle-class poverty, which must not be admitted. Charles takes no notice of the fact that his wife and child are almost starving, and Sophia's increasing desperation has to be hidden as she has no network of support and advice. The attitude of the nurses in a charity maternity hospital to the poor patients, and the unthinking callousness of Sophia's employers when she takes a job in the country as a cook–housekeeper, imply a critical social awareness on the part of Barbara Comyns, but this is undermined later when Sophia, about to marry rich Rollo, looks forward to ringing a little bell to summon a servant. The novel is an expression of indignation that a middle-class young woman such as Sophia, who can appreciate the theatre and meals out, should be treated as a mere servant by the family who employed her, rather than a critique of class divisions in society.

On the surface, Sophia appears a passive victim, suffering her fate without striking back. Yet I find that Sophia, while appearing as victim, is actually wily and manipulative, somehow putting everyone else in the wrong. The effect is heightened because Sophia is the narrator of her story; she controls the material and can control the effect it has. The novel is narrated in a babyish, 'faux-naïf' style, as if Sophia were a young child, and it opens with Sophia telling her story and getting the inevitable reaction:

> I told Helen my story and she went home and cried. In the evening her husband came to see me and brought some strawberries; he mended my bicycle too, and was kind, but he needn't have, because it all happened eight years ago, and I'm not unhappy now.[20]

The opening words tell the reader exactly who is the victim, and we are prepared to view Charles as the villain right from the beginning.

The reader is given no time to decide from what viewpoint she will regard events. Throughout the novel, Sophia manipulates the reader's sympathies, leaving her no choice in her interpretation of events. Sophia is the pathetic victim; her story will have the same effect on us as it had on Helen and her husband. Yet Sophia portrays herself as unaware of the way sympathy can be gained by telling her 'sad story', and when she meets Rollo, he too is treated to the story of her life:

> Then I told him about Fanny and all about Peregrine and his disgusting wife, and any other odds and ends of awful things I could remember doing. He heard them all, but it only seemed to make him love me even more. We became engaged to be marrried.[21]

Tears, strawberries, a husband – Sophia's 'sad story' produces some very pleasant rewards. This passage also demonstrates another aspect of Sophia's character: her belief (pretence?) that it is really she who is in the wrong, that when she tells her story it is really a confession of her guilt, and she claims she is surprised when her listeners treat her as an innocent victim. It is a technique which Barbara Comyns uses in other novels to extract sympathy for her victim women.

The role of the helpless victim can be used to bind people to the victim in pity and guilt and Sophia frequently uses the strategem. I find it difficult to believe that Barbara Comyns was unaware of what she was doing, but I am unsure where her own sympathies lie. Perhaps she too, like Sophia, hides from herself her own anger, or perhaps she is, more subtly, portraying a woman who could play the helpless victim, while cunningly ensuring that even if she was trapped, others should not escape guilt-free. There is one intriguing interpolation in the text that suggests the latter interpretation. While working as a cook in the country after she has left her husband, Sophia adopts a young foxcub who does not take to Rollo and behaves badly when he is around, on one occasion biting him. Rollo insists that Sophia get rid of Foxy before she marries him. She takes Foxy to the woods and leaves him:

> In the night I heard him barking in the garden and went out to him in my nighty and he jumped up into my arms, so I took him back and had him in my bed all night. But early in the morning I took him a long way away, several miles. I carried him all the way.[22]

Her parting from Foxy leaves her feeling 'too sad to cry'. Foxy appears to represent that cunning part of Sophia's character which enables her to retain her femininity while at the same time ensuring that anyone who behaves badly to her will be seen in the worst possible light. Sophia also thinks that the reason Foxy is so aggressive towards Rollo is because he doesn't like men, and this makes it even more likely that he represents Sophia's anger against what the men in her life have done to her. It is not uncommon for women writers to project their heroines' inadmissible emotions on to the natural world. Sophia can eventually give up Foxy because, married to Rollo – the perfect husband – she no longer has need of this wily side of her nature and her anger against men is dispersed.

Foxes, of course, do not just personify cunning. They also symbolise the wild, untenable, non-law-abiding side of human nature. Interestingly, a later novel of Barbara Comyn's, published in 1987 but apparently written in the 1950s, is entitled *Mr Fox*.[23] In it, the heroine – another Comyns 'victim' – has an ambiguous relationship with a Mr Fox, who is a kindly and not-too-successful 'wide boy'.[24] Through his help, the heroine survives the austerities of the war years, but it is her revelaton of his presence in her life that destroys her chance of happiness with another man. Again, the suggestion is that it is the 'foxy' aspect of female coping skills that is unacceptable and that men prefer female 'victims' who do not scheme to survive on any terms.

Sophia, in *Our Spoons Came From Woolworths*, seems to be aware of this and plays the game so as to appear completely at the mercy of the men in her life, while ensuring that her victim status gives her power over others. It is, unfortunately, a power game that only gives Sophia minor satisfactions. It may temporarily induce others to do things for her, or to feel sorry for her, but at no point does it empower her to take active control of her own life. She is never an agent, only the passive recipient of good or bad fortune.

## Marriage, the family and femininity

Not all writers were pessimistic about marriage. Elizabeth Goudge's fiction enshrines all the postwar beliefs about women: her heroines are 'true' women who fulfil themselves as wives and mothers, providing a steady centre for their more volatile men. Her heroes are often flawed, with some weakness they have to learn to overcome, and they are aided in this by the love of a good and wise woman. Goudge constantly emphasised the need for resignation to the role of wife and mother, even when this required considerable self-sacrifice. However, her novels are not gloomy; they belong firmly in the comedic range, and her endings are always happy. She made no apology for this, once stating:

> I know that happy endings are sometimes inartistic, and certainly, not always true to life, but I can't write any other kind. I am not a serious chronicler of the very terrible contemporary scene, but just a story teller, and there is so much tragedy about us everywhere today that we surely don't want it in the story books to which we turn when we are ill or unhappy, or can't go to sleep at night. We must escape somewhere.[25]

She is also essentially a moral writer and there is a didactic quality to her writing. This is how women should be, she seems to say, pointing with approval to heroines such as Lucilla, Stella and Sally.[26] Her heroes, on the other hand, are imperfect, and she suggests it is up to their women to devote themselves to helping them attain wisdom and to be their final reward at the end.

There seems little to choose between Elizabeth Goudge's fictional treatment of women and that of contemporary male novelists, but there are curious contradictions. Brought up in a strictly Christian tradition (her father was in the church) she learned her storytelling skills from her mother and the family's cook, who filled her head with folk and fairy tales. The philosophical underpinnings of her novels are a mixture of traditional Christian beliefs and fairy lore, with a generous dash of Manichaean heresy, and although she appears to endorse the Christain view, it is the fairy element that has captured her heart. Her attitude to Christian belief is often ambivalent and her overt allegiance to Christianity is subverted by her mixing it with earlier pagan beliefs. Her characters generally have their mystical experiences, not in a church or Christian sacred place, but in woods: in, effectively, the 'green' world,[27] which is pre-Christian. She herself said she didn't like church services, and she held some naïve beliefs in ghosts, spectral singers and even fairies, thus rejecting the church establishment in favour of her more idiosyncratic beliefs.[28] A spinster herself, who at one time wrote that she had 'lived to "thank God fasting" for the single state',[29] she wrote wholly approvingly of marriage and of the traditional role of women in marriage. A Labour supporter with considerable social awareness of the fundamental injustice of society and a deep compassion for the poor, she was smitten with love for the aristocracy and for those of, what she called, 'gentle birth'. Many of her lovers and her 'good' characters have somewhere in their background noble blood and she correlates this with the nobility of their characters. She shows sympathy and insight into the sufferings of the dispossessed – her description of the conditions in Newgate prison during the Napoleonic period is a masterly combination of vivid picture-making and compassion for the prisoners, brutalised by their surroundings[30] – but she seems unable to make the connections between cause and effect that lie behind socialist philosophy.

These contradictions, coupled with a genuine storytelling talent and a gift for the description of people and places, form a body of fiction that openly makes conventional statements about women and their role, but at the same time subverts those same statements by making her good, conforming women not only somewhat unreal, but at times slightly repellent. For example, Lucilla, in the Eliot trilogy,[31] is beautiful and beloved by all. Yet her worship of her youngest son and her grandson David is contrasted with her selfish exploitation of her daughter Margaret. Margaret, plain and un-loved, takes on the full burden of the running and maintenance of Damerosehay so that Lucilla can lead the gracious life she feels is her due. Margaret also has to face the fact that for all her devoted service and hard work, she cannot command love as Lucilla, without lifting a finger for anyone, can, and she asks the agonising question, ' "Why must it be only women of charm who can know the fullness of life?" '[32] It is a question which Elizabeth Goudge, throughout her fiction, tries to avoid answering.

While appearing to condone Lucilla's attitude to her plain and clumsy daughter (Lucilla is, after all, entitled to her gracious lifestyle by dint of her beauty and noble birth), Elizabeth Goudge's real feelings about the unfairness of the treatment of plain women slip through the text and an almost bitter note is heard, though she seems to recover and continues to present.Lucilla as the ideal of womanhood. Yet even while portraying Lucilla as a good woman, Elizabeth Goudge undermines the picture over and over again. Lucilla's rejection of her son Hilary and her daughter Margaret on the grounds of their plainness (she thinks of Margaret as a 'frump') is contrasted with their selfless devotion to her, and there is a sharp ironic tone in the following passage which describes Lucilla's attitude to the servant problem:

> It was strange how few domestics were attracted by the thought of living in a marsh; or by the prospect of cooking for children and dogs. Lucilla thought it very sad that the hearts of the proletariat should be so singularly unsusceptible to the beauties of the country, to the loveliness of child nature and the charms of canine character. She mourned a good deal over this unsusceptibility, which she felt to be a not altogether reassuring characteristic of modern national life. Margaret had no time to mourn. It was all she could do to get the work done.[33]

The passage is almost worthy of Barbara Pym, but its tone clashes with the prevailing tone of the novels, which is romantic and sentimental, not ironic. Perhaps there were two writers struggling to get out in Elizabeth Goudge: the romantic, sensuous, but traditional storyteller, and the acute observer of human failings. The spirit of the period she wrote in is accepted and fostered in her fiction, but every now and again she allows questions about its assumptions to slip through the text.

Elizabeth Goudge's duality as a writer is reflected in the use of doubles in her novels. Sometimes these doubles are two people, as in the case of the white and the black witch in *The White Witch*;[34] at other times it is the same person who displays two contradictory facets. Her frequent references to the old Manichaean belief in the warring forces of good and evil in the world, and her portrayal of divided characters, result in the conflict in her novels being portrayed as a fight between these two forces. The confrontation between good and evil is sometimes portrayed fairly simplistically, as in *The White Witch*, sometimes more subtly, as in the characters of Lucilla and Nadine in the Eliot trilogy.

Of all her fiction, the three novels that make up the Eliot trilogy – *The Bird in the Tree, The Herb of Grace* and *The Heart of the Family* – are the most concerned with exploring Elizabeth Goudge's ideas on marriage and women's role in it. The novels span the period from just before the Second World War to 1951, and they reflect some of the changes taking place during that period. The final novel in the series, published at the beginning of the fifties decade, is the most uncompromising in its imposition of the wife/mother role as the true path to womanhood. One of the central themes in these Eliot novels is the conflict between two of the women: Lucilla, the head of the Eliot family, the 'good' wife, and Nadine, the wife of her son George, the 'bad' wife. Just as the black and white witch are opposed in *The White Witch*, so Lucilla and Nadine represent opposing forces, not, as in that novel, of absolute good and evil, but of the good wife and mother versus the bad wife and mother. The life-and-death struggle between them is based on Lucilla's determination to ensure her son George's happiness, even at the cost of Nadine's. There is also a suggestion that the differences between Lucilla and Nadine are not absolute; both are extremely beautiful women who always put men first in their lives, both are married to husbands considerably older than themselves who cannot awaken passion in them, both transfer this passion to a son, and, in Lucilla's case, to her grandson David as well. Both have had the same temptation: to leave their husband for another, younger lover, abandoning the children. The difference is that Lucilla has accepted her sacrifice as right from the beginning; Nadine is less wholehearted.

I must assume that the evidence of Elizabeth Goudge's fiction – her happy endings, her emphasis on the primary importance of the wife/mother role, coupled with her prevailing tone which is didactic and romantic – is that she did believe that this *was* the best role for women. She wrote many of her novels in a period during which this belief was loudly voiced, and her immense popularity with the reading public probably owed as much to her acceptance of these beliefs as to her talent as a storyteller. The novels about the Eliot family were particularly popular, and the third, *The Heart of the Family*,[35] was written, according to Elizabeth Goudge, in response to a demand from her readers to continue the story of the Eliots. The claustrophobic nature of that family, the almost total isolation in which they lived their lives, with even the men's working lives only shadowily conveyed, the semi-feudal relationship they have with their servants and the portrayal of village life as a rosy bucolic frolic, must have fed the dreams of many who found the postwar world harsh and dismissive of their middle-class expectations.

A reader today would probably find Lucilla's selfish autocratic ways unendurable, and sympathise more with the less perfect, but more human, Nadine. Equally, in the same novel, Sally's total self-abasement in her marriage to David, is depicted by Elizabeth

Goudge as truly womanly, whereas it might now be interpreted as spineless and even masochistic. Perhaps Elizabeth Goudge's postwar readers might have felt differently, but some may have noted the contradictions which surface oddly from time to time, as for example in the almost schizophrenic nature of the following observation (made twice in the novels) when Elizabeth Goudge's sharp eye results in a sharp pen, which is immediately self-censored:

> But David, standing where all the Eliot men always stood, in front of the fire so that none of the warmth could reach their female relatives (though to do them justice they did not think of this, Lucilla not having the heart to point it out) . . . [36]

This is a curious interpolation in a text that wholly agrees with the notion that women's true end in life is to serve their men self-sacrificingly. The short passage itself reads awkwardly, as if two forces were pulling in contrary directions. Later there is a revealing glimpse of Lucilla's real motives in manipulating those around her 'for their own good':

> Lucilla's lovely blue eyes were alight with love as she smiled upon her obedient daughter-in-law. That horrid tight feeling that came about her heart when people opposed her eased a little. It was a nasty feeling, and people would never oppose her if they knew how nasty it was. [37]

For a moment the tyrannical monster peeps out from behind the lovely, selfless mask of Lucilla's maternal love, but the insight is as quickly relinquished. On the other hand, plain, clumsy, unloved Margaret is never portrayed as anything but what she appears to be: lovingly self-sacrificing and devoted to her family. Lucilla, whose love for the male members of her household makes her use all her skills of dissimulation to spare their feelings, allows her daughter, Margaret, to be aware of her contempt and impatience towards her, and this further undermines the reader's approval of Lucilla and, by extension, her views on marriage and women's duties.

These ambiguities and contradictions are only a very small part of Elizabeth Goudge's fiction, but they do suggest reservations in Elizabeth Goudge's own mind about the redemptive views she appears to hold. Her endorsement of conventional views about marriage didn't prevent her from portraying some of her fictional marriages as not completely happy,[38] and these flawed marriages seem more real than the happy ones, such as Stella's and Zachary's fairytale marriage in *Gentian Hill*. It is not happiness Elizabeth Goudge is extolling, but duty; acceptance and self-suppression are a woman's lot in marriage and rebellion is frowned upon.

Even though not all marriages portrayed in postwar fiction were unhappy, what many of the women novelists suggested was that, even when a marriage was happy, attitudes to a woman's place in the family were subtly corrupting. The family could become a prison for a woman, and if she was unable to escape, she needed to find a socially acceptable strategy to exercise power. One such strategy was to use her 'femininity' to make sure that others shared the prison with her, and she could do this by enslaving and controlling husband and children. This is what happens in Susan Ertz's *Charmed Circle*.[39] At the beginning of the novel, the reader is introduced to what, at first, appears to be the perfect family. The Prentisses and their children lead charmed lives, with Myron and Ruth devoting themselves to each other and to their children, shutting out the rest of the world so that they can create the perfect family. Slowly the reader comes to realise that at the centre of this perfection there is a moral vacuum and the first faint whiff of decay strengthens into something more nauseous. Gradually cracks appear in this idyllic family life – not in the relationship between Myron and Ruth, but in the failure of their children to grow to maturity. The 'charmed circle' of the title is, of course, the family: totally inward-looking, selfish, lacking in any social awareness, assuming its right to all the good things of life and refusing to accept responsibility for the results of its self-absorption. Initially everyone colludes in keeping the Prentisses happy and undisturbed; Syl may say with bitterness, '"They never in all their lives looked an unpleasant fact in the face"',[40] but Syl himself has played a major part in ensuring that they didn't have to. The charming Prentisses turn into monsters before our eyes, their happy marriage and mutual absorption portrayed as gross flaws. Myron and Ruth's fight to keep the family circle intact results in two tragic deaths (one of them their younger son's) and their daughter's failure to become a mature woman. Only their elder son, Halley, escapes their net. He does this by doing what none of his family have been able to do: he accepts responsibility for his own acts and, once he gains self-awareness of his faults, he can grow and become mature.

Susan Ertz uses Halley as narrator to reveal to the reader her own attitude to the social irresponsibility and self-delusion of the moneyed and the privileged. Halley, noticing humorously and affectionately that his parents claim to be no richer than other people, reflects:

> The wealthy, or at least the more refined wealthy, like not only to minimise their wealth but to minimise to themselves the power and privilege that wealth brings and the gulf that exists between those who have far more than they need and those who have far less.[41]

The reader, less seduced by the charm of the Prentisses, is chilled. Halley's perception of his family alters, particularly when he sees his parents' callous reaction to Fred's suicide, for which they are largely to blame, and he begins to understand how these apparently loving and unauthoritarian parents create fear and the need for secrecy in their children. For the children know that the one unforgivable crime against the family is to attempt to leave it, and their half-hearted attempts to lead their own lives have to be based on deception and lies. It is not that the Prentisses overtly punish their children for their bids for freedom; it is just that yielding to their parents' wishes will make life 'highly agreeable', the reward for obedience being comfort and safety. Disobedience might mean expulsion from the family and an insecure and comfortless existence. Again it is Halley who sees what is wrong: 'we swam without directives, without guidance, in a degree of warmth which perfectly suited us; primitive, uni-cellular creatures, our every need supplied'.[42]

Halley does escape, and at the end of the novel turns down his father's plea that he return to America to become again a member of the Prentiss family. But Susan Ertz does not like simple, happy endings, and the final paragraph suggests that perhaps Halley's escape has not been as complete as suggested:

> I knew that in spite of everything I loved them all, and as I drove back to Chelsea I wondered whether, perhaps, there might not be a good deal of truth in what my father had been saying; whether, perhaps, taking the long view (and if Selma agreed), I ought not to make up my mind to go back. Only in that way could I help to close the ugly gap in the circle made by Julian's death.[43]

Implicit in this novel is a strong critique of the ideology of the 'family' when it is used to impose patterns on people's lives and to exclude those who do not conform to it.[44] The novel had particular relevance in the postwar world, now examining the rise and fall of fascism and its emphasis on such ideologies. It also shows how a powerful woman, denied a legitimate outlet for her intelligence and strength of character, turns into a monster. Ruth Prentiss resembles Lucilla, in the Goudge novels, in her manipulative strategies. Her son, Halley, describes her as 'softly implacable', a good description of his mother, who, while retaining her femininity and ensuring that everyone will do anything for her, particularly her husband and sons, allows no criticism to reach her and no pity to sway her. The soft marshmallow exterior conceals a steel core and she coldly exploits the love and devotion of those around her. The ideal of family life, so prevalent in the postwar period, is held up for examination, its bland mask stripped away to reveal what narrow conformity to the roles imposed in family life can lead to. In some ways it prefigures Friedan's *The Feminine Mystique*[45] in its awareness of how the idealisation of the wife and mother not only mutilates the woman herself but leads to the emotional crippling of her children.

Another woman corrupted by adherence to the ideal of femininity is portrayed in Mary McMinnies' *The Visitors*.[46] Like Lucilla, Milly is the type of woman who does not need to lift a finger to inspire devotion. Not only men fall into her net, women do too. However, Milly uses her powers of seduction to feed her own vanity and acquisitiveness and the results of her meddling are catastrophic to everyone but herself. Milly's power lies in the fact that not only is she beautiful, but she knows what men require from women and she supplies it. From within the protection of her marriage, she flirts and teases, well aware of the techniques she uses. The lessons in the art of being 'feminine' have been well learned and Milly knows exactly what she is doing. Here she is talking to herself:

> You are naughty, Milly. She giggled. Naughty was a word she rather enjoyed as applied to herself or her actions; entirely acceptable, implying femininity, coquetry, innocent misdemeanours to be forgiven with a loving kiss – it covered so much.[47]

Men have often found the child-woman immensely seductive and women have learned to play this role. Milly is no fool; she knows the rewards for feminine irresponsibility are solid, those for responsible adulthood in a woman doubtful. She is also aware that her charming irresponsibility is a construct and that she will be absolved of all blame for its harmful consequences. She does not even have to be responsible for looking after her home or her children, as her husband's diplomatic status ensures that these duties will be carried out by paid employees. Milly can only continue to play her game within the protective confines of marriage. No demands are made on her, no decisions required. It is not possible to blame Milly entirely for the tragedies she causes, for the men collude in her irresponsibility.

Mary McMinnies' novel challenges the acceptance of the ideal of femininity by exposing the way Milly's successful personification of this ideal causes anguish, betrayal, and even the death of two women – one a totally innocent victim, the other, almost a Milly 'double', uses all the wiles in her power, but fails because, unlike Milly, she is unprotected by a husband and is vulnerable to the political uncertainties in postwar communist Europe. The cause of these tragedies is Milly's feminine ignorance about the country she is in and the danger she, a privileged foreigner protected by her husband's diplomatic status, represents to those who have to survive in a politically repressive regime. Milly, and the adoring admirers who surround her, have ignored the fact that 'innocent misdemeanours' are what children are guilty of; an adult woman's actions have considerably greater consequences.

## Happy marriages

It seems, then, that the picture of marriage as represented in these novels is one of disillusion, unhappiness and even mutilation. Even when the marriage is happy, the woman has had to sacrifice something, and it is suggested that the very skills that have enabled women to get a husband can ensnare them – spiders caught in their own sticky webs. This is not, however, the whole picture and it is interesting to look at the fictional happy marriages that do not harm either the woman or those around her.

One light-hearted description of a well-balanced marriage is Margery Sharp's *The Tigress on the Hearth*,[48] but even this novel is subtly subversive, for the happiness of Hugo and Kathi is based on a form of gender-crossing. Kathi is everything that femininity decrees she should not be: quick to action, intelligent, physically imposing (with a thirty-inch waist, 'all solid muscle', that refuses to be compressed as nineteenth-century fashion dictated) and totally incapable of lies or subterfuges. However, these aspects of her personality have to be 'bowdlerised', and her character 'stripped of all unfeminine energy',[49] in order to make her acceptable to Hugo's family and to nineteenth-century Devonshire gentry. But though Kathi seems to have adapted to English life, leaving the more debatable aspects of her tough Albanian ways behind her, intrinsically she remains unchanged and continues to act decisively, even murderously. Aware that he cannot change Kathi's character, because she has not been brought up in a society which connects femininity with frailty and dependence, Hugo realises that he will have to lead the sort of life that will not provide occasion for Kathi's more alarming actions on his behalf. Margery Sharp makes her ironic intention clear when she has Hugo write some pamphlet homilies, entitled *Letters to a Young Man*. One of these pamphlets, *To a Young Man About to Marry*, carries this passage:

'Remember . . . that the Female nature is timid, passive, unwilling to act alone; lay down a plain course of conduct and your Wife will accept it not only with submission, but with gratitude. The good Gardener does not let his Rose-Tree ramble at will, but trains and prunes her to be the glory of his Garden.'[50]

Hugo is not writing tongue-in-cheek; he genuinely believes this to be the case, for his upbringing and all he has been taught tell him this is so. He is symptomatic of a masculine inability to see women as they are, even when married to women who challenge such stereotyping. His view of the relationship in their marriage is based on a romantic ideal: Kathi's is based on a realistic appraisal of Hugo as the weaker vessel, in need of her ability to act decisively. It is a view which was widely accepted in Hugo's England because, as Margery Sharp says, 'the rising tide of Victorian morality' was with him. The irony is more pointed because Hugo and Kathi remain devoted to each other, Kathi bearing eight children and fulfilling perfectly her role as wife, mother and hostess, without in any way feeling trapped by the role. Her unswerving love for Hugo remains, but her 'tigerish' qualities are no longer needed to defend him. In other words, her 'femininity' is expressed in her love and loyalty to her husband and children, rather than in a 'role' imposed by society.

Margery Sharp likes to write about the difference between men's and women's moral thinking. The unorthodox conclusions reached by her women characters are perfectly logical, and based on deep moral convictions, whereas her men characters flounder because their convictions are based on conventional stereotypes and are the results of mere reflex action rather than individual judgements based on experience. Consequently they find they cannot success-fully challenge their womenfolk and instead have to accept another aspect of female logic: that it results in decisive, if often uncon-ventional actions. On the other hand, though her women possess characteristics considered masculine, they are never surrogate men. Indeed they are often model wives and mothers even while retaining such unfeminine traits. Her tone is humorous rather than satiric, but by investing her women characters with 'unfeminine energy' she challenges the concept of femininity current in the postwar period.

Other writers also used humour to attack contemporary images of women. Barbara Pym subverts the conventional picture of the happy housewife heroine in *Jane and Prudence*.[51] Jane and Nicholas are happy together, despite Jane's sadness at the loss of romance and poetry in their relationship, but this is in spite of Jane's total inadequacy as housewife or supportive clergyman's wife. Hating housework and cooking, Jane conspicuously does not fulfil her wifely duties, although she daydreams about being such a wife. Her daydreams unfortunately are often based on fictional representa-tions of marriage, especially Victorian ones. Nicholas may at times wish he had a more conventionally supportive wife, yet even Jane's worst gaffes only arouse mild irritation. Jane, unlike Kathi, has been subjected to the pressure on women to conform to a false ideal and therefore, although she is unable to be different, feels guilt at what she sees as her own 'lack'.

These happy marriages portray wives with characteristics which distance them from the conventional images of the period. Kathi's masculine energy and Jane's total inadequacy as help and support to her husband exist within stable unions, suggesting that men are wilfully blind to what they really want from their wives. On the other hand, these are fictional representations of marriage and, it could be argued, not to be found in real life. If the latter is the case, then perhaps these pictures of 'happy' marriages are the most subversive of all.

## A limited offer

The picture that emerges from reading these postwar novels is one of basic unease about marriage itself – or rather, conventional ideas about marriage. What was being enjoined on women – passivity, the 'background' role – was not just seen as offering little in the way of happiness, but as contrary to women's real needs – and men's, for that matter. The choice of marriage, one that in the postwar decades was the choice that the overwhelming majority of women were making, is seen as one that does not necessarily lead to fulfilment for women. The men they choose to marry may seem to offer the opportunity to enter a wider world, but the offer is limited, and once the woman changes from desired object to possessed chattel, that wider world seems farther away than before. What these novels appear to be saying is that true female autonomy is rarely possible through marriage. Conventionally, a beautiful heroine is pursued by one or more handsome heroes and the story ends with her choosing which she will marry, by saying 'yes'. These novels dissect the implications of that uninformed 'yes', which, at the time it was said, seemed to promise nothing but happiness. The writers portray their heroines choosing lovers and husbands, and describe the qualities they looked for, what they avoided and how they chose between discretion and romance. The simultaneous pull in two such contrary directions becomes even more equivocal when behind the decision of whom to accept lurks the temptation to say 'no' to all.

# 3

# Odd women

'You don't mean it cruelly, I know, but "odd" means someone who is left over when the rest are divided into pairs.'

'My dear, when I say "odd" I mean someone – remarkable, someone strange, someone out of the ordinary.'[1]

The position of the unmarried woman – unless, of course, she is somebody's mistress, is of no interest whatsoever to the readers of modern fiction.[2]

One of the characteristics of traditional stories is that living happily ever after is always seen, for women, as living happily as a married woman. In these stories the unmarried woman, if ugly, is seen as a witch, if beautiful, as an evil force. Ugly women – witches – live on their own, often in grotesque houses, like the Russian witch Baba Yaga, who lived in a house that had chicken legs and could walk around. Their activities take place at night and are connected with the moon, black cats, toads, spiders. Their unmarried status is linked with their antisocial behaviour, which frequently results in harm to others. Beautiful single women, like the Snow Queen, are attractive but deadly, associated with ice and cold, sexually frigid. The witch in *Snow White* combines the beautiful and the hideous in one person. Behind these stereotypes lurks the fear and hatred men feel for women uncontrolled by them. The fear is often masked in contempt and ridicule and the suggestion is that these women are evil, either because they have been sexually rejected by men, or because their frigidity impels them to reject masculine love. These stereotypes, often disguised, still haunt male fiction, whereas women writers, some of whom are spinsters themselves, view the matter of singleness quite differently.

There are two types of single women in women's fiction of the period: those who choose to remain unmarried, and those who, desiring marriage, find themselves single and have to make the best of it.

## Making the best of spinsterhood

The latter category is most memorably evoked by Barbara Pym, particularly in the character of Belinda. Barbara Pym herself did not marry, though she was attracted to several men and continued to have love affairs until late in life. Her sexual attraction to men and her affection for them did not blind her to the realities in relationships between women and men, nor to how much women's attraction to men is exploited. With ironic detachment she wrote humorously about this exploitation in the six novels published in the 1950s. During the long period of her enforced silence in the 1960s and early 1970s – 'enforced' because she continued to write novels and submit them for publication during this time – her view of this exploitation darkened and her *Quartet in Autumn*[3] strikes a more disturbing note than her earlier novels. She had learned by then more about the attitudes of men – *and* many women – towards the unmarried, ageing woman, and this knowledge informs her last two novels, *Quartet in Autumn* and *The Sweet Dove Died*.[4] However, during the 1950s she handled her subject matter lightheartedly. Her women fail to marry, lose their lovers, long for unattainable men, but carry on their lives in a positive way, finding consolation in the single state where they can. The character of Belinda, in Barbara Pym's first novel, *Some Tame Gazelle*,[5] is the forerunner of many middle-aged single women in her fiction. These women are divided between those who had perhaps wished to marry but not succeeded, and those who had remained single, perhaps not so much from choice as from the lack of a strong enough desire to marry.

*Some Tame Gazelle* portrays two middle-aged sisters, Belinda and Harriet, living comfortably together, even though both assume that what they really want is marriage. However, both turn down marriage proposals – Harriet repeatedly – and it is apparent that though, superficially, this may be because the suitors themselves are unsatisfactory, the truth is that neither really wants to change her comfortable and happy life. Belinda is uneasily aware that her image of herself as a rejected woman, one 'left on the shelf', is a false one; Harriet is clearer about her motives. Rejecting one suitor, she reflects on how little desire she has to change the 'comfortable life of spinsterhood' for what she sees as the 'trials of matrimony'.[6] These 'trials of matrimony' are represented by the description of the marriage of Belinda's former lover. Not only is it a deeply uneasy one, but the man Belinda has persuaded herself she wanted to marry, viewed at close quarters, is hardly the ideal husband: demanding, petty-minded, and disloyal to his wife, he is an unattractive alternative to Belinda's happy life with her beloved sister. So Belinda is like many other Barbara Pym heroines, who may appear to long for love but settle for keeping their independence. Society may have prescribed a marginal role for them, but they refuse to see their lives as meaningless, finding ways of making themselves indispensable to men. Some, like Belinda and Harriet, provide creature comforts; others, educated women, some of whom like Barbara Pym herself have been to university, prefer to play the 'handmaiden' role to the 'great' men in their lives, mainly church-men and anthropologists. They type these men's theses, compile their indexes, even knit and cook for them.

There is something sad in Barbara Pym's portrayal of women who are still trapped into having to define themselves by referring to their usefulness to men, and even the humour and irony she uses in her fiction fails to dispel this picture of women living at the margins of society, their talents and skills ignored. She is, however, painting a realistic picture of the lack of opportunities for even well-educated women in the postwar years. On the other hand, though her women characters' consciousness may not be raised, they are not unaware or uncritical of the role society prescribes for them. When Edwin Pettigrew, in *An Unsuitable Attachment*, talks about getting an assistant to do clerical work for his veterinary practice, he com-ments to his wife:

'I had thought of getting a young man . . . though perhaps in a way it's hardly a job for a man. One feels that anything to do with card indexes is more in a woman's line.'
'You mean it's slightly degrading?' said Sophia.
'Oh no,' Edwin protested. 'A card index may be a noble thing, especially if it has to do with animals.'[7]

Barbara Pym has used Sophia to sum up masculine attitudes to women's work and she shows Edwin expressing the self-deceiving posture taken up by so many men. These sort of barbed remarks occur throughout her novels as she gently but firmly pokes fun at masculine assumptions that women's true role is to serve them, the masters of creation, and she refuses to take seriously what men see as serious and important, portraying their lofty unconcern with the practical and mundane as essentially ridiculous.

Barbara Pym was writing of her generation, many of whom failed to marry because of the loss of young men in the two world wars. Her single heroines do not see themselves as sad, useless creatures, on the margins of society, but at the centre, essential to the functioning of their parishes, with their vicars and curates as ornamental in function, something there merely to give point to the women's activities. This world of churchmen is a curiously feminine one, the men inhabiting it seeming more prone to the stereotyped female faults than the women. Both sexes see themselves as superior to the other, the women because of their surer grasp of the practical and everyday, the men because they are men. However, in spite of the femininity of the world of churchmen, it is rigidly committed to separate roles for men and women and quite clear that the woman's role is inferior. The tensions between these contradictions provide Barbara Pym with material for a great deal of fun. Other novels depict the world of anthropologists, which Barbara Pym became familiar with in her work for the International African Institute. Here the gender distinctions are not so marked – there are women anthropologists who have their own research – but even so, the women are generally seen as secondary to the men and only the older single women are accepted on an equal basis.

Barbara Pym's single women do not just have to endure men's thoughtless slighting, but also their married women friends' bland assumption of superiority. Ironically probing the gulf that lies between the married and the single woman, Barbara Pym wrote sometimes from one point of view, sometimes from the other. Her single women see marriage as a more satisfactory state than it actually is; the married women assume that women who have not married are natural spinsters, perfectly happy with their lone state, and if they do not enjoy filling their lives with small services to the community, then they should. They are always amazed when their single friends suddenly announce they are about to marry. A typical reaction is Wilmet's shock on learning that her sixty-nine-year-old mother-in-law was to marry: ' "But she was Rodney's mother and my mother-in-law – how could she ever be anything else?" '[8] As a spinster herself, Barbara Pym often has single women resenting or quietly rebelling against the stereotyped responses and assumptions of men and married women. By giving us the thoughts of single women such as Mildred Lathbury, Ianthe Broom and Belinda, she strikes a blow for all those 'excellent women' whose lives are regarded as marginal and whose inner feelings are so misunderstood by others.[9] Her married women patronise and slightly despise their unmarried sisters, even while accepting their services, as in this conversation between Mrs Gray and the unmarried Mildred:

> 'What do women *do* if they don't marry,' she mused, as if she had no idea what it could be, having been married once herself and being about to marry again.
> 'Oh, they stay at home with an aged parent and do the flowers, or they used to, but now perhaps they have jobs and careers and live in bed-sitting rooms or hostels. And then of course they become indispensable in the parish and some of them even go into religious communities.'
> 'Oh, dear, you make it sound rather dreary,' Mrs Gray looked almost guilty. 'I suppose you have to get back to your work now?' she suggested, as if there were some connection, as indeed there may well have been, between me and dreariness.[10]

Barbara Pym is also sharp about the fact that it is single *women* who are expected to provide all the voluntary services society needs, not single men, who are allowed to lead as selfish a life as they wish. Even if the men do perform any service, she casts doubt on their altruism. ' "I had observed," ' Mildred reflects in *Excellent Women*, ' "that men did not normally do things unless they liked doing them." '[11]

Using humour, irony and an occasional flash of satire, Barbara Pym rehabilitated the image of the faded dowdy spinster of the parish, giving her a dignity and courage that she lacks in other fiction. Her single women never whine; they accept the patronising tones and deep misunderstanding of their feelings with a self-deprecating humour that makes them attractive characters. Barbara Pym shows her women dealing with their secondary status by envisaging themselves as indispensable, with the men incapable of achievement without their support. To a large extent this may be true, but the women fail to see the trap in the 'power behind the throne' idea. The problem with Barbara Pym is that she seems to accept this arrangement of gender roles, and although she is clear that the men are getting away with the lion's share (this is conveyed in her use of food as an indicator of the way men commandeer scarce resources),[12] she does not seem to envisage any change. She is not complacent, like Elizabeth Goudge, but nor is there anger or overt criticism, or even a suggestion that things could, and should, be different. It is perhaps unfair to criticise her on those grounds. She appears to have been temperamentally incapable of bitterness and used humour and irony to defuse anger or pain in her own life.

Barbara Pym's single women are middle-class, often comfortably off, certainly not desperately clinging to existence as Miss Bohun does in Olivia Manning's *School for Love*.[13] Initially Miss Bohun appears to be the usual stereotype of the older, single woman, the archetypal witch. The reader first sees her, through a young boy's eyes, as a repellent and monstrous woman, resembling a praying-mantis. Her character is as unattractive as her appearance. Turning the uncertainties of refugee-crowded Jerusalem towards the end of the Second World War to her own advantage, she exploits anyone and everyone – even the orphaned Felix – packing them into her comfortless house and charging exorbitant prices for her rooms. She is prepared to go to any lengths to ensure her survival, calculating not just humans' usefulness to her but even a cat's. But as the novel unfolds, this portrait of Miss Bohun becomes more complex, less easy to dismiss unthinkingly. The witchlike exterior is penetrated to reveal a lonely old woman whose calculations have to be balanced against her need for love. However, warped by the bitter struggle for survival on her own, she destroys Felix's gratitude, her gifts to people only repel them, and her dream of 'a happy family' in the house, with everyone loving everyone else, is spoiled by her need to grasp at material security.

Olivia Manning's realistic portrayal of the deformation of charac-ter necessary to survive economically when the woman is neither young nor beautiful, is made less negative by the very tenacity with which Miss Bohun clings to life. Even so, it is a bleak vision of the ugly single woman and this bleakness is accentuated by the choice of viewpoint in the novel. Miss Bohun is seen, and judged, through the eyes of a growing boy. This allows the author to record the ambiguities of Miss Bohun's character which the viewer, a young male already susceptible to female beauty, eventually resolves uncompromisingly. Olivia Manning does not leave the reader with this damning view and, at the end of the novel, allows another, and different, view to be expressed, choosing an old man who has suffered loneliness and neglect himself to suggest to young Felix that he may be blind to the reasons for Miss Bohun's conduct because of his youth and inexperience. Rebuking Felix for his harsh judgement of Miss Bohun, Mr Jewel tells him that she's nothing but a 'lonely old woman': ' "All she's ever wanted is for life to give her something, just to show she's not out of it all, not neglected. We're all human; it's not for us to be too hard on one another. You'll find that out some day." '[14] Felix lacks the charity and compassion that has led to Mr Jewel's more complex understanding and dismisses his insight, seeing himself as the mature judge of character, and Mr Jewel as childlike. The reader can make her own decision: whether to accept Felix's view as the 'true' one or, through Mr Jewel's eyes, watch Miss Bohun's witchlike characteristics stripped from her, leaving nothing more menacing than a frightened and pathetic old woman struggling desperately to survive. Olivia Manning's vision is bleaker, she is less compromising than Barbara Pym about the realities facing such women as they grow old (though Marcia Ivory in *Quartet in Autumn* comes near to such bleakness), and she is more realistic about the way such women are seen and judged by those around them.

## Challenging the stereotypes

Both Barbara Pym and Olivia Manning have, to a certain extent, conformed to the conventional view of spinsters as marginal women, struggling in the backwaters of life to give meaning to their lives, but always at the edge of a man's world. Other writers of the period wrote across the grain of accepted beliefs about unmarried women, presenting them as powerful and autonomous individuals. To do this they had to challenge the ideology of the postwar period which not only equated womanliness with the ability to catch and keep a man, but considered that a woman who did not marry was a ridiculous object, something to be dismissed with contemptuous pity or criticised for her avoidance of the responsibilities of married life. Because a woman's duties were defined as marital and domestic, and the giving and sharing in family life was considered not just her responsibility but her sole purpose in living, the single self-sufficient woman was viewed with suspicion. The outward expression of social disapproval masked a fear of powerful un-attached women who did not fit the conventional 'old maid' stereotype, a stereotype which was reassuring because it was associated with passivity and powerlessness. The autonomous single women who appeared to have *chosen* to avoid marriage or to remain celibate were threatening, not just to men, but to other women. In the past, women on their own have run the risk of society turning against them and accusing them of witchcraft. In the twentieth century these accusations were replaced (thanks to the popularisation and, in some cases, misinterpretation of Freud and his disciples) with the slur of mental illness, especially in the case of celibate women and lesbians.[15] The heterosexually active woman who did not tie herself to one man, but actively sought her pleasure, was labelled a 'nymphomaniac'; the powerful celibate woman was 'repressed' or suffering from a masculinity complex.

If women writers wanted to write about such women in the 1950s they had to find a way of exploring the implications for women of being without men in a society which saw woman as 'other',[16] a shadow of the man she was linked to. At the same time they had to avoid alarming their publishers or readers. Because of the backlash against feminists they could no longer write the type of novel that had as a heroine a woman who was identified with women's rights. The use before 1940 of heroines who were successful in the professions or in business was not now possible, because the role of breadwinner, a strong element in the concept of masculinity, was barred to women. However, there still remained a large readership for books about single women, and the postwar woman writer could count on a faithful public if she found a successful formula with which to explore the possibilities for women of achieving power and autonomy, not through marriage, but through their own efforts. Women writing in this period not only often chose to write about women on their own, but by making these women nuns, intel-lectuals, widows, spinsters, artists and even witches, they under-mined the negative images these categories of women held in the dominant ideology. They also chose to write about the harmony that could exist in friendships between women and, in Kate O'Brien's novels, even about communities of women.

Kate O'Brien's first novel was published in 1931 and she was still writing in the postwar period. She is the most overtly feminist of all the writers I mention, and her fiction forms a link between the old feminist ideals and the new awareness of the conflict between autonomy and the need to love and form human relationships. Two of her novels, *The Land of Spices*[17] and *The Flower of May*,[18] have similar themes: the choices for young women at the beginning of the twentieth century in view of the fact that neither education nor the right to work were automatically theirs. The plots have certain similarities. Women are the key characters, the older women influencing the young ones. The older women are either intellectual and independent, sometimes also ambitious and powerful, or they represent the conventionally accepted woman's role. The younger women are ambitious, and fight for the right to spend time exploring the possibilities of their own natures and abilities. In both novels the girls have been educated in convents, and during, or at the end of, this education, realise that society's view of their future role as women clashes with their own wishes and expectations of a wider life. These young girls want the chance of further education or experience. Their goals are not necessarily definite; it is just that they want to have the opportunity to see what their potential for a full intellectual life can be. Their entry into this wider world is threatened by the forces of society, lack of money and parental pressure and it seems that there will be no way of avoiding the trap of the marriage market. Their escape from this trap and their emergence into freedom is aided by an older and celibate woman whose life-story has been one where an earlier mistaken choice, or force of circumstances, has prevented her from achieving her own ambitions and therefore has made her particularly sympathetic to those of the younger woman.

In *The Land of Spices*, Anna Murphy's struggle to get herself eduated is aided by the powerful Reverend Mother, who takes Anna's side against her family, particularly her strong-minded grandmother who opposes Anna's plans. The Reverend Mother's victory, and the way it is achieved, is typical of Kate O'Brien's own beliefs about the strength of female alliances. The Reverend Mother wins her battle with Anna's grandmother over Anna's right to choose her own path because, as the head of a convent that is not even answerable to the Bishop of the diocese for the decisions it makes, she uses the one card that cannot be trumped – her freedom from the rules of male power. Kate O'Brien makes it clear that the grandmother, powerful though she is, is dependent on male support. Like many women, her authority is not autonomous, but based on deferring to, or colluding with, powerful men. In *The Flower of May*, Fanny's wish for a full education is frustrated by more subtle means. Brought up in an Irish Catholic society, which saw the obedience of daughters as unquestionable, she is trapped, not just by the conventions of the time, but by her love for her family and the deep roots she has in it. In her case, it is the enemy within that has to be conquered. Again, it is a strong celibate woman, Fanny's unmarried aunt, who gives Fanny the one thing necessary for freedom of choice: economic independence. What is celebrated in the novels is the power of female friendship, what the modern feminist would call 'sisterhood'.

Kate O'Brien often wrote of strong characterful nuns, breaking not only the stereotype of the passive, unworldly recluse, but giving a positive value to celibate women. Her knowledge of nuns and convents was drawn directly from her own experience. Educated herself in a convent, she also had two aunts who became nuns, and Kate, as a young motherless girl, had frequently visisted them under the free and easy relations her aunts' convent kept with the outside world.[19] Unlike later women's novels, such as Antonia White's and Edna O'Brien's,[20] she drew a positive picture of convents, their all-female composition providing a powerhouse in which young girls could grow without having to measure themselves against male expectations. The roots of Kate O'Brien's fiction lie squarely in the older feminist ideals: her emphasis on the restrictions that marriage, particularly early marriage, places on the intellectual and spiritual growth of young women; the joy that dedication to an intellectual and spiritual ideal can bring; and her tenacious belief that not only should women be able to choose freely, but that it is important that they fight to overcome the restrictions that prevent them from doing so.

In *That Lady*[21] the female support does not come from an older woman, but from a woman servant and a daughter. The reversal underlines the tenacity of women's devotion and love for other women, but at the same time emphasises its material powerlessness when none of the women have real power. *That Lady* is a fiction based on some sparse historical data about the widowed Princess of Eboli, punished by Philip II of Spain for her link with his scheming minister, Perez, and Kate O'Brien uses the few available facts to explore the paradox of an apparently powerful woman, 'the most powerfully placed female in Spain', who is completely at the mercy of the men in her world. Without the sheltering walls of the convent to protect her and lacking the political shrewdness and Machiavellian capacity to plot and manœuvre, Ana becomes the victim of men's fear of women who break stereotypes. Her enemy is not just Philip, who imprisons her, but all the men who turn away and fail to come to her defence. Finally, walled up in a windowless cell, separated from her faithful servant, she has only her daughter as company. When she dies, her daughter, certain lessons well learnt, enters a convent. Even so, Kate O'Brien refuses to accept that women's subjection to men is necessary. Imprisoned, cut off from life, Ana de Mendoza resists Philip, sees her lover briefly one last time, and then awaits death, her body imprisoned, but her mind and her spirit free. During her imprisonment, reflecting on the paradox of her powerless power, she tells Bernardina, her servant, and her daughter, Anichu, that she wished she'd been a man, not because she is denying her femaleness, but because she realises that only then would she have had real power.

In all three of these novels, the love of men is seen as somehow impeding full growth. Fanny comes to realise that love is not for her yet, that it will have to be avoided until she has gained more insight and knowledge, while Ana de Mendoza's love for Perez has put her in mortal danger and results in her imprisonment. Love of family, too, limits the choices women can make. Fanny struggles to achieve her ambitions, but her love for her parents makes it impossible for her to be ruthless. Yet Kate O'Brien's heroines possess courage and tenacity and do achieve autonomy, even when, as in Ana de Mendoza's case, they are physically confined. Her 'message' is that the enemies of such autonomy are ignorance and passivity, its allies education and the support of other women.

Even the conventional Elizabeth Goudge was tempted into portraying a powerful single woman, using one of the most negative stereotypes of single women, the witch, whom she turns into a positive moral force for good in her novel, *The White Witch*.[22] Froniga, the white witch of the title, has paranormal powers: second sight, knowledge of the future and the gift of telepathy. Half Romany and half 'gorgio',[23] she belongs partly to the 'green world', partly to the straight world. She lives in her small, neat cottage, cultivating healing plants and herbs, on the edge of both worlds, not completely one with either, rejected by the adult Romanies and viewed askance by the settled villagers. She is part of the natural world where all things, even inanimate objects, possess life and can transmit power. She is a healer, proud of her craft and contemptuous of the medical knowledge of her day.

Elizabeth Goudge's novel is set against the background of the civil war which led to the execution of Charles I. Once again the contradictions in her thinking result in a confused treatment of her themes. Though she presents both sides of the civil war, her sympathies appear to be conventionally pro-Royalist and, surprisingly for the daughter of a Church of England cleric, pro-Catholic. Yet this stance is undermined by Froniga's central position in the novel. Her pagan power is more impressive than even Parson Hawthyn's, and the male world of battles and struggles for power seems irrelevant and trivial compared to the woman's world where Froniga practises her magic skills and fights the elemental forces of evil. At the end of the novel, Elizabeth Goudge satisfies her desire for orthodoxy by having Froniga give up her spells and her magic powers, retaining only her knowledge of herbs and healing.

Goudge may have been trying to present a portrait of a powerful, celibate woman in such a way as to avoid the antagonism such women create. Perhaps she thought that if she linked Froniga's character to old myths and archetypes of Woman as Nature, and even to pagan ideas about the power of virgins (carried through to the Christian Virgin Mary), she would defuse some of the fear of single women. At the same time she suggests the other, darker side of a witch in the character of the black witch, Mother Shipton, whom Froniga has to overcome. When the struggle between them comes to a climax, with the two witches representing the fight between good and evil, Elizabeth Goudge's ambiguity confuses the apparently clear struggle between light and dark. Mother Shipton ceases to be a separate person and becomes an aspect of Froniga herself, which she has to conquer but not kill. She does this by 'absorbing' the other woman into herself. Undermining this archetypal woman who, like the Indian goddess Kali, represents opposing forces, is the character of Froniga herself, subject to human feelings, longing for love and only finding it in looking after two Romany children and through her involvement with Jenny, who is her spiritual heir and to whom she teaches her skills.

As a single woman herself, and one who had made a very successful career as a writer, it is possible that Elizabeth Goudge was struggling to express her feelings about her own life and its significance. She was influenced by Shakespeare, and this shows in her use of woods as refuges from the real world, where people can go in order to find themselves and resolve conflict. There is a faint echo of Prospero putting aside his magic at the end of *The Tempest* in Froniga's relinquishing of her magic powers. Elizabeth Goudge may also have been influenced by the suggestion in *The Tempest* that magic power and the power of the storyteller to create imaginary worlds were not dissimilar, for she saw herself as belonging to that older tradition of storytelling which mixes reality and fantasy, moving from one to the other completely naturally. Froniga is almost a storyteller herself, not just influencing events and shaping them, but at times being able to step outside the confines of self, the 'I' in narrative, to experience 'oneness' with other people, whose presence she can feel before they are visible and whose traumas and deaths she experiences even while physically separated from them. Again in Elizabeth Goudge's fiction there seems to be a self-censorship which prevents her from exploring what surely, as a creative artist herself, she must have found interesting: the nature of the woman artist. Other writers were less reticent, and I discuss their portrayals of women artists in Chapter 7, 'Women and Work'.

## Lesbians and passionate friends

Whether it was censorship or self-censorship that led to an almost complete absence of lesbians in women's fiction during this period is hard to tell. The silence about lesbianism was twice broken by Kate O'Brien: once in *Mary Lavelle*,[24] where one of the minor characters is a lesbian, and in her final novel, *As Music and Splendour*,[25] where one of her two main protagonists is a lesbian. Otherwise there appears to be silence, though some novels portrayed women whose friendship had definite elements of homosexual love, notably Susan Ertz's *The Prodigal Heart*.[26] The silence did not extend to male fiction, but lesbianism was not generally treated sympathetically by men writers, though Colin MacInnes, for example, does attempt a more friendly portrait of a lesbian in *Absolute Beginners*.[27] However, even she is still a stereotype.

Kate O'Brien struggled to say something about homosexual love that would break the stereotypes of homosexuals as perverts or 'inverts', and would show them to be human beings who were not grotesque, or in some way neurotic. She wrote openly of deep friendships between women, and also of the passionate friendship and sexual attraction young girls feel for each other and for older girls and young women, distancing it, however, by calling it by its German name, 'schwärmerei'. *The Land of Spices* portrays a male homosexual, and one of the main themes of the novel is how his daughter, who became a nun as a result of her shock on finding out about his homosexuality, gradually ceases to condemn her father, seeing him at the end as what he really is, a good man whose sexual orientation is towards his own sex. Kate O'Brien was always interested in forms of sexual love that transgressed religious and social rules. Adulterous love appears in several of her novels, and of course, as a Roman Catholic, especially an Irish Catholic, she knew that any form of sexual love outside marriage was condemned as morally wrong. Yet over and over again she created heroines who break the rules and at the same time command our sympathy. She never overtly refused to accept the Roman Catholic teaching on sex, but she undermined the importance attached to sexual morality by the Church by making those who transgressed sympathetic characters, and those who applied the rules vigorously, sterile or fanatical. All her heroines are deeply moral women, who think carefully about the ethical choices they make. They are also active sexually, choosing the men they want and often making the first sexual advance. It was inevitable that she would want to write about the most misunderstood and most proscribed sexual love at that time. Her first attempt is not very successful. In *Mary Lavelle*, Agatha Conlon is a tortured, neurotic lesbian, torn between her sexual attraction to women and her devout Catholicism. Although she is sympathetically portrayed, Kate O'Brien did not seriously challenge the negative image of lesbians current at the time. She made amends for this when she later made a lesbian one of her central characters.

Kate O'Brien's last novel, *As Music and Splendour*, has two women as its main protagonists: Clare Halvey and Rose Lennane. Both ignore the social restrictions on women's sexuality and, more seriously for them, the religious taboos as well. Rose's rebellion takes the more conventional form of having lovers, but she gives up her second lover when he decides to marry and keep Rose as a mistress; adultery is something Rose's religious conscience cannot allow. Clare falls in love and has a passionate affair with another woman, knowing that her church condemns such love. There is nothing neurotic or bitter about Clare, only sadness that her love for Luisa has to be hidden, even from her closest friends. She also has to endure the condemnation of friends who guess what her relationship with Luisa is and take up stereotyped attitudes. Particularly hurtful is her friend, Thomas's, reaction. Thomas, in love with Clare himself, represents the world's reaction to lesbianism. Kate O'Brien, by creating a heroine who, while lesbian, is a normal, well-balanced and deeply *moral* human being, challenges that stereotyped image of the lesbian. Clare and her lover, Luisa, are also beautiful and graceful and both are sexually attractive to men – thus questioning the image of a lesbian as a physically unattractive woman who has no choice but to turn to another woman for sexual gratification.

*As Music and Splendour* is often considered a flawed novel, not one of Kate O'Brien's best. Certainly it is not an easy read, and there are times when the moral and political stance of the writer interferes with the novel as a work of art. It is also rather long-winded and repetitive in its handling of some of its material. But Kate O'Brien wrote the novel at the end of a highly successful and acclaimed career as a novelist. She knew her craft, and cannot be accused of failing through lack of skill. After reading this novel I asked myself two questions: What was Kate O'Brien trying to do? And why has she failed? To begin with, she set out to break not one, but two stereotyped images of women. The first was her challenge to the image of lesbianism; the second was her determination to portray women for whom their work – as professional singers – was central to their life, with love playing an important but secondary role. Her women singers' passionate commitment to their art, their acceptance of the discipline and sacrifice it entailed, is a revolutionary treatment of women's lives – perhaps more disturbing to male fictions about women than the theme of lesbianism. (I have written in more detail about this theme in Chapter 7.)

My dissatisfaction with the lesbian theme is that although Kate O'Brien is quite specific that Clare is a lesbian and that her relationship with Luisa is a sexual one, she avoids confronting many of the real problems lesbians encountered. By placing her lesbian lovers in a context which removes them from country, religion, family and 'everyday' life, and by only allowing one character, Thomas, to express some of his feelings about Clare's lesbianism – and those brief and less virulent than expected – she avoids exploring what being a lesbian in a hostile environment really meant. Clare's isolation is stressed, but her knowledge that her love for Luisa is condemned by the Catholic Church is made less significant by her equating this condemnation with the Church's attitude to heterosexual adultery and fornication. She ignores, or chooses to avoid confronting, the difference between the virulence with which the Roman Catholic Church attacks homosexuality and its more relaxed attitude to heterosexual misbehaviour. Also, by not allowing Clare to discuss her love for Luisa with other women, particularly her close friend Rose, Kate O'Brien does not explore the contradictory attitudes of fear and anger that many women evince towards lesbians. The reasons for these silences were probably many, and it is perhaps unfair to criticise Kate O'Brien for a brave attempt to create a lesbian woman who was not a caricature. The ideology of the time, the double standard of morality that allowed more freedom to male writers writing about sex, her own religious upbringing and her love for her family, still living in Ireland, must all have been constraining factors. *As Music and Splendour* may not be a great novel, but it is interesting in what it attempted to do, and its failures are probably more an indictment of social values current in the fifties, than of Kate O'Brien as a creative writer.

Other women writers of the period were more cautious in their approach to love between women. But even though the portrayal of close and passionate friendships between women stops short of sexual love, some novels seem to be writing covertly about lesbians. Susan Ertz's *The Prodigal Heart* is a good example of this. The 1951 Book Club edition has a book-jacket illustration which suggests that this is a conventional love story between a woman and a man, and the title of the book would seem more appropriate to a Mills and Boon romance, but both title and illustration mask the real theme of the novel. Though superficially the love story of Robert Lyddon and Medwin, it is really about a passionate triangular relationship between three women, with Robert merely acting as a catalyst. The two older women, Miss Lyddon and Mrs Gresham, live in the same house and employ Medwin as a live-in secretary. All three women are living without men; one has never married and the other two are widows.

It is a curious book, not quite certain what it is about. On the surface it is about Medwin, thirty-two years old, widowed and with a daughter, who works to support her family and who meets and falls in love with a handsome young man. But the essential passions are those between the women, and all that happens in the novel is regulated by the past and present feelings these women have for each other. Their relationships are flawed by the wish to dominate or totally possess the loved woman, and only Medwin is free to love without these desires. Her problem arises because she does not want to be the exclusive property of either Mrs Gresham or Miss Lyddon. The novel is full of strong female bonds: Medwin's love for her daughter, her sister and her mother; Louise's feelings for her niece, Medwin; Miss Lyddon's and Mrs Gresham's feelings for each other. Even the shadowy Gwen Jones, Medwin's predecessor, is the victim of her love for Miss Lyddon. The men, in comparison, are shadowy or unsatisfactory. Medwin's father is weak and selfish and precipitates the crisis that leads to the break-up of the relationship between Miss Lyddon and Mrs Gresham. Medwin's dead husband has mainly served to leave her with a daughter, and her lover, Robert, is the archetypal hero of romantic fiction. The relationships between the men and the women are described in conventional, almost woman's magazine style, and fail to come to life, but the relationships between the women are real and vivid. They form the mainspring of the novel, while the men only serve to precipitate events, usually in the form of damaging the women's relationships.

It is difficult to know whether Susan Ertz was trying to write about lesbian love but disguising what would certainly have been unacceptable in her time by tacking on the conventional heterosexual love stories. The feelings the women express, and their reactions to each other, suggest more than friendship. Jealousy, the desire to dominate and control the loved one, the grief that follows the discovery of love transferred to another: all are manifestations of something deeper.[28] In addition, the heterosexual love affairs are flawed in some way: Miss Lyddon's lover had left her on the flimsy basis that she was involved in a lesbian relationship with another woman, and it is uncertain at the end of the novel whether Robert will give up his wife for Medwin.

## 'Odd' women in postwar women's fiction

It is not surprising that single women should feature in so many novels of the period, despite being ignored by official commentators and institutions. In the 1950s there were around two million more women than men, one and half million being spinsters over the age of twenty-five. Several of the novelists writing autobiographically, mention, often with affection and appreciation, the presence of unmarried 'aunts', who gave all sorts of services to their married relatives and who appeared at times of family crises to keep the household running. Kate O'Brien wrote a whole book celebrating her aunts, and Elizabeth Goudge mourned their passing.[29] In more recent fiction, 'women alone' figures are more likely to be divorced or separated wives, single mothers or lesbians. Spinsterhood as a concept of women living at the margins of others' lives, appears to have almost disappeared. This perhaps ignores the fact that there are still such women and that society takes for granted that they will sacrifice themselves if there is a family crisis, taking on the burden of an ageing or sick parent while their married sisters and male relatives plead other responsibilities. Being single was perhaps made more painful in the postwar period by the overwhelming silence about unmarried women and their relegation to the unimportant and insignificant. Even later commentators on the period have tended to marginalise such women, including Elizabeth Wilson in her book *Only Halfway to Paradise*,[30] which only mentions them in passing and does not even have an entry for them in the index. Women's magazines had little to say to them, assuming that their unmarried women readers would be young and looking for a marriage partner. Only in the fiction of the period were these women represented, their problems analysed and their emotions given importance.

However, singleness for women was seen as problematic. Barbara Pym, for example, gave the image of the spinster an individual human face, but she did not significantly alter it. She still saw singleness as essentially a negative state, one to be made the best of, but not one actively sought by women. Her single women often sigh after love and, if the opportunity offers itself, will marry the most unappetising men. I cannot feel anything but disappointment that the intelligent and witty Mildred Lathbury should marry such a prig as Everard Bone, and even Mildred herself feels the price may be too high. However, she still sees marriage as a better state than singleness. Kate O'Brien on the other hand went further and made a positive statement in favour of singleness, seeing it as the *only* way women can really grow and reach their full potential. She does not underestimate the need for love, but her heroines are capable of turning their backs on a loved man if he threatens their autonomy. Her single women are among the most positive creations in the fiction of the time, and the happiness and fulfilment they find compares favourably with that of married women. Yet even when she portrayed spinsterhood as a positive choice, an avoidance of the stunting that marriage entails, it was not treated as an easy option. Kate O'Brien's most successful spinsters are nuns. By withdrawing from the male world into a totally female community they are self-governing, safe from the intrusions of men, and can undertake those journeys of the spirit that the world considers appropriate only for men. The French Order of nuns she depicts is autonomous – but are convents really not as subject to male domination as any other institution? The Pope, the final arbiter, is a man, representing patriarchal power, and the history of convents demonstrates that successful and independent convents are those most at risk from male intervention.[31] There is also a danger of 'ghettoisation', which Kate O'Brien does not fully explore. Elizabeth Goudge returns to an earlier historical period to explore the dilemma of the single woman, and her heroine has to have magical powers and be mythically linked with earlier Nature goddesses. Finally, the subject of lesbianism was still a taboo area, and this results either in the ultimately unsatisfactory portrayal in Kate O'Brien's fiction, or in the masking strategies used by Susan Ertz.

All these writers have problems creating strong, celibate women. They find it difficult to portray them openly, without subterfuge or reticence. I cannot help thinking that this suggests an awareness, perhaps merely subconscious, that these women were the most dangerous heroines of all. If so, this would explain the self-censorship it is possible to detect in some of the portraits. I suspect that Elizabeth Goudge, for example, was not conscious of this self-censorship, but that Kate O'Brien may have been. *That Lady* is a very feminist statement about the silencing of unattached powerful women. Still, the writers obviously wished to avoid the determinism of nineteenth-century women novelists and in doing so created some memorable single women. This in itself was a notable achievement in a period that was otherwise silent about women who did not marry and that only saw women in relation to men.

# 4

# 'Remember Madame Bovary': infidelity

There is a certain inertia that prevents most married couples taking decisive action to end a marriage. Frequently some catalyst is needed, in fact often sought, to provide the excuse as well as the energy to break up a marriage. In the immediate postwar period there was a steep rise in marital breakdown and the divorce rate began to climb.[1] The reasons were many: marriages begun in the artificial atmosphere of war; long separation during war, with husbands away on active service and wives getting used to making the family decisions; the feelings generated by the war that life afterwards had to be better and fairer for all. Certainly the expectations of women had been raised, and in the general questioning of social values that immediately followed the war years it was not surprising that marriage itself should be subject to evaluation. Though this period did not last, swiftly turning into the elevátion of marriage as women's 'career' during the 1950s, these ideas did not just die out but continued to flicker, here and there, almost unobserved. One sign of this smouldering was the public debate about divorce, which continued to be a major preoccupation during the fifties, despite the fact that the divorce rate had begun to fall.[2] Elizabeth Wilson suggests this was because criticism of marriage itself was largely eschewed and the problems relating to it could only surface in discussions about divorce.[3] Divorce, though still thought of as a major problem, became less socially reprehensible and also more available to ordinary people. There was continuing pressure to reform divorce laws, but the nature of the reforms was muddled because of the ambivalence in the attitudes expressed – not least by some feminist groups. 'Broken' marriages were cited as the cause of a host of social ills, with the blame falling on women, especially if they were mothers, and though adultery was now grounds for divorce for the woman as well as the man, the concept of 'the guilty party' remained. Unfaithfulness in marriage was therefore a serious matter from the legal point of view, as both partners could use it as a means of parting from the other. But the legal equality was not reflected in the social, economic and emotional penalties for infidelity.[4] The discovery of an unfaithful partner inevitably meant different things to a man and a woman, and the fiction written by women was perhaps more sensitive to the ramifications for women than fiction written by men. There was also, of course, a difference as to whether the woman was the 'offending party' or whether she was the 'victim'.

Attitudes to adultery still reflected the old 'double standard' of sexual morality. This meant that a husband who had lovers was viewed more benignly than a wife, the underlying assumption being that if the man's sexual needs were not being provided for adequately within the marriage, he was entitled to seek satisfaction elsewhere. Consequently, to whatever guilt the wife may have felt, social opprobrium added its weight. Ideas about the nature of female sexuality were still very contradictory. Wisps of the Victorian attitude, summed up in the adage, 'Ladies don't move', intermingled uneasily with press coverage of the 1948 and 1953 Kinsey Reports[5] and with news stories. Elizabeth Wilson[6] mentions cases where either a wife's refusal to fulfil her husband's sexual demands, or her too-frequent demands for sexual gratification, could both be considered valid reasons for granting a divorce on the grounds of cruelty. Consequently, although the law had changed, social attitudes to female adultery remained.

**Infidelity as self-assertion**

Social attitudes did not prevent women novelists from taking a more charitable view of adulterous wives, but even so, their fictional representations of erring wives did not provide much comfort. Flaubert's *Madame Bovary* became almost an archetype for some women writers at this time, Emma Bovary's character and fate haunting the stories of faithless wives. '"Remember Madame

Bovary"' , Kitty says to Harriet in *A Game of Hide and Seek*.[7] Kitty
is trying to persuade Harriet to turn her back on her childhood love,
Vesey, and accept the more solid reality of her sixteen-year-long
marriage to Charles (the choice of whose name is unlikely to be
coincidental).[8] Harriet doesn't listen to her. To be with Vesey is the
only thing that she has ever wanted with intensity; the rest of her life
has just been a drifting – into an unsatisfactory job, a passionless
marriage, a detached motherhood. Vesey, whom Harriet has not
seen since she was eighteen, comes back into her life when she is
middle-aged, and at that stage when women often question the basis
of their daily life and their goals. Harriet is not Madame Bovary; her
feelings are more subtle, more riddled with guilt, and her love for
Vesey has nothing of the materialistic about it. What she does have
in common with Emma is the aimlessness of her life, which has left a
vacuum Vesey can easily fill. There are reversals, too, to the story.
While Emma Bovary sought to escape the coarseness of her daily
life in provincial France – her final tragedy brought about more by
her fatal money entanglements than her adultery – Harriet has a
comfortable and graceful living style with Charles and will have to
leave it for a dingy and depressingly poverty-stricken existence with
Vesey. In fact, Vesey sees this background as more inimical to his
interests than Harriet's husband. What Harriet thinks of as 'middle-
aged comforts' are what Charles can give her, but not Vesey. What
Vesey offers, Harriet thinks, is an end to loneliness.

   This loneliness is captured in a bedroom scene between Charles
and Harriet, which suggests that the dulling habits of marital sex,
where the closest intimacy masks a lack of any feeling other than
habit and the assumption of automatic access to the woman's body,
are a factor in Harriet's yearning for Vesey.[9] The description of
Harriet hurrying to avoid being seen naked by her husband because
of her dread of the implied intimacy, is contrasted with a second
bedroom scene which begins in a sleazy room, certainly lacking in
those middle-aged comforts Harriet has come to rely on. This time
Harriet is with Vesey, and though again she does not wish to be seen
naked, this time it is for a different reason:

> She saw so clearly that her youth was gone. Her body had bloomed and
> faded. She brought to Vesey all the signs of middle-age, the blurred
> outlines and the dullness of the flesh. She thought of undressing at night,
> her waist pinched, her sides creased and reddened from her corset; the
> brightness of girlhood softened, dimmed.[10]

Here, Harriet is not shrinking from indifference but from disappointment. The damp chill of the weather, the gloominess of their surroundings, Harriet's guilt and fear of being found out, and her sadness that Vesey has missed the best of her, the 'brightness of girlhood', prevent her from seeing this meeting as a second chance for her love for Vesey.

*A Game of Hide and Seek* ends ambiguously. Harriet goes back to Charles, promising she will stay with him, but the novel ends with Harriet returning to the sick Vesey and taking him in her arms. The reader is left wondering whom Harriet has betrayed: her husband or her lover. For this novel is as much about betrayal as about marital infidelity. Vesey betrays his earlier feelings for Harriet, Harriet betrays her feelings by her marriage to Charles. Harriet's daughter, Betsy, betrays her mother to her beloved teacher, Miss Bell. Vesey's mother constantly betrays her husband and her infidelities affect Vesey's character and outlook. The only true relationship in the novel is between Harriet's mother and her friend Caroline, a loyalty and friendship which has as its basis their feminist past and the support they gave each other as suffragettes. Contrasted with this political and emotional solidarity, the male world of business appears full of betrayals: Reggie's of Tiny, both Reggie's and Tiny's of Charles. The deceptions are strengthened by self-deceptions, deliberate turnings-away from the truth, as if the truth were too painful to contemplate.

Deception and self-deception are themes that Elizabeth Taylor turned to several times. Many of her characters are unaware of their real needs and this influences the decisions they make. At times it also makes them deceivers. Equally, those guilty of self-deception are ripe for deception by others. This is especially the case when they choose lovers or marriage partners. Nor are just women capable of this self-deception: men too project on to their lovers and wives the characteristics they want to find. For example, in *Palladian*,[11] Marion's self-deception has led to his failure to see the truth about his dead wife and her faithlessness. Violet is more shadowy than the other unfaithful wives because she is interpreted through the memories of her lover Tom, Marion her husband, and her Nanny, but her absence dominates the novel. Marion, sunk into melancholic inertia, and Tom, trying to blot out his grief by sinking into drink and lust, are no help to Violet's child, Sophy, whose birth has killed her mother. She attempts to recreate her dead mother by snippets of Nanny's reminiscences, supplemented by large doses of her fertile imagination. Elizabeth Taylor suggests that the failure of the characters in *Palladian* to see truly, leads to sterility: the death of the psyche. Images of death haunt the novel: Tom's grotesque drawings, the decaying manor house, cats crunching into dead mice, even the roots of trees and flints in the earth suggesting buried bones. The dead Violet continues to haunt the living, coming between Marion and Cassandra. It is not until Sophy's death that Tom releases Marion by telling him of his dead wife's betrayal and that Sophy was not Marion's daughter but his.

The story has elements of *Wuthering Heights*; indeed Tom refers to himself at one point as a Heathcliffe figure. Like Cathy, Violet did not marry where her heart was. Impatient for life, she married Marion, not Tom, her real love. Her death in childbirth has left Tom, like Heathcliffe, distraught with grief, but the vengeance he takes is on himself rather than on the world. Violet's unfaithfulness had arisen from the same situation as Harriet's: an adolescent love affair that continued after a passionless marriage. However, Violet is cast in the mould of the traditional faithless wife – beautiful, selfish and materialistic, afraid of age and the loss of beauty – whereas Harriet is a sympathetic portrait of a less calculating, more tormented woman.

Violet represents that contradiction between physical beauty and inner vacuity that Elizabeth Taylor frequently explored. A beautiful appearance can mask an inner ugliness: the toad hidden behind the leaves. In her novels Elizabeth Taylor often described the shock a sudden revelation of horror has on the discoverer, suggesting that all beauty is suspect and linking beauty with deception and betrayal. In *Palladian*, Cassandra had questioned her father's use of the now clichéd line, 'Beauty is truth, truth, beauty . . .'[12] Violet had been beautiful, but a deceiver, and Marion's memories of a great love are false. Marion should have known the truth, but Violet's beauty had blinded him, preventing him from seeing her as she really was. Violet's child, Sophy, is also prevented from knowing the truth about her mother by death and silence, and has to invent facts about her mother to make her real. Those who knew her mother see these inventions as lies, or as a form of self-deception, but sometimes Sophy curiously apprehends a truth which is not necessarily a fact. For example, Tom dismisses Sophy's claim that the poppies she laid on her mother's grave were her mother's favourite flower, yet she is later perhaps justified by the cameo brooch that used to belong to Violet and that Marion gives to Cassandra. The cameo is a portrait of a woman with an owl and poppies. Yet again, two versions of the truth clash: Tom's, which is that Violet always wore the brooch; and Marion's, that it was his mother's and that Violet rarely wore it. That the flower which links the two episodes should be the poppy, the emblem of oblivion, only emphasises the underlying message that memories cannot be relied on and that truth is not necessarily a fact. By making the truths in the novel ugly, and their revelations to be about lies and betrayals, Elizabeth Taylor removes the easy complacency of platitudes about Beauty and Truth.

Violet is unusual in that she never seems to hesitate in her adultery. Many of the fictional wives contemplate adultery, but few carry it out. Elizabeth Taylor does have characters who habitually deceive their husbands – Mrs Veal and Vesey's mother, for instance – but they are minor characters.[13] When the woman is a major character, women writers seem to prefer to show her tempted, but vacillating. Despite awareness of Madame Bovary's story, there are few resemblances to be found between her characters and those portrayed in women's postwar fiction.

Milly, in *The Visitors*,[14] does eventually take a lover, but not before her first attempt is thwarted because Abe Shulman, shrewdly aware of Milly's machinations, evades her. The story seems a conventional one of the bored, erring wife and the more noble man, tempted but determined not to betray the husband, his friend. With Milly, baulked in her attempt to seduce Abe, turning to the unattractive Herbert Wragg, Mary McMinnies suggests that the identity of the lover is not important. Milly is destined to be an unfaithful wife; she is like Emma Bovary in this at least. The differences are illuminating: Milly is in love with her husband; her instincts as a mother are stronger than her sexual desires; and, most significantly, she escapes unhurt. Milly is not punished for her adultery. There is a moment in the novel when it seems that she might be – that her two children will be killed as a result of her absence the night she spends with Wragg – but her author has her arriving in the nick of time to save them. Most ironic of all, one person benefits, and he is the only person who is not harmed in some way by Milly: Herbert Wragg has at least one memory of a sexual encounter which is pure bliss and he remains grateful to Milly for the experience.

This lighthearted, non-condemnatory attitude to female infidelity is also apparent in Barbara Pym's fiction. Her determinedly untragic approach to women's disappointments in love extends even to the subject of infidelity. Wilmet, in *A Glass of Blessings*,[15] vaguely longs for a lover, feeling the staleness that has crept into her marriage, but the desire is confined to daydreaming and a wish to return to the romantic times of her youth. Comically, she turns down the opportunity of an affair with the straightforwardly male Harry, preferring to dream about Piers, who behaves most unsatisfactorily. The final revelations – of Piers's homosexuality and her husband's mild flirtation with another woman – merely cause Wilmet to feel a rueful sadness, not pain. Wilmet is no Emma Bovary, and she settles for what she has: a reasonable, if dull, husband and a friendship with Piers and his lover, Keith. Similarly in the potentially tragic triangular relationship between Helena, her husband Rocky and her colleague Everard, in *Excellent Women*.[16] the strongest emotion registered by Mildred, present at a meeting of the three, is social embarrassment. There seem to be no social rules for such an encounter and it is Everard, the potential lover, who loses his nerve and escapes. Again, there is a reasonably happy outcome: Helena and Rocky settle their differences and Mildred embarks on a promising relationship with Everard.

The unfaithfulness of wives is taken more lightly by women writers than by men and there is not the same desire to see the woman punished. Even the conventional Elizabeth Goudge saves her fictional heroines from destroying themselves, making Lucilla and Nadine, both on the verge of abandoning their husbands, turn back at the last moment. She does not underestimate the pain it causes, and indeed it is many years before Nadine can meet her lover without deep emotion, but Elizabeth Goudge prefers to use the experience to strengthen her heroines and to provide material for her need to justify marriage.

Boredom, overpowering sexual attraction, or challenging of the double standard: none of these reasons quite explains why a woman is unfaithful to her husband. In the power struggle between husband and wife, the weapon of a lover is a woman's means of asserting her individuality. Apart from the escape from the dreary domestic routine into the romantic adolescent world of doomed passion, it is also a challenge to the husband's ownership of his wife's body. She demonstrates her autonomy by making it available to a rival male, asserting her right to award or withhold sexual favours. To an essentially femininine woman, powerless in a masculine world, it is indeed tempting to set that world at odds by subverting the patriarchal order through infidelity. Unfortunately it is not self-empowering because the woman is not rebelling in a way chosen by herself. By accepting men's definition of women as bodies, owned or not owned, given or withheld, women remain trapped in that definition and have not truly freed themselves. The patriarchal order is not disturbed by such challenges, as it has a whole mythology to deal with them and ways of punishing women who forget they are 'property'. For example, in *The Doves of Venus*[17] Petta's string of infidelities in the end leads to despair and she never confronts the central dilemma of her life. Equally, Sophia in *Our Spoons Came from Woolworths*[18] takes Peregrine as a lover when she is angry with her husband, Charles. She gives up Peregrine when Charles behaves well but returns to him when Charles reverts to his old selfish behaviour. Her infidelity is a direct expression of her anger at Charles, but instead of strengthening Sophia it merely lands her in another and worse mess. Deserted by Charles, she turns to Peregrine, only to be rejected in turn by him. None of these wives has the courage of Nora, in Ibsen's *The Doll's House*, who asserts her right to explore what possibilities there are for her, unencumbered by husband and children, or even a lover. Nor are they fully conscious of what they are doing. The circular movement from husband to lover and, often, back to husband, changes nothing.

If this is what writers are aware of, their indulgence towards unfaithful wives becomes more understandable. If they see it as an important gesture against a social order that diminished women to helpless children, the infidelity ceases to be a true betrayal. As children must rebel against parents, women have to rebel when they are confined in roles that emphasise their dependence and power-lessness. This is confirmed by the fact that the husbands these women betray are not evil monsters but kindly men who want to protect their 'defenceless' women. In *The Visitors*, Larry is a good and moral man, but he sees nothing dangerous in Milly's rootless life and her ability to use her charm and beauty to get her own way; in *A Game of Hide and Seek*, Charles does not deny Harriet anything, but he sees her mainly as an embellishment to his life, a symbol of his male success and a boost to his self-confidence; in *Palladian*, Marion's arid intellectuality cannot satisfy Violet and she also has nothing to distract her or give her life meaning. Both

Harriet and Violet have drifted into marriage because they could think of nothing better to do. In *The Doves of Venus*, Petta, despite her independent fortune, cannot live without a man to define her. These women are treated as children and are never called to account for their actions as adults, and therefore they cannot be held wholly responsible for those actions. They are rewarded as young women for immaturity and punished or disdained for attempting to grow into maturity, making it even harder for them to persist in their efforts to become responsible adults. Punishment meted out to children must always take account of their understanding of the nature of their misdemeanour and the provocation under which they operated. Women writers extend the same understanding to their fictional adulteress heroines.

**Betrayed wives**

However, when it comes to writing about the infidelity of husbands and lovers, a more serious note is struck. Then the pain and sense of abandonment the woman feels are portrayed in detail and the reader's sympathy is engaged. One of the most disturbing novels about the effects on a woman of a husband's infidelity is Elizabeth Jenkins's *The Tortoise and the Hare*.[19] In it, Imogen stands by helplessly while her husband, Evelyn, becomes more and more enmeshed in an affair with Blanche Silcox. In her novel Elizabeth Jenkins turns upside down many of the assumptions about feminine attraction, sexuality and unfaithfulness in marriage. The stereotyped situation – successful middle-aged man leaves ageing wife for a younger and more attractive woman – is jettisoned. Imogen is everything that the ideology of femininity required: beautiful, devoted to home and husband, unassertive, living only to serve the man in her life. The woman who threatens her marriage is a plain, even 'frumpish' woman in her fifties, assertive, knowledgeable about the world and masculine in her tastes. It is because of this that Imogen finds it impossible to believe that Blanche has replaced her in her husband's affections. The novel is a subtle portrayal of the inevitability of the tragedy that eventually overwhelms Imogen, and her refusal, against all the evidence, to see what is happening or, once seen, to take steps to prevent its course.

Imogen has grown up with assumptions about beauty in women

which she is painfully to discover are mistaken. As a lovely young woman among other lovely women, she had shared their belief that whatever gifts a man brought – physical magnetism, money, status – his reward was a beautiful woman. The greater the man's gifts, the more beautiful a woman he deserved. It was a belief strengthened by the ideology of feminity that prevailed in her time. Imogen fulfils all that she feels is expected: she is decorative and elegant, she bends her will to her husband's, has no life apart from him and presides over a comfortable and well-run home. Yet she fails in two points that will prove damaging: she is not totally reliable about practical matters, often forgetting to carry out minor but important tasks with which she has been entrusted, and she fails sexually. The latter failure only assumes an importance after Evelyn comes to know Blanche. Imogen responds to her husband's lovemaking and is happy in his embrace, but she fails to achieve orgasm, her response romantic rather than passionate. When the cracks in their relationship appear, Evelyn makes her aware that he is disappointed, and she not only senses that she is missing something herself, but that she is also being 'subtly belittled and condemned because she did so'.[20] These cracks, and Imogen's failure to change as her husband has, are the first weaknesses that Blanche can use to draw Evelyn to her. Her grasp of worldly and practical affairs, her ability to provide exactly the comforting and supportive back-up that he needs, and her passionate sexuality, are lures that Evelyn cannot resist. Imogen's blindness to her danger only aids Blanche in her slow encroachment on the Gresham household.

Imogen has an even more deadly weakness which will aid Blanche in her plans: a perverse blindness to what is happening under her nose. She tends only to notice those things that are of personal relevance to her and she is constantly being surprised by facts she would have been expected to know. Her blindness about Evelyn's fascination with Blanche is a result of this lack of observation and her romantic ideas about sexual attraction. Evelyn himself suggests that Imogen's knowledge of what attracts a man is totally wrong, that beauty is not the main factor. There is a more significant warning in Evelyn's story about his mother sending him to school with shoes instead of boots, thus impressing on her son for ever more that she was a 'fool' and that, by extension, all women who did not understand and share the priorities of the masculine world were 'fools'. Evelyn never fails to stress the differences between the totally feminine Imogen, uninterested in anything that happens in the world beyond her family, and Blanche, totally at home and involved in that world, and he makes his approval of Blanche's attitude quite explicit.

Imogen ignores her instinctive awareness of danger. She notices small indications of the disaster that is about to overtake her, but is incapable of altering her perception of her marriage as a happy and secure one. Elizabeth Jenkins makes use of the pathetic fallacy to represent Imogen's state of mind. Throughout the novel the weather is clear and calm, with brilliant sunlight and warmth even in the winter, where snow brings clarity and light. Superficially Nature does not seem to reflect the human passions, but Elizabeth Jenkins uses the metaphor of the river, apparently quiet and harmonious, to suggest that below its surface a hidden force is working, its relentless movement suggested when 'now and then a small leafy spray, a straw or a dead rush was seen to float by'.[21]

Imogen represses her unconscious knowledge, partly from fear of pain, but also because she dreads making a move that will precipitate events. The tragic inevitability of events is stressed by the description of the calm river ending in the turbulence of the weir when the final tearing apart occurs. Once over the weir, Imogen cannot return and can only be carried helplessly on. The simile turns into a metaphor: Imogen *is* the river and is as subject to natural forces as it is.

The river imagery intensifies the reader's awareness of Imogen's passivity and helplessness, her feminine incapacity to *act*, even when she does learn the truth. Throughout, the feminine conditioning to which she has been subjected, the qualities she has been taught as desirable to men, act against her and make it inevitable she will lose. Like the river, the flow of her life is predetermined. She has been conditioned to accept unquestioningly contemporary views of femininity, and her refusal to accept the evidence of Evelyn's unfaithfulness arises primarily from her failure to see what her friend Cecil perceives clearly: that Blanche can give Evelyn everything that he needs and wants, in spite of her plainness and 'masculinity'. Imogen cannot confront Evelyn because she fears his cold rage. On the few occasions that she attempts the lightest criticism of the time he spends with Blanche, his defensive anger frightens her into silence. She also shrinks from Evelyn's destructive criticism of everything that she is and does. Too civilised to kick and beat her physically, Evelyn lays about her with a verbal and psychological violence which, while leaving no bruises, strips Imogen of her one defence: belief in her own power to attract and hold a man.

I can only guess at Elizabeth Jenkins's own point of view. Imogen's passivity, a fault that would generally not endear her to a reader, is offset by a genuine care and sensitivity to others, and her vulnerable innocence, while making her a victim, gives her a claim on our sympathies. The novel is narrated in the third person, but the events are filtered through Imogen's thoughts and feelings, ensuring that the reader will identify with her increasing distress and pain. Although Imogen's passivity is viewed with dismay by her friends, they seem unable to do anything about it: Paul can only suggest that she 'endure', Hunter sees no happy outcome, and even the devoted Cecil cannot offer any comfort to her despair. At the end, with Paul dead and Cecil married, Imogen has to face life alone, stripped of everything that gave it a meaning, aimless and despairing. Evelyn's insensitivity is emphasised by his failure to understand the pain he inflicts on Imogen through his infidelity and desertion, as well as by the contrast between his delight at the ease with which he has got rid of Imogen and her misery at being rejected. Blanche's attitude is only an extreme example of everyone else's, Imogen's friends included, who avert their eyes, detach themselves and do not attempt to defend her. No one criticises Evelyn and only Cecil finds harsh words for Blanche. They behave like people in a crowded street turning away from one human-being being battered or mugged by another, refusing to become involved. This cowardice, and the implicit assumption that when a marriage goes wrong it is the woman's fault, results in Imogen's total isolation.

Elizabeth Jenkins may compromise at the end – without some hope, the novel would be very dark indeed – but she has been otherwise uncompromising in her suggestion that passivity and living through others is fatal and that reliance on beauty is a delusion. She is also uncompromising in showing how no one can help Imogen because Imogen will not help herself, cannot help herself. Once she loses confidence in her power to attract Evelyn she makes false move after false move. Hunter sums her up:

'women who are attractive in that sort of way, it's their *thing*. They never think about anything else, practically. That's why they're such good value, up to a point. But an affront to that side of them, and they're beaten to the floor. It wouldn't occur to them to try to patch things up.'[22]

Elizabeth Jenkins also depicts the hard truth that once a woman ceases to fascinate a man she might as well be dead as far as he is concerned. Evelyn has no compunction about what he does to Imogen and he never shows compassion or understanding of how he has destroyed her. He takes it for granted that he is entitled to cast her aside as a useless, marred object – spoilt, like the worn Sheffield plate and the cracked Harvester mug that Imogen loves – and take a more practical and useful wife.

Elizabeth Jenkins chose to see Imogen's defencelessness against Blanche as a result of her unthinking reliance on beauty and her passive femininity. Unable to express her feelings, she remains silently suffering to the end, her attitude summed up cruelly by her son Gavin: '"She never does. She just *suffers*."'[23]

Antonia, in *The Long View*,[24] also just suffers, but although her passivity has prevented her from doing anything effective to halt the decay of her marriage, Elizabeth Jane Howard suggests that this passivity has its roots in Antonia's adolescence, in her betrayal by her first lover and, above all, in her rejection by her father: a primary rejection that has perhaps set a pattern of expectation in Antonia where she sees rejection of herself as inevitable.

Both *The Tortoise and The Hare* and *The Long View* show how once a beautiful woman loses confidence in the power of her beauty, she is without resources, unable either to defend herself or even to express her anger and outrage. The anger turns back, destructively, on herself and the betrayer is not confronted. This inability to express anger is effectively conveyed at the moment when Imogen finally loses her self-control but can only manage to utter '"How *dare* you!"' repeatedly before she chokes on her tears and is unable to say another word. Speechless and sobbing, she is put to bed and treated like an invalid rather than an angry woman. Her unexpressed anger not only leaves her with a sore throat and loss of voice, as if she had indeed been shouting, but pushes her into self-destruction.

In these novels, both Elizabeth Jane Howard and Elizabeth Jenkins reject the fallacies current in the 1950s, suggesting that everything these betrayed wives have been shaped to be, the feminine virtues they have been led to believe are what a man wants, and their unthinking acceptance that Beauty not only gets but *keeps* the Prince, are shown to be lies. Nor is this the most bitter lesson they will learn. The men to whom they have entrusted their lives and happiness will not just desert them, they will turn on them with bitterness and contempt. Having been encouraged to remain dependent children, they find their dependency is held against them. The rejection they suffer is rooted in their 'femininity' and passivity, the first preventing them from expressing anger or taking direct steps to put an end to their husbands' infidelities, the second ensuring that even when they feel anger they can find no way of expressing it and it turns inward against themselves.

However, fictional betrayed wives need not be vulnerable. If a woman is secure in herself, if she has created an identity which has nothing to do with her dependent role as wife, it may be possible to survive. In *A View of the Harbour*,[25] Beth's life as a romantic novelist is almost more real than her everyday one, which she sees as an interruption of her job as a creative writer. Beth is never tested, because her complete blindness to what is happening is almost a defence against a final cataclysm – may in fact prevent it happening. There is no question of a self-fulfilling prophecy in her life.

Beth never for one moment suspects that her husband and her best friend have fallen passionately in love. Like Imogen, she is surrounded by people who begin to suspect the truth, above all her daughter, who turns against her father because of it. Beth's unawareness of her danger is unlike Imogen's; she has no pretensions to beauty and, far from living only to serve her husband, she is a haphazard and inefficient home-maker. Beth's eyes are turned inwards to the fantasy life she expresses in her romantic novels. She has a novelist's eye for the detail of human behaviour and has been described as a perceptive writer, but when a young man says to her daughter that her books are 'witty and observant', Prudence retorts, '"My mother? She never made a joke in her life. And she's as blind as a bat."'[26] Prudence is right in one respect: Beth *is* blind as a bat when it comes to perceiving the feelings between the two people closest to her, her husband and her friend. She accepts their avoidance of each other at its face value, believing the emotion between them to be dislike, and it seems that no evidence would alter her unswerving trust in both.

The triangular relationship between Beth, her husband Robert and her best friend Tory has conventional and unconventional aspects. The conventional is represented by Robert falling in love with a woman who is all that his wife is not: beautiful, elegant, an impeccable home-maker and deeply feminine in her response to men. Tory has never done anything except be a wife and mother, a role she has carried out with such style and distinction that it has masked her innate egoism. Her passion for Robert is authentic and their propinquity as neighbours means that they have the daily torture of seeing each other. Robert too is the conventional betraying husband: tired of his wife and her shortcomings as a wife and mother, at a crisis in his working life when everything seems dull and grey. Inevitably he is drawn to the excitement an affair with a beautiful woman offers. The unconventionality of the situation is that this is *really* a triangular relationship, for the sexual love between Robert and Tory is matched by the love and friendship between Tory and Beth, who have been friends since schooldays. Between them since childhood there has been 'only clarity and candour and intimacy' and Tory knows that it represents the only true aspect of her nature. '"If I throw away Beth,"' she thinks, '"I throw away my best chance of happiness."'[27] Beth stands between both of them, but it is Tory who finds her an impassable barrier. Robert is torn – but mostly by the feeling that his picture of himself as an honourable man is jeopardised. Typically, he blames Tory for his infatuation, accusing her of being the temptress, the light woman, telling her, '"I have never behaved like this before, or stooped to such petty deceptions."'[28]

Taking the male point of view, Robert blames Tory for his feelings, not himself; he is in the grip of a passion that she has stimulated and he cannot be held morally responsible. Without Tory, he suggests, he would be an honourable man, a good husband. However, it is Tory, the woman he has accused of frivolity, selfishness and lack of care for others, who tears herself away from temptation in order to preserve her friend's happiness, and sacrifices herself to a dead-end marriage. In this way, Elizabeth Taylor not only indicts Robert's self-deception and moral duplicity, she also rejects the assumption that less blame attaches to male infidelity than to female. Tory is the really honourable character and, unusually in fiction, places her love for Beth above that for a man. This is, of course, heresy. To suggest that a heterosexual woman, particularly one like Tory, can feel more loyalty and more unselfish love for a woman than for a man, is deeply subversive to the notion that women are natural rivals for the favours of men. And not only does Tory give up Robert, but she makes the renunciation final by marrying a man who certainly cannot bring her any happiness. Worst of all, she moves away, distancing herself from Beth, the one person besides her son whom she truly loves. Elizabeth Taylor's comparison of the behaviour of a man and a woman in an adulterous affair is uncompromising in its suggestion that women are more moral than men and more courageous.

The theme of loyalty and betrayal permeates the novel and, as in *A Game of Hide and Seek*, the strongest bond of loyalty is between the women, Tory and Beth. Throughout Elizabeth Taylor's fiction the affection and loyalty that women feel for each other is tested and found to endure. As Tory says to Beth:

> 'But nothing with men is so good as our friendship. If women love one another there is peace and delight, fun without effort. None of that wondering if the better side of one's face is turned to the light.'[29]

Beth also differs from the other fictional passive, suffering wives in her assertion of her individuality. Beth knows who she is and does not want to change herself. This is revealed in a passage where Tory, torn by her feelings of guilt, tries to glamorise Beth by persuading her to use make-up and wear the sort of clothes that are more like Tory's – in effect, to play the feminine game. At first Beth goes along with the idea, allowing herself to be uncomfortably corseted and prettied up, but she quickly rebels. She knows this 'persona' Tory is foisting on her is not her and that she would be uncomfortable with it. Also, although Beth never suspects anything of Robert's feelings, she cannot avoid noticing his increasing asperity with her – to any other woman a warning sign – and she does not hesitate to criticise him, suggesting that his upbringing as a polite and well-mannered boy must have 'exhausted' his politeness because he is often rude to her. Exhilarated by the expression of her anger, she goes on to talk about his 'patronising airs' towards her writing. Not only does she turn his aggression back on him, but she confounds him, because although Robert can criticise her, he never envisaged that she could regard him critically or dispassionately.

Tory is aware of Beth's inner strength, knowing it is rooted in her writing, which she suggests to Robert is 'the Beth'ish thing'. ' "She is the only happy person I know,"' Tory goes on. '"Nothing people do can ever break her."'[30] Tory's certainty here contrasts with her concern not to betray Beth, and suggests that her sacrifice was not to avoid destroying the indestructible Beth, but to avoid destroying Beth's trust in her and the one true unselfish love she has ever felt.

### The role of victim

*A View of the Harbour* demonstrates that it is not infidelity itself which is the key issue. It is a symptom rather than a cause of marital breakdown. The 'victim' need not even be a woman, since the failure of a marriage can be triggered by one or both partners failing to play the role expected of them. Being a victim implies passivity – stereotypically a female characteristic – but intrinsic to the novel *A View of the Harbour* is the idea that if a woman is not a passive sufferer, if she is, or becomes, active, an agent in her own life, she cannot be destroyed.

Another novel, *Artist Among the Missing*,[31] suggests that passivity is a *role*, not something that is inherent in women. Viola has played the role of the passive, dependent wife, but her rebellion not only allows her to assume control over her own life, but reverses the power relationship in her marriage. In *The Tortoise and the Hare* Isobel represents the feminine, intuitive and artistic aspect of cultural life, rejected by Evelyn in favour of the masculine, materialistic and practical side as represented by Blanche. Olivia Manning, in *Artist Among the Missing*, reverses this feminine/ masculine dichotomy, making the husband represent the artistic and intuitive aspects and the wife the materialistic and practical side. The novel charts the painter, Geoffrey Lind's, gradual disintegration into insanity while in the Middle East during the Second World War. An encounter with a dog, presumed to be rabid, triggers an acute crisis in Geoffrey's life. Falsely imagining himself to be on the verge of rabies, he becomes self-obsessed, perceiving the real world as a hostile place where 'intelligence and sensitivity' cannot survive. He is subjected to electro-convulsive therapy at the hands of the army, only interested in quick cures, and becomes almost lobotomised, his memory uncertain and his fear of the pain of reality unresolved.

Viola, helpless and uncomprehending, cannot help. Having

chosen to remain childless, she enjoys the responsibilities of her work and her social life in Cairo. The move from Greece under the threat of the Nazi invasion has led to Geoffrey ceasing to paint, while for Viola it has opened up an independent and enjoyable life instead of the merely wifely role she performed in Greece. She flowers in Cairo, while he withers. Their role reversal is completed when Geoffrey becomes totally apathetic and she embarks on a love affair for purely sexual reasons. Viola is sorry for Geoffrey and feels a certain responsibility for him, but at the same time she resents his dependence on her, perceiving him as a barrier to her freedom. Her infidelity, though it indirectly causes serious repercussions in their lives, does not materially affect their relationship. The real break has more to do with Viola's rejection of Geoffrey's negative reaction to life. She equates it with his suppression, in the early part of her marriage, of her 'embryo personality'. Theirs is a partnership which resembles the relationship of the sun and the moon: while one waxes the other wanes. Having lived in Geoffrey's shadow in Greece, with no life of her own, bored and dissatisfied, she has no wish to return to that subservient position and has little patience with Geoffrey's claim that the move from Greece has killed him as a painter. She has enough artistic sensibility to see that in Cairo and the Middle East there is sufficient material to satisfy any painter. What she fails to understand is that if the inner vision is damaged or missing, the artist cannot use the material; that art is not merely a transferring of images to the canvas.

Olivia Manning's special talent in all her novels is to write about intense private lives intimately and sensitively, while at the same time setting those lives in public events and showing how those events affect not just the exterior aspects of their living, but their interior landscapes.[32] Viola's infidelity, Geoffrey's obsession with the dog, are merely symptoms of the effect that the war has had on them. The mad dog is for Geoffrey a manifestation of a mad world where his values are marginalised and trivialised. It is no accident that Olivia Manning makes his final descent into madness a result of the crude attempts of the army, a war machine, to cure him. Geoffrey is broken by the war, by the second-rate nature of authority in war conditions and by the failure of sensitivity and intelligence.

On the surface, Viola appears to be the devouring woman, obsessed with her own superficial needs, failing to be the true support of her artist husband. She signally fails to fill the role of the wife of a famous man. Her affair with Clark is purely an affair of the senses, but its main significance lies in the fact that Clark is a soldier, thus linking Viola's emergence into light directly to the war. Clark has a more sinister role to play. His insensitivity has originally helped to drive Geoffrey into his paranoiac fears and it is his intervention that places Geoffrey in the hands of the army doctors. It is not a personal malice that Clark feels for Geoffrey but the impersonal hatred of the material military mind, which only desires to push into oblivion what it cannot understand and therefore fears. All military thinking, it seems, is in essence fascistic and its enemy is the artist. Like Imogen in *The Tortoise and the Hare*, Geoffrey is identified with the natural world and, animal-like, does nothing to alter the course of events. ' "I'm so alone I'm nothing," ' he says to Viola, ' " – so I can become anything: a fish or a snake or a leaf or a tree, and when I become them, I paint them." '[33]

*Artist Among the Missing* is a reversal of the usual pattern of conflict between the insensitive, materialistic, active male and the over-sensitive, intuitive, passive female. Here the woman inhabits the 'real' world of work and is active and dynamic – *sane* – while the man is confined, out of touch, unable to function in a world where the traditional macho values predominate. This reversal illuminates the old argument about whether female passivity is inherent or acquired, by showing a woman thriving in a macho world and a man being destroyed by it. Geoffrey's destruction is not the result of his artistic sensitivity, but because a world which embraces solely male values of aggression and insensitivity can be as hostile a place for a man as for a woman and can produce virtually the same behavioural pattern: passivity, withdrawal, madness. Geoffrey is as much a casualty of war as those physically destroyed or maimed: he is 'missing' even though not dead.

The role reversal in the marriage also suggests something else: that marriage is a power relationship and the most difficult thing to attain is a balance. It is significant that as Geoffrey weakens Viola becomes stronger. It is as if there was a need for one or the other to be the passive victim and it suggests one reason why men are so determined to retain patriarchal patterns of power in society: they can use them to buttress their personal weaknesses in private relationships.

## A woman-centred double standard

The themes that emerge from these novels about infidelity are not just those of betrayal and deception. They deal with the relationship between powerlessness and the suppressed anger of the powerless person – usually a woman. They also make a gesture of acceptance towards the idea that women's infidelity has a lot to do with motiveless lives, boredom, a feeling of ineffectiveness. The imprisonment of women in childish dependence can result in the sort of immaturity that prevents a woman making a stable relationship and therefore moving from man to man, as Petta does in *The Doves of Venus*. Men too suffer from this incapacity to make stable relationships, but although there is also an element of immaturity in them as well, this 'Don Juanism' can be the result of contempt and dislike of women, even perhaps a suppressed homosexuality. In addition, their sexual adventures are a source of congratulation and envy among other men, while such sexual adventuring in women not only ensures the contempt of men, but condemnation by other 'respectable' women, who feel their own men threatened by such adventuresses. The double standard prevailed even here, with men gaining admirers for the behaviour which socially isolated a woman. This makes a reversal of the usual attitudes to male and female adultery in these postwar women's novels even more striking.

What are the reasons for women writers' lenient treatment of straying wives and their harsh indictment of unfaithful and deserting husbands? While it is true that an abandoned wife suffers not just the loss of a husband but economic hardship as well, this is not a central theme in any of these novels. Sophia in *Our Spoons Came from Woolworths*[34] is perhaps an exception, as her poverty and struggle are real, but her life as a deserted wife is no worse than her married life with a feckless husband. Indeed it is arguable that, with a secure roof over her head and enough food, she has greater economic security on her own. She has gained economic stability even though she is still in a dependent position. In fact it is notable that few of the deserted wives in this middle-class fiction suffer major economic hardship as a result of being deserted. Imogen will receive sufficient income, Antonia retains her elegant home and there is no question of having to get rid of her servant or lower her lifestyle. Even Beth, threatened by a possible desertion, has an income from her novel-writing, and her lack of interest in material comforts suggests that minor hardship would not overwhelm her. Tory, who herself was deserted by her husband for a younger woman, lives elegantly and comfortably and there is no suggestion that she suffers financial hardship. The emphasis in these novels is much more on the emotional battering, the self-depreciation that failure in marriage inflicts on women, and on the social isolation and motiveless life that will result from being once more a woman alone.

There are several possible reasons for this emphasis. Perhaps the writers were challenging the assumptions behind the 'double standard' of sexual morality by reversing it. Certainly it does not seem that overwhelming sexual attraction is the main motivating force where the women or the men are concerned. It is noticeable that the unfaithful wives do bear some resemblance to Emma Bovary in that their lives are devoted to domestic duties, to being wives and mothers. Nor are these domestic duties very onerous ones as, belonging to the wealthy middle class, they generally have at least a woman who 'does' for them. They seem trapped in the same situation as their upper-middle-class Victorian sisters, and although they may be freer to use their time productively, as they either have small families or no children at all, they seem unable to do so, frittering it away on pointless activities.

The same is true of the betrayed wives, making their sudden manless existence even more pointless than their married state. The inequality in marriage, the ideological pressure on women to value themselves solely in reference to their ability to retain a man, is portrayed as making failure in marriage more psychologically devastating for them than for men. If in addition they have been encouraged to remain childishly dependent, they are unable to take steps to ensure their survival when abandoned. There is therefore a case for the different women-centred double standard expressed in these novels, which insisted that a husband's infidelity and abandonment of his wife was less tolerable than a wife's similar behaviour. The reason given for this viewpoint is that a woman who has been treated as a child, who has been rewarded for her immaturity, and punished or suppressed for any move towards adulthood, is less to blame for her behaviour than the society which has subjected her to this treatment. If men begin by rewarding irresponsible immaturity in a woman, they cannot suddenly change their minds when the childish chatter begins to pall. Nor can they be allowed just to cast aside a woman who has expended all her energy on making herself a desirable object when someone younger and fresher appears on the scene. As Tory says, justifying her uncompromising insistence on a generous income from her deserting husband, ' "A man cannot be allowed to reserve a woman's beauty for himself until it is gone, and then throw her on to the market again with nothing left to sell." '[35] The cynical reference to the 'market' and 'selling' underlines the feminine woman's role as product, an object to be bought or sold or thrown into the bin when cracked or stained, whose lack of selling appeal may result in her being left 'on the shelf'.[36]

It is not so much that the writers set out to justify the behaviour of unfaithful wives or defend women who behave like egotistic children. The novels used the theme of infidelity to explore the inequalities in the institution of marriage that led to the necessity to take a different moral line on infidelity, depending on whether it was the wife or the husband who was unfaithful. Ultimately the theme of infidelity is about power in marriage, about ownership. While women are viewed as objects, or only in relation to men, and while the women themselves accept the parameters men decide for them, their rebellion will be futile and self-defeating. They have to challenge the concept of ownership by owning themselves and by having power over their own lives. Beth, in *A View of the Harbour*, owns herself and she can, when pushed, express her anger without fear. Helena, in *Excellent Women*, also can be happy with Rocky because she has a profession. Her threatened infidelity was really only an attempt to regulate Rocky's unselective dispersal of his charm to any woman he comes across and to establish her priority in his life. Evelyn and Blanche, in *The Tortoise and the Hare*, will make a successful marriage because there is a balance of power between them and Blanche is as essential to Evelyn as he is to her. And, as Cecil shrewdly points out, Blanche will see to it that if Evelyn's affections should wander, she will take effective action to put a stop to it.

When these women novelists wrote about infidelity they were often really writing about marriages which were already cracking, and they treated infidelity as symptom rather than cause. The ending of a marriage, they suggested, has less to do with guilty and innocent parties than with something essentially wrong in the marriage relationship itself. They demonstrated the dangers that lie in the cult of passive femininity and a reliance on personal beauty, suggesting that women should defend themselves by becoming active agents in their own lives, by growing up. It was a message totally at variance with the usual 1950s' view and handed the responsibility for women's lives back to the women themselves, even while groping towards the realisation that in periods that repress women's striving towards independence and isolate them from each other, few women will be able to draw on sufficient strength to be able to accept such responsibility.

# 5

# Ugly sisters

Now that her first surprise had passed, she felt a sudden acute envy of the girl. It seemed that all she had been given herself – beauty, an unexpected fortune, the attention of countless men – was as nothing compared with the intelligence that would enable this plain girl to turn her back on a world where beauty and money held all the cards. She was simply side-stepping the whole damn-fool set-up.[1]

Pamela Hansford Johnson tells of an episode when she was only four years old and playing with a pretty girl playmate. She overheard a woman remark to her mother, 'She seems such a clever little girl. What a pity she is so U-G-L-Y.' Unfortunately Pamela Hansford Johnson's cleverness meant she could spell at this age and she therefore understood the cruel remark. Her mother, challenged to explain the remark by the young Pamela, claimed she was mistaken, that the woman had not said she was ugly, thus confirming to Pamela that to be ugly was inadmissible. Later, at a friend's house, she heard the same juxtaposition of 'clever but plain' ascribed to her.[2] I once heard a friend's daughter, sitting beside her two more beautiful sisters, quote what a nun had told her about beauty: 'You can't be both good and beautiful,' she announced triumphantly. Both young girls had been subjected early to one of the basic lessons in femininity: that while beauty and cleverness or goodness are incompatible, beauty remains the essential female characteristic. On the one hand, women need no other qualities for success with men, and the female quest being the acquisition of a husband, they merely have to display their loveliness to achieve their goal. On the other hand, if they lack beauty, they cannot be truly feminine but must compensate by being either clever or good.

Real life may not be as predictable and, as they grow older, girls notice that ugly ducklings can grow into swans, plain women marry and even grotesque women can achieve power and control over their lives. Beautiful women may feel cheated; they find that being chosen by a man for their beauty alone is not as satisfactory as they had expected. Beauty is an effective lure, but it too easily turns into a trap. And the nightmare the beautiful woman faces is the possibility of the destruction of her most prized possession and the certainty of the ravages of old age. What initially seems a disaster for a young girl – a plain face – may turn out to be, at best, a liberating factor.

Unfortunately fiction often seems to confirm that plain or ugly women will not just be unattractive in appearance, but in character too. The original ugly sisters in the Cinderella story are an extreme example of the role that women who lack beauty are conventionally expected to play. How, then, could a love story have a plain woman as a heroine, given the role generally played by unattractive women in such stories? Traditionally in fiction, plain women in love are depicted as grotesque or ridiculous. Even women writers generally prefer to have their heroines beautiful. One instance of the difference in the fictional treatment given to a beautiful woman in love and an ugly one is in Mary McMinnies' *The Visitors*,[3] where Milly is forgiven everything because of her beauty, and the governess, Miss Raven (a resonant name), is made not only ridiculous but menacing, her sexuality viewed as an obscenity. There have been attempts by women writers to write sympathetically about plain women in love. Charlotte Brontë, after all, deliberately set out to create a plain heroine when she wrote *Jane Eyre*, but how many readers visualise Jane as anything but attractive? Women writers have continued to equate love and sexual attractiveness with beauty, particularly from the 1960s onwards.

The attitudes of women writers to plain women may be influenced by whether the writer is herself a beautiful or a plain woman. Elizabeth Jane Howard and Elizabeth Taylor, both lovely women, have no insight into the feelings of unattractive women; Kate O'Brien, also beautiful when young, has only one heroine who is disfigured, but she is immensely sexually attractive. It isn't surprising that in *The Unspeakable Skipton*, Pamela Hansford Johnson not only created a successful ugly woman in Dorothy

Merlin, but also wrote perceptively about the terror women may feel at the loss of beauty in old age. Barbara Pym, a plain woman, fills her novels with mousy women dressed in brown, whose lack of the distinction of ugliness ensures their invisibility.

### 'Excellent women'

Barbara Pym's plain women are, in the phrase she uses ironically, 'excellent women'. They have chosen to be not clever, but good. These 'excellent women' perform all the menial tasks that men scorn and it is assumed that that is what they are there for. If they cannot be decorative they can at least be useful and can try to convince themselves they are irreplaceable in someone's life. They learn to cope with their insignificant fate and resign themselves to being ignored, even to being almost invisible. Mildred Lathbury, in *Excellent Women*,[4] is a typical example. Ruefully she accepts that Everard Bone will not recollect her face, that Rocky will only remember her as a dispenser of tea at moments of crisis, and that even those who know her well will not notice her appearance.

One of the characteristic marks of the excellent woman is that she frequently dresses in brown shapeless garments, or prefers others' cast-off jumble-sale offerings. It is as if the excellent women put on this disguise – knowing that brown is the most reticent of colours, the least likely to shock or draw attention – so that they can scurry about their business, their eccentricities and little failures in conformity hidden by their camouflage. Their brownness not only allows them to merge into the background, it also removes from them any distressing signs of femininity. '"You know what women are"', one male character says to Dulcie in *No Fond Return of Love*, and Dulcie cannot help feeling 'that she was somehow a woman manqué, who could not be expected to know what women were'.[5] Excellent women only emerge from this disguise when they *want* to be seen, generally by a man. Hunting a man is different from other forms of hunt in that the hunter must be seen, clearly and vividly, by the prey. This is why, in *Excellent Women*, Mildred changes her appearance when she goes to see Everard, why Jessie Morrow, in *Jane and Prudence*, paints her face and wears the type of dress she is never seen in to attract Fabian Driver, why, in *A Glass of Blessings*,

Mary Beamish suddenly shows an interest – inexplicable to the blinkered Wilmet – in clothes.

Against the neutral background of these plain women, the more glamorous women flutter and preen themselves, doing nothing for others and reaping all the rewards, while their mouse-like sisters mop up behind them and provide tea and sympathy for their temporarily heartbroken men. In *Excellent Women*, Allegra Gray behaves abominably yet pays no price for it, leaving behind a saddened brother and sister and a filthy kitchen when she goes on to improved prospects. In the same novel, Helena Napier behaves childishly and selfishly, flirting with another man and shamelessly using Mildred's services to repair the damage she has done. As a reward for her kindness, Mildred is left with the unsatisfactory Everard, while Helena gets back the delicious Rocky, leaving Mildred reflecting sadly on the fact that the common assumption that good housewifely qualities were what attracted a man was far from the truth. This is a common theme in Barbara Pym's fiction. Repeatedly she shows women with a high level of domestic skills being passed over by men in favour of less able, but more sexually attractive women, such as Allegra and Helena.

Barbara Pym writes about genteel people, but her tone is mock-genteel, her narrators appearing to accept the genteel mores while subtly undermining them. It is not true to say she is like Jane Austen: her tone is sharper and her view of men considerably less charitable. There are no Mr Knightleys in her world. She constantly deflates the pomposity and selfishness of men in their relations with women, while at the same time showing the way in which women, particularly plain women, trapped by their need to love, attach themselves to the male world, by making themselves indispensable. To preserve a sense of their worthiness, they invest their hand-maiden activities with an importance which they really lack, trying to blind themselves to the fact that 'wifely qualities' are not as important as beauty, though repeatedly this unfair preference is demonstrated to them. When Julian Malory expresses his humiliation at being taken in by the lovely Allegra, Mildred keeps her thoughts to herself, reflecting only that he had been deceived 'like so many men before him, by a pretty face'.[6]

But even though Mildred is aware that uncritical adoration is the lot of the beautiful woman, while expectation of services is the lot of the plain one, she is still subject to female guilt at turning her back on a demand for her help. Her critical intelligence rightly interprets Everard's invitation to dinner at his flat as an invitation to do the cooking herself, not to mention the washing-up afterwards, and she hardens her heart to the picture of him leafing helplessly through a cookery book to find out cooking times. '"Men are not nearly so helpless and pathetic as we sometimes like to imagine them, and on the whole they run their lives better than we ours,"'[7] she reflects, but this does not prevent her from feeling she has behaved callously, and it is inevitable she will eventually enter the trap and find herself with her hands in the washing-up bowl, even though she knows her services are less appreciated than the presence of a beautiful woman would be. Jane, in *Jane and Prudence*, reflecting on the thankless nature of the domestic round, thinks that perhaps Miss Doggett was right when she said scornfully that men 'only want one thing':

'Typing a man's thesis, correcting proofs, putting sheets sides-to-middle, bringing up children, balancing the housekeeping budget – all these things are nothing really,' said Jane in a sad and thoughtful voice.[8]

Margaret, a plain spinster in Elizabeth Goudge's Eliot trilogy,[9] is also an 'excellent woman'. Ungrudgingly she does all the hard unglamorous work that her mother, Lucilla, does not wish to soil her hands with, virtually bringing up Lucilla's grandchildren. However, for all her painstaking unselfishness, she does not receive the same reward as the beautiful Lucilla, who 'had had all the beautiful and gentle tasks, such as having prayers said and filling Christmas stockings, and had had in consequence a far greater love'.[10] Resigning herself to what seems to be an immutable law, she finds a source of satisfaction in taking over the Damerosehay garden, expressing her passion in the riotous colour of the autumn flowers she grows, despite Lucilla's disapproval of such unrefined excess. Margaret has a source of power and creativity that cannot be taken from her, and this compensates in some part for the unfair fate that has her less loved than she deserves.

## Plain women who triumph

Plain women, however, do not *have* to efface themselves modestly. They can ignore their own plainness and use force of personality to dominate the men around them. Take Dorothy Merlin in *The Unspeakable Skipton*:

> The woman was short and meagre, perhaps at the beginning of her forties. She was dark-skinned, and the hair wrenched back from her box-like forehead into a bun had a surface fuzz which the violence used upon it had been unable to repress. Her eyes were prominent, her nose was small and hooked. She looked like some distraught bird chained by one claw to a perch. She was obviously the dominating member of the group, not just because of her difference, that is, she was a woman, but because there was domination in her personality.[11]

Here Dorothy is seen through the eyes of the man who will become her arch enemy, Daniel Skipton. She is certainly no self-effacing brown woman, apologetic about her appearance and modest about her gifts. Constantly holding up her twin achievements – the production of seven sons and her success as a poet and playwright – she dominates and bullies the three men who accompany her, using her rage and her privileged position as creative artist and mother to get her own way. She is everything a woman should not be: loud-mouthed, vainglorious, bullying, uncaring of her husband and openly contemptuous of his friends. She refuses to mask her ugliness in brown and instead wears brilliant colours which only emphasise her grotesqueness. Yet the men fawn and creep round her and in the end it is her husband, Cosmo, who defends her from Daniel Skipton's evil plans. Dorothy's unpleasantness is balanced by the repulsiveness of the men around her. The 'unspeakable Skipton', Cosmo, Duncan and Matthew, with their perverted sexual tastes and search for pornographic titillation, seem to deserve all that Dorothy can hand out to them in the way of punishment, balancing her monstrousness with their obnoxiousness.

The character of Dorothy Merlin was so popular with readers (presumably many of them women readers) that Pamela Hansford Johnson was encouraged to write two sequels, *Night and Silence. Who is Here?* and *Cork Street, Next to the Hatters*,[12] but in the first Dorothy is merely a 'voice off', and in the second she is diminished, reduced to a caricature and defeated by Cosmo's hatred and her own ill-health. Her triumphant ugliness has paled into a ridiculous and pathetic silliness. In *The Unspeakable Skipton* Dorothy still has a demonic quality, reminding Daniel of a 'rampant dark demon' in an Italian painting. While Barbara Pym's plain brown women lack passion and colour, Dorothy has not suppressed her capacity for strong feelings. Her triumph is the triumph of a woman who refuses to be constricted by the usual fate of plain and ugly women. Instinctively she realises that the harpy and the witch are powerful objects of fear and she plays on the moral cowardice of men to ensure that this power is not challenged.

Generally speaking, though, fictional plain women do not easily succeed in impressing men. This may not necessarily be a tragedy. Olivia Manning, in *The Doves of Venus*, suggested another viewpoint by looking at some of the results of this dichotomy of plainness and beauty. She uses Tom Claypole to express the dismissive attitude taken by some men towards plain women. Tom is only interested in beautiful young girls, but this is because his wealth and his servants provide all his material needs and, as an old man, he can afford to indulge himself. His view of women is therefore uncompromising. He dismisses his niece, Nancy, remarking that because of her plainness she will never find a husband. Tom is not so much a male chauvinist as a man 'imbued with so complete a certainty of masculine ascendancy, disputation could only be a joke'.[13] Girls are only there to be the doves of Venus, 'little soft white doves . . . silver doves that carry our thoughts',[14] who should use their charms to gain material rewards. He has no time for Nancy's complaints about unequal pay and small portions of food for women, seeing this as perfectly justified. If women couldn't please men, then they were superfluous and Tom did not care what happened to them. But the plain, bespectacled Nancy has her own life, earns her own living and even has a lover.

The beautiful but ageing Petta represents what happens to women who allow themselves to become the doves of Venus. Her views on beauty are the feminine complement of Tom's, and this has led her to ignore her plain daughter, Flora, seeing in her more of her despised ex-husband than herself. Petta has deliberately neglected her daughter, rarely seeing her after leaving her husband, and it is only because of a fit of boredom that she envisages herself teaching her daughter the skills of a beauty. But the value she places on her own beauty has not prepared her for the radical change from her first patronising view of Flora as a 'short, stout girl' to an awareness that the plain Flora feels pity for her. She realises that Flora has something that she has never had, nor thought she needed, and that this gift – intelligence – would indeed 'enable her to turn her back on a world where beauty and money held all the cards'.[15] Flora's cool rejection of the life Petta offers makes Petta reassess her own values and beliefs. Both these plain young women, Nancy and Flora, have gifts that may not bring them easy lives, but will give them independence and power.

Petta has made the common mistake that beautiful women often make: she has assumed that plainness is a total disaster and that beauty is the only key to happiness. In the same way Imogen, in *The Tortoise and the Hare*,[16] cannot believe there is a sexual element in the relationship between Evelyn and Blanche because Blanche is a plain, middle-aged woman who follows masculine pursuits and shows a lamentable lack of taste in her clothes. Some of the women's fiction of this period is aware of the complexity of needs that men require women to meet, suggesting that though beauty may be the initial spur, its holding quality does not last if the man finds his other needs unfulfilled. Imogen, like Petta, blinded by her belief that beauty is enough, fails to interpret all the signs of Evelyn's passion for Blanche, closing her ears to the warnings that first Paul, then Evelyn himself, give her about her failure to appreciate the type of women men really fall in love with, Evelyn himself stating clearly how little he values her type of female beauty. Talking of another beauty, Zenobia, he says:

> 'women as a whole, in my opinion, attach too much importance to the effect of beauty on men. If they used their eyes, they'd see it isn't beauty that is the attraction. Consider that woman [Zenobia] as a case in point – she can give a man a knock-out blow, but once the chap has picked himself up again she can't do anything else.'[17]

As Imogen comes to realise that Evelyn is passionately in love with Blanche, she begins to reassess her own values, coming to see that her beauty links her with Zenobia, a sultry temptress who is more of a parody than a threat. It takes another plain woman, Imogen's friend Cecil, to appreciate how dangerous Blanche is. Despite Blanche's poor taste in clothes and her masculine behaviour, Cecil senses the passionate sensuality of Blanche's nature, like 'an indrawing draught of a furnace', which will give Evelyn a sexual satisfaction he has never experienced with his wife. It was only as a young man that he was attracted to Imogen's beauty;

he has aged and changed and now sees only her flaws. Blanche can offer him more solid, masculine pleasures – material comforts, 'a whole way of life, a gratification of needs which he would no more readily give up than a famished man will forgo food and warmth'.[18] Blanche entraps Evelyn – as both Jessie Morrow and Mary Beamish entrap their men – by studying his needs and supplying them, instead of passively waiting for the adoration that a beautiful woman expects as her due.

Elizabeth Jenkins emphasises the insubstantiality of physical beauty in two of her sub-plots. Hunter's marriage to the beautiful Zenobia has ended and, older and wiser, he looks for more solid qualities, finding them in plain Cecil, whose independent character and moral strength promise a more lasting happiness. Similarly, Paul regrets marriage to a wife much younger than himself, a result of his attraction to her physical grace and beauty, and the marriage is only held together by her self-absorbed indifference and his good manners. It is merely an empty convention.

Plainness in a woman, initially considered a misfortune, can in fact be a hidden blessing. Because she cannot automatically rely on her looks to get her through life, a plain woman has to develop what talents she has. In the novels of this period, it is noticeable that many of the plain women are more active and more prepared to take realistic steps to achieve what they want than their beautiful sisters. The failure of the Ugly Sisters in Cinderella was due to their unpleasant character. If they had developed their talents they would not have needed to chop bits off their feet in a vain attempt to convince the Prince they were really the beautiful, small-footed Cinderella. In real life plain women are more realistic and practical. The skills they acquire stand them in good stead all their lives, and when age dims any sexual attractiveness they may have, the investment they have made in more durable attributes pays off. Plain women can perhaps face old age with more equanimity than beautiful women; they have had a lifetime to build their defences against the casual cruelties and neglect they suffer and to create a sense of worth in other qualities they have developed. This is not so for beautiful women, who come to old age unprepared for their sudden loss of power. Beautiful women are used to being forgiven, their defects of character ignored, their presence always noticed – especially by men. Their fall from grace is keenly felt, because at the time it occurs they have passed that period in life which teaches flexibility, and their response to sudden invisibility is desperate.

## Old age and the loss of beauty

A sympathetic portrayal of such an ageing beauty can be found in Pamela Hansford Johnson's *An Avenue of Stone*.[19] Helena had been a beautiful woman, used to getting her own way, but now, at sixty-seven, she has to face the cruelties of the ageing process. Like Snow-White's stepmother, she rejects the truth her mirror tells her, refusing to believe that the image reflected in its glass is really her. The 'fat old girl with a lot of white hair and a jowl' isn't her, it's someone else. She looks at other old women, thinking, 'That old lady . . .', then remembers with a shock that the same woman is younger than her. Helena's younger self is imprisoned in an aged body, making her pursuit of love and her attempt to be once again a desirable woman appear ridiculous. She is not just fighting old age but the death of the heart. Defiantly, against all common sense, she forces back the grotesque mask of old age with a passionate declaration that she is not dead yet:

> 'I am sixty-seven,' Helena said, and with the words the years seemed to fall one by one like stones down a well. She added, after a time, 'and not dead yet. Damn it,' she said desperately, 'not dead yet!' For the moment, her flesh glowing, the fire of some inner conflict shining behind her eyes, she looked like a strong young woman, amateurishly disguised as an old one, badly wigged, the wrinkles unexpertly drawn in with a lining pencil.[20]

Her love for Johnny, a younger man, brings only brief satisfaction; its more serious result is self-deception, what her stepson Claud sees as a 'dulling' of her once brilliant personality. She not only fails to recognise her own image in a mirror, but is also blind to the fact that the behaviour she condemns in another woman is a mirror image of her own. The woman she sneers at for running after Johnny is no more ridiculous than she is.

Helena could easily have been portrayed as yet another painted and bedizened old woman, fantasising about her brilliant past, much like those painted masks that ageing film star goddesses so often become, their vanity preventing them from seeing that they too are subject to mortal decay. Pamela Hansford Johnson uses a male narrator, Helena's stepson Claud, who has known and loved Helena in her triumphant beauty. Although he begins by deprecating her behaviour, representing the conventional male standpoint, he gradually comes to understand the desperate fear of loneliness that underlies it. Helena's courage in resolutely refusing to be defeated by the diminishment old age forces on her gains her stepson's loyalty and love and he sacrifices his own freedom to stay with her in her lonely old age. The reader sees Helena through Claud's eyes; and what might in real life repel – the sight of an aged, painted woman pursuing a young man – has its tragic and human dimensions exposed and we can respond to Helena's desperate courage with understanding and compassion.

It is more difficult to sympathise with Petta in *The Doves of Venus*. Her selfishness is that of a spoiled beauty who has always had her own way and, now ageing, begins to lose her grip. Petta has lived all her life depending on men. It is not a question of money, because Petta has her own fortune; it is an emotional dependence about which Petta herself seems to feel some ambivalence because she frequently threatens suicide, destroys her relationships and ends by sinking into self-disgust. She has allowed herself to become a plaything, a 'pet' as her name suggests, and now that the plaything is showing chipped paint and can be compared with newer, more fascinating toys, Petta finds herself being discarded – even by men at the bottom of the heap – and has to use her seductive skills on men she despises. As she slips further and further down, she starts to see what the younger women of the next generation have, what she could perhaps have had herself. Consumed with self-pity, aware of the barrenness of her life, but unable to see how she can change it, she continues to grasp at whatever man she can find, deluding herself into thinking that love will make her flower again, and denying the image in the mirror which tells her she is only an 'old bag slipping out for a pint'. Like Helena she cannot accept the end of her beauty: 'She was not old: she was a girl hidden behind a mask',[21] and, like Helena, she has a desperate courage. This, and a glimpse of Petta as a young girl, humanises her.

Both Pamela Hansford Johnson and Olivia Manning write compassionately about the death of beauty, the moment when a woman who has been used to nothing but admiration from men suddenly notices there is no sexual element in the looks men give her – even if they look at her at all. The rewards for beauty only last as long as that beauty lasts. Petta, looking at Ellie's 'smooth magnolia' face, wishes she had youth again, with the knowledge she has now, thinking vengefully of the hell she would put men through. Petta, like Helena, has learnt nothing; she still thinks the game can be played with the woman winning. Olivia Manning makes her point clear by showing how the cold and conscienceless Tom Claypole and Quintin Bellot go on winning to the end, Tom with his money, Quintin with the charm which makes him a masculine, and therefore successful, version of Petta. This is the bitter side of beauty, when the gift turns into a curse.

Throughout *The Doves of Venus* the theme of old age intrudes into Ella's and Petta's reaching for life and love. Just as Petta's end seems to cast a shadow over Ellie's hopeful beginning, so Petta herself remembers seeing a faded beauty, grotesquely dressed, her face reflecting despair, when she herself was young and at the height of her attraction. The memory has haunted her, puzzlingly linking her with the older woman at the end of a triumphant reign over men. It is like some *memento mori*, a skull painted in the corner of a portrait of a rich and beautiful young woman to suggest that old age and death await all, and that beauty is only temporary. Helena's final despair was relieved by the unselfish love of her stepson; Petta has no one, and the novel leaves her vomiting into a urine-smelling lavatory after an abortive suicide attempt.

There is one glimpse of the young girl Petta that suggests another possibility. The child of an impoverished Irish aristocratic family, she was wild and free, climbing walls, swinging round the stable from hook to hook. The world's opinion of dirty, wild girls is expressed in the contempt shown by the English colonel's wife, a contempt for a child from an 'inferior' race, who was not 'just what a little girl should be'. There is a reminder that the tomboyishness of female adolescence is punishable, and the lesson of feminine conformity has to be learnt painfully. Olivia Manning's awareness of the way history, too, affects how a woman might see herself, hints that Petta, the maimed, diminished woman, might have remained that proud 'Petronia Berengaria Vanessa Kilkane, of Kilkane House', a descendant of Irish kings, if she had not been humiliated by her first brush with the power some wield over others.

Power is one of the underlying themes in *The Doves of Venus*: the power that beauty bestows, the power men have by virtue of being men. The power of men is based on something more solid than the power of beauty, even though lack of beauty makes a woman at best invisible, at worst a butt for contempt or ridicule. In Petta's life the imperial power of the occupying English was merely replaced by the sexual power of men. Olivia Manning's message is clear: beauty is not enough and the plain women – Flora, Alma, Nancy – may have more enduring qualities that will outlast their youth.

## Marred beauty

These are, however, mostly uncomfortable portraits of plain or ugly women, showing them either accepting, or eventually being beaten by, their failure to attract men's unquestioning homage. Even Blanche Silcox in *The Tortoise and the Hare* has had to wait until middle age to get a husband. A more complex situation arises when the woman is not ugly, but has been disfigured. Ana de Mendoza, in Kate O'Brien's *That Lady*, is one-eyed, what the Spanish call *tuerta*. She covers her deformity with elegant eye-patches, using her disfigurement to create an odd and disturbing beauty. Her feelings about her marred face are ambivalent. Looking at her reflection in the mirror, she thinks, 'I am marked for the grotesque' and she sees her face as 'halved and split into blackness'.[22] Kate O'Brien uses the theme of darkness to express the split in Ana's life, the struggle between the secret hidden 'black' half of her face and the outer, more conventional 'great lady' that Ana represents in the world of sunlight. The darkness wins, but in a curious and ironical twist, Kate O'Brien represents the victory of darkness as Ana's triumph.

Ana's blackened eye-socket is the direct result of her challenge to the stereotyped role laid down for her as a woman; she lost her eye in a duel with a pageboy at the age of fourteen, an age when she should have been totally immersed in feminine activities. She is heavily chastised for her transgression, but her spirit is not completely broken. Throughout her life she continues to think and behave according to her conscience and her feelings, not according to a feminine role. Though her marriage has been a happy one, it has lacked something that Ana, at the time of her husband's death at the beginning of the novel, has not yet defined. The novel is about her search for that something that her *dueña* and close friend, Bernardina, has glimpsed, a 'lack' in her, something that she seems to have lost or never been able to express. Kate O'Brien links her heroine's disfigurement to her 'lack'. Initially her blemish saps her confidence, making her unable to confront life directly without a husband. This had been the source of her husband's power over her, but once that power is removed, Ana can see how her physical mutilation mirrors the mutilation she has undergone in marriage:

> whilst he was there she had never been able to be anything but exactly his, as he made her. She was, it seemed, mutilated, *tuerta* – depleted in some sense she would never discover by the perfect taking over and direction of her life.[23]

Her husband's protective custody results in a fear of freedom, which causes her panic-stricken attempt to enter a convent. When, therefore, she is expected to take her place in the world, her first free decision – to take a lover – is also self-limiting. Despite her initial delight at discovering sexual pleasure for the first time, she still suffers from a 'lack'. She finds that her power as the great Princess Eboli is a mirage too. Powerful though she is, in court etiquette she is a widow, an 'unprotected' woman, who is not allowed either to attend functions or to hold them herself. Eventually her widowhood and the removal of male protection force her to return to her fourteen-year-old self by transgressing man-made laws governing what women should or should not do. The blinded half of her face comes to symbolise the real Ana and she only discovers her true self in misfortune and darkness. She ceases to listen to men's voices telling her what to do and listens to her own uncompromising inner voice. Shaw might have seen her as a Saint Joan, with the same wilful disregard for any but her own inner convictions.

Kate O'Brien has used the marred image of feminine beauty to suggest that it is only by breaking the image, spoiling it, that women can achieve true autonomy. Ana's patched eye set her apart from other women, just as her uncompromising search for truth alienated her from the times she lived in. She found that she had to hide what appeared a fault – her blind eye – by a patch, just as she had to hide her strength and intelligence. Her seeing eye deceived her because all it saw was the surface of things; when the daylight is excluded from her final prison, it becomes irrelevant and the blinded eye can come into its own. Kate O'Brien is not the first writer to use the theme of blindness to express enlightenment, suggesting that it is only by shutting out the distractions of the world that the inner self can be revealed.

## Removing the mask

Plain or ageing women have always been subject to unsympathetic stereotyping, and this was certainly the case in the 1950s, a period which equated successful femininity with sexual success in getting and keeping a man. Yet in some of the fiction published at the time, the false images of plain and ageing women are subverted by the author's choice of viewpoint. Sometimes the women are seen through the eyes of a character who is unsympathetic or 'blinded' in some way. This blindness of vision can occur because the viewpoint is male, but equally women can also misinterpret what they see, so thoroughly have they absorbed the images of women current in their society. Where there is love, as in the case of Claud's love for Helena in *An Avenue of Stone*, the mask of ugliness becomes transparent and ceases to distort. Where there is hatred, as in Daniel Skipton's view of Dorothy in *The Unspeakable Skipton*, the woman turns into a gargoyle and the only corrective is the view taken by other characters round her, or by the author herself revealing the falseness of the viewpoint. Sometimes it is not just a question of love or hatred. The flawed viewpoint can be the result of youth, unthinking acceptance of false concepts of femininity, or lack of empathy with those who are 'different'. By starting from the prejudices and assumptions many of us hold about unattractive or ageing women, and then gradually revealing these women to be more complex and, surprisingly, more successful than the stereotype would suggest, the writers make the reader re-evaluate the way *she* sees such women.

There is an ambivalence in many of these women writers' approach to beauty. Aware of its transience, they seem to be saying to beautiful women, 'Beware!'. At the same time, although their plain women can draw on inner strengths to create out of their marginality something positive, they still have to accept the pain of rejection. For example, Barbara Pym's 'excellent women' convince themselves of the importance of their ministrations to men, and this view is bolstered by a delicate contempt for the male character, so obviously unable to survive without them. But at the same time, their longing for the love of a man betrays them into giving up their independence. Both of Pamela Hansford Johnson's heroines, Helena and Dorothy, despite their loss of sexual power, bind men to them in loyalty, but Olivia Manning reminds us that this is not generally the lot of the ageing or ugly woman, and success for plain women is tempered by what they have had to endure. Even so, what all the novels do is to question the contemporary view that femininity and desirability were the sole keys to success.

# 6

# Children: 'strange unexpected flowerings'

> No warmth fell from her over her children. Even their ages, the fifteen years between Prudence and Stevie, suggested that they were haphazardly conceived, incidental to her, strange unexpected flowerings.[1]

When women writers create child characters they often have two viewpoints from which to work: their own childhood, and their adult experience as the prime carers of children. This can result in child characters being seen simultaneously from both sides of the adult/child divide, with the adult's and child's worlds running parallel and only occasionally touching. The child's perception and innocence is balanced by the adult's knowledge and experience, leading to a paradoxical mixture of insight and obtuseness on both sides. Child and adult are like two nations who appear to share a language and are therefore lulled into supposing that the differences between them are minor. The misconceptions and mutual incomprehension to which this leads can be a source of comedy or tragedy.

During the postwar years, motherhood was believed to be one of the defining attributes of femininity, an intrinsic element in being a woman, and it was therefore natural that women perhaps found it more difficult to accept the complacent generalisations of men as to what the relationships between mothers and children were or should be. Bowlby's and Winnicott's theories,[2] and the belief that motherhood should exclude any activity that appeared to conflict with its sacred duties, so much a feature of the ideology of family life during the period, seem to have had little influence on how some women novelists portrayed mother/child relationships. There are no platitudinous madonnas or evil stepmothers in their fiction. Instead the complex nature of human relationships in general is reflected in the way parents and children interact, with personality and temperament determining the nature of adult and child relationships.

The way children are portrayed in the fiction of this period depends to a certain degree on whether the writer is herself a mother or not. Barbara Pym, Kate O'Brien and Elizabeth Goudge were childless. Children are virtually absent from Barbara Pym's fiction; the few who do appear are young adults, the children of friends and relatives of her heroines, who try to see these grown children as versions of themselves when young, but who are bemused by the differences between their young selves and the young women of the postwar world. They remain detached observers and are not emotionally affected. Kate O'Brien's portrayal of childhood and young adulthood is derived from her own experience, and again, like Barbara Pym, her emphasis is on young women in transition from childhood to adulthood, but her viewpoint is different from Barbara Pym's in that she sees through the eyes of the emergent young women. I suspect that much of her writing is semi-autobiographical, portraying her own struggle to be an autonomous person against a background of a loving, but dominating family, and a Catholic upbringing which set very narrow limits to a young woman's adult choices. Barbara Pym and Kate O'Brien wisely limited the presence of children in their fiction to what they knew of first-hand. Elizabeth Goudge's child characters are another matter. She seemed to suffer from what I can only describe as an anglicised Shirley Temple-itis. Her children, especially her girl children, are often unbelievably angelic; wise beyond their years and subject to semi-mystical experiences. She fails in her attempts to write about the imaginary worlds which young children easily inhabit because she tries to make these worlds significant in a quasi-religious way. Occasionally her observation triumphs over her sentimental exaggeration, as in the earlier portrait of Nadine's twins,[3] who initially exhibit that demonic rejection of the world of adult rules that all secret alliances of children show to some extent, but which is accentuated in twins. Unfortunately, this pair of ear-splitting wreckers fade into another example of Elizabeth Goudge's sentimental approach to child characters.

The writers I am more interested in examining are those novelists who portrayed children from the dual viewpoint of adult and child, especially those who were mothers themselves. Subject to the clear, uncompromising judgement of their own children, the latter realise that though children lack adult self-deception, their judgement is often hard and merciless, and these writers use the contrasting views of adults and children to shift the reader's perception of character. I have already mentioned the use Olivia Manning makes of this device in *School for Love*,[4] where Miss Bohun is seen, with a mixture of clear vision and absolute judgement, through a boy's eyes, until the very end of the novel, when the viewpoint shifts to a man who is as old and as lonely as Miss Bohun, and whose understanding of the real springs of her behaviour turns her from gargoyle into weak human being. The child's view in these novels is used to make a simple uncompromising judgement of adult actions, and to demonstrate how children view themselves as a separate species, grossly misjudged and unnecessarily hampered by adult prejudice.

**Through a child's eyes**

Although in many of the novels children are marginal to the main themes, unless they themselves are the protagonists, some writers use the child's viewpoint to illuminate the questionable basis of adult assumptions and their relationships, not just with the children, but with each other. Because children are socialised as much through what they observe as through overt teaching, the process of this type of socialisation can be examined to explain some of the less happy consequences of children's initiation into adult life.

In *The Tortoise and the Hare*[5] Elizabeth Jenkins uses the character of a young boy, Gavin, to explore how adult male attitudes to women are inculcated, almost unconsciously, at an early age. Gavin, and his friend Tim, are not only clearly drawn characters in their own right, but their presence in the adult world has an effect on that world. The relationship between Imogen and her son, Gavin, must be one of the most painful mother-and-child relationships portrayed in fiction. Evelyn's rejection of Imogen in favour of Blanche is immensely damaging to her self-esteem. She could perhaps have borne her replacement by a younger woman who still represented the values she held, but her expulsion from Evelyn's world is linked with Evelyn's preference for the masculine choice of action over feeling, the practical over the imaginative. The behaviour of her son, Gavin, makes the masculine rejection bitterly clear. Gavin, at the age of eleven, is quick to pick up and identify with his father's attitudes. As a young male he looks to his father for clues to what a powerful male should be. If this includes a dismissive and contemptuous attitude to his mother, Gavin, unreflectingly, imitates this attitude. Imogen sees the connection, but not its significance. She accepts and even admires Evelyn's attitude to her, because he is her husband and fifteen years older, but jibs at the same behaviour in her son. Imogen fails to see that it is *because* she accepts it from Evelyn that Gavin feels he too can treat her in the same way; she is merely reinforcing his view that the feelings of women such as his mother are of no consequence, and his expressed contempt for Imogen's passivity turns to annoyance and resistance when she tries to make him do anything. When there are clashes of will between them, Imogen does not use her authority as adult and parent to strengthen her control but descends to the same level as Gavin, so that their outbursts are on the level of quarrels between children rather than a responsible parent insisting on respect or obedience from a refractory child. Inevitably she fails to gain Gavin's co-operation and this becomes yet another reason for Evelyn's dissatisfaction with her.

Evelyn is much easier in the use of his authority, exercising it quietly and confidently, so that Gavin, and even Tim, accept what he says. He is not conscious that it is his behaviour that is making Imogen's role as mother difficult, persuading himself that his son is merely demonstrating a natural male reaction. His lack of support for Imogen's authority is made overt in the scene where Imogen has imposed a punishment on Gavin for his insolence towards her. Evelyn makes it clear to both that he considers Imogen's reaction a huge joke and he sides with Gavin, persuading Imogen to restrict the extent of her punishment. He seems totally unaware that he is using the child as a weapon against Imogen, something that Imogen, when her turn comes, recoils from doing. Imogen, painfully aware of Gavin's indifference to her, knows that when the break comes between Evelyn and herself, Gavin will not want to live with her. Resignedly she agrees to Gavin remaining with

Evelyn and Blanche. Gavin's reaction to the news of his mother's departure is ambiguous, though. He has for so long taken her presence for granted, has so completely imbibed his father's view of her, that he has never imagined that she could act as an independent person and go away. The shock is like a concussion, and Evelyn, regarding his son's reaction, realises that some unforeseen and indefinable damage has been done to him.

Elizabeth Jenkins uses the character of Gavin to reflect clearly the disregard a male world has for female values. Gavin's scientific interests, which make him want to know how the physical world functions, are nearer to Evelyn's practical view of the countryside as something to be exploited. Evelyn despises Imogen's aesthetic and emotional response to the living plants and creatures that make up the country, implying that what is merely decorative, like Imogen, is useless. Because Imogen's values are considered female, they must therefore be inferior. Elizabeth Jenkins subtly suggests this is not the case by portraying another couple, Paul and Primrose, where those values are reversed, with Paul having the same aesthetic sympathies as Imogen. It is also significant that Gavin's young friend, Tim Leeper, who joins Imogen in her lonely exile, also rejects the world of male values represented by Evelyn, Blanche and Gavin, and it is his act of faith in Imogen that brings her back from despair.

In *The Tortoise and the Hare* Elizabeth Jenkins shows how the male sense of superiority is constructed and how difficult it is for a mother to challenge it or change it. The values that Imogen represents will come to be linked in her son's mind with weakness and failure, and there is little chance that this impression will be altered by his boys' boarding-school or his home life with Blanche and Evelyn. The loss of these values, Elizabeth Jenkins suggests, could be crippling.

Gavin's shock at learning that his mother is a separate human being with a will of her own is so characteristic of children's view of their parents that several writers refer to it. The realisation is often connected with pain, with revelation, and with growing up. In Elizabeth Taylor's *A View of the Harbour*, Prudence has to come to terms with the fact that parents aren't 'sub-human' but do have emotions that may prompt them into betrayal of each other. Intuitively, she guesses at her father's infatuation with another woman. Still too much of a child to see things other than in black and white, she assumes the worst, and her judgement is implacable: her father is the betrayer. Robert, loving his daughter, is saddened by a realisation that he has lost her, that she will never come back to him. Prudence, though, is not damaged by her awareness of adult deceit and self-deception. Despite her initial shock and revulsion, the revelation releases her into independence and adulthood. She rejects the security of home as soon as she realises the shaky basis on which it is built.

### Surviving in a hostile terrain

Prudence is not alone in her capacity to survive the inconsistencies of the adult world. Very often children use adults' involvement in their own problems to extract advantage for themselves. Elizabeth Taylor sees children as survivors, quick to perceive the realities in the games adults play, especially when they are seeking children's support. In *A View of the Harbour*, for example, when Robert and Beth play that favourite parental game, 'Who Understands the Children Best?', it is the unperceptive, detached Beth who wins, only strengthening the notion that being too emotionally involved with children leads to blindness. Beth is also less in need of her children's approval than the guilt-ridden Robert, and therefore in a stronger position.

The undeclared wars that can exist in a family have their darker side, but Elizabeth Taylor often takes an amused, ironic view, particularly of children's manipulative genius. Constance, for instance, in *The Sleeping Beauty*, 'had an instinct, always useful, though often contemptibly used, of knowing what answers went down well'.[6] Children are perceptive observers of the power relationships in marriage, and when foiled in their plans to outwit parents, turn to emotional blackmail without a tremor of guilt. But perhaps the most slyly manipulative of all fictional children is Sigi, in Nancy Mitford's *The Blessing*.[7] Not only is Sigi undismayed by the rift between his father and mother, but quickly apprehends positive advantages for himself in the need both parents have to retain his love and loyalty. His strategy almost leads to the divorce of his parents and his duplicity is only accidentally revealed. Sigi is not a monster, only an extreme version of the way children can use the parental need for childish approval to manipulate any discord they discern in adult relationships.

No break-up of parents or stress in marriage is without its effect on the children, but Elizabeth Taylor is more realistic about their essential toughness and resilience. Children's instinctive movements are towards life and happiness, and if the sadness is there, it is pushed to the background – Tory's son, for example, only briefly expressing what his parents' separation means to him.[8] Elizabeth Taylor's children often accommodate themselves to the adult world they inhabit by using their ability to create and live in an imaginary world. Sophy, in *Palladian*,[9] copes with her motherless childhood by creating a fantasy of a mother on whom Sophy is the only expert witness. It is an imaginative strategy which enables Sophy to come to terms with her loss and to deal with the silences about Viola which both her father and her uncle do nothing to break.

## Home as a haven

Despite Elizabeth Taylor's faith in children's ability to survive, other writers take a less optimistic view. In *The Long View*[10] Elizabeth Jane Howard digs deep into parent/child relationships, showing the psychological destruction parents can wreak on their children, almost without being aware of it. Antonia is not a totally happy child, but her life has enough satisfactions to ensure that she is not unhappy either. As she reaches adolescence, though, the desolation of her parents' marriage is revealed to her in a series of brutal awakenings which end in a horrifying rejection. Her mother's persistent infidelities and her father's isolation in an academic coldness make both of them disregard the effect their hollow marriage will have on their child. When Antonia first realises the significance of all the men who become her mother's 'friends', especially the man who has first made love to her, her sympathies recoil from her mother and she longs to console her father and protect him from what she sees as her mother's callous triviality. She reaches out to her father only to discover that her simplistic view of guilt and innocence in her parents' marriage is inadequate. In a shocking scene, Antonia's father rejects her not merely as his child but as a *woman*, pouring out his twisted hatred for all women. Antonia, open and vulnerable in her love and admiration for her father, has no defence. She cannot turn to her mother, who totally disregards her daughter most of the time, her derogatory comments on Antonia's appearance and personality betraying a hostile jealousy of her daughter's youth. She even undermines Antonia's womanhood by telling her that her father had not wanted a daughter, but a son. The twisted, skewed views both her parents have of Antonia eventually turn her into an Ice Princess. Antonia's insight into the horror of her parents' lives does not free her; she defines her perception of their power as the 'machinery of terror'[11] and she pulls round her an excluding blanket of indifference. Antonia cannot help herself, cannot use rage or rebellion to reject the negative images of herself that her father and mother have foisted upon her, and inevitably she becomes a victim. One after another, all her relationships are blasted, including those with her own two children. Distanced from her son, she cannot even help her daughter whom she watches, helplessly, make an emotional mess of her life.

Antonia's childhood has been spent in the countryside, which Elizabeth Jane Howard uses to represent Antonia's true nature. Her innocence and spontaneity merge easily with its undemanding rhythms. Shortly after her confrontation with her father, Antonia leaves her home and the countryside and never returns. She turns her back on its shimmering beauty and its invitation to sensuous delight and calm pleasure, surrounding herself with the more controllable comforts of an elegant and refined life: a town house, good food, foreign travel, beautiful man-made objects. These cut her off from her innocent childhood and adolescence, and her failure to return to it emphasises the barrier that now exists between the original Antonia, destroyed by her parents' mutual hatred and contempt, and the artefact created by her husband, Conrad; she is another Eve who has eaten the Tree of Knowledge and is therefore banished from Paradise.

Sometimes children escape the potential destruction their homes can cause, either through strength of character or by finding someone else who provides what they need. In *The Tortoise and the Hare*,[12] the Leeper household is run solely for the benefit of the adults in it, and the three children live in neglected chaos, ignored and virtually unloved by their parents. The two girls are almost savages, but the boy, Tim, finds in Imogen, his friend Gavin's mother, the one person who can fulfil his passionate desire for order. The neglectful Leepers are well-to-do middle class – in fact the 'Yuppies' of their time. Their neglect arises from selfish dedication to their own interests and amusements. Nor is the Leeper marriage an unhappy one; it is merely that two human beings who should have remained childless, have unthinkingly coupled and produced a brood which they proceed to ignore. Elizabeth Jenkins spoils her message a little by stereotypically blaming the mother more than the father, whereas both are equally irresponsible.

All these novels explore the conventional 1950s' belief in the home as a safe haven for children. Because of the indifference and ignorance of parents, sometimes compounded by their damaged personalities and relationships, these are marriages which provide dangerous environments for children. The comfortable assumption that the worst disaster for children is a broken home is challenged by descriptions of marriages that allow no place for children's needs. Although the effects of these neglected childhoods may last into adulthood, the novels are not tracts in support of Bowlby's theories of motherhood. In fact, the ideology of motherhood and of 'happy families' is subtly undermined. All these mothers are at home, constantly with their children. Apart from the Leepers, the children are fed, clothed and sheltered more than adequately. Parenting, it is suggested, is not a natural instinct, not even in a woman, but a world that only saw women's destiny in terms of wife and mother allowed no possibility of a woman asking herself if she really wanted children, and rarely encouraged her to envisage any other role for herself. This refusal to treat women as other than breeding machines, whose physical attractions will ensure them a good stud, is brutally expressed by Antonia's father when she tentatively asks his advice on what she should do with her life. Brusquely rejecting any other human attributes she may have, he tells her that, like most young women, 'marriage and all that goes with it' will be her sole 'métier'.[13]

In the postwar outcry against working mothers and 'latchkey children' there was a class bias; once again the middle classes were attempting to impose their moral imperatives on another class whose behaviour and rules arose out of very different life circumstances. Yet none of the novelists suggests that it is the working class that fails its children. The belief that the middle classes bring up their children better than others is questioned by the portrayal of these middle-class homes, where the wives have little to do but attend to themselves, and where the presence of nannies and servants and the practice of sending boys away to boarding school, distance mother and child. The immature, dependent women in these novels have not sufficiently emerged from childhood themselves to make adequate adults, let alone mothers. The ideal of femininity is portrayed as fundamentally antagonistic to the ideal of motherhood. The first encourages narcissism and the relegation of anything that does not directly relate to men to a secondary status; the second requires a mature, balanced and independent judgement and an ability to provide security which will not stifle. The only type of woman who can give this sort of security is one whose self-image is not damaged, whose life is not devoted to everyday trivia and who is not destructively self-sacrificing.

## Separate lives

Although the novelists I mention did not generally make children central to their novels, two wrote vividly about the secret, separate world often created by children in a large family. Both writers had childhood experience of being part of such a family, though only one was a mother herself.

Barbara Comyns's two novels, *Who Was Changed and Who Was Dead*[14] and *Sisters by the River*,[15] give a child's-eye view of an adult world which is not just lacking in logic but at times cruelly irresponsible. Barbara Comyns's novels are spoiled by her 'little girl' style of writing, a style which avoids confronting the fact that this is not a child writing but an adult trying to re-enter a child's world. Her children, like her adult women, seem strangely passive and unspeculative, even though she must have been aware that children need to make sense of their world, and most children try to find ways of controlling it. Her child characters, like her heroines, do not overtly challenge authority, becoming instead secretly manipulative. If a reader can overcome irritation at a style of writing that does not change whether it is describing adult or childish reactions (and there are, no doubt, many readers who like her style), the novels are not only perceptive about children but often capture the helplessness children feel before adults' brutish callousness. This is especially so in *Who Was Changed and Who Was*

*Dead*, a novel which is full of violent deaths and catastrophic events seen largely through the eyes of the Willoweed children. There are unforgettable pictures: the kitten drowned in the flood, with the bone of its tail exposed; the butcher's appalling suicide; and, above all, Emma's discovery of the crawling, burnt body of Toby – '"He smelt so dreadful, and he crawled . . ."'[16] Barbara Comyns creates a cruel and heartless world whose chief victims are young women and children, but there is little rebellion in her fiction, merely a fatalistic determinism.

Despite her imaginative creation of a child's world and the individuality of her children – a refreshing change from Elizabeth Goudge's – Barbara Comyns's novels are marred by the way she seems to wallow in the fate of her victim heroines, most of whom are either suffering or mad. These are, after all, middle-class families she portrays, not the poor, the landless or the workless, and her acceptance of their suffering passivity and their self-pity contrasts unfavourably with novels – such as Maureen Duffy's *That's How It Was*,[17] – which recall childhoods which really were underprivileged but which showed women fighting against the multiple disadvantages of class, gender, poverty and ill-health to achieve something.

Nancy Mitford's children are a refreshing contrast. Her four novels featuring Fanny and her Radlett cousins appeared between 1945 and 1960, and her point of view shifts from a child's-eye view of the adult world to an adult's view of a child's world.[18] Adults and children regard each other with uncomprehending frustration, the children's main objective being to circumvent adult plans for them and to survive the madnesses adults are capable of. If you can get over the prejudices that the antics of the aristocracy can raise in many of us (I include myself), the eccentric Radlett family, seen through their orphan cousin Fanny's eyes, are marvellously comic creations. Despite her irritating tone and style, Nancy Mitford is not an uncritical admirer of the Radlett girls and their upbringing. In fact while describing their undisciplined lives, she makes explicit her belief that the education of girls is a liberating and empowering influence, and throughout the quartet of novels, the poor choices made by the Radlett girls, especially Linda, are blamed on their lack of a formal education. Fanny is luckier; her guardian, Aunt Emily, is totally devoted to the principle of girls' education and ensures that Fanny receives a good one. This enables Fanny to see the differences between her and her cousins; she attributes their inability to concentrate on anything for any length of time to the lack of disciplined study in their lives that education would provide. They are intelligent, imaginative and often original, but full of sudden enthusiasms and as sudden boredoms.

The Radlett girls have grown up in a household where male values hold sway; where men are men, and women are there to serve them. The description of the Radlett house emphasises its function as a place for men, for it is not so much a home as a rather cold and comfortless place from which men sally forth to pursue their hunting, shooting and fishing activities and return to in order to eat, sleep and shelter from the elements. The difference is made even more pointed by the picture of Lord Merlin's house: elegant, graceful, warm and filled with beautiful things; a feminine home even though it is run by a man. The Radlett girls grow up in a home where, though they are allowed the freedom to run wild, their futures are never considered, as it is assumed they will marry and live the same sort of life as their mother. Their father, Matthew, holds the traditional male view of women's education, rejecting Aunt Emily's ideas. Later, Fanny's future husband will represent another, minority male view of educated women, when he tells Fanny that he disapproves of the uneducated Radletts and could never marry such a girl. The failure of Matthew Radlett to provide a structure or discipline for his daughters' lives (the sons, of course, are sent away to be educated) and their mother's acceptance of her husband as the decision-maker, are implicitly criticised, particularly as Fanny makes connections between Linda's upbringing and the rootless, impulsive life she takes up as an adult. At the same time, Fanny can enjoy the time she spends with her Radlett cousins, benefitting from the unstructured freedom as a balance to her quieter, more orderly life with Aunt Emily. Later in life, returning to Alconleigh as a married woman, she views the younger Radletts' behaviour with a good deal less tolerance, seeing the dangers in its anarchic rejection of discipline and its fundamental immaturity.

As in Barbara Comyns's fiction, the countryside is the setting for the children's lives, but Nancy Mitford's countryside is less extreme than Barbara Comyns's, which tends to veer from the lyrically beautiful to cruel horror. Nancy Mitford describes the countryside as it is; it does not serve any symbolic function in her novels. Her children explore it, enjoy it, but suffer no traumas from what they see or hear. What is wrong with the Radlett way of life, much as

Fanny loves and enjoys the members of the family, is a result of human attitudes and beliefs, of action taken or not taken by parents and guardians. The way these failures affect the children depends too on those children's characters and temperaments. Fanny feels that all Linda's misfortunes could have been avoided if her parents had been more vigilant and prevented her disastrous first marriage, but the novel also suggests that something deeper, the 'Matthew view' of women as secondary in importance and only of value in their relation to men, is as much to blame.[19] Fanny's own marriage to her beloved Alfred can survive the rough periods because of the confidence she feels in herself as a result of an upbringing which emphasised women's values rather than men's.

## The ideology of motherhood

With the exception of Elizabeth Goudge, all these writers ignore the conventional views of motherhood current in the postwar world. One went so far as to satirise such views openly. Pamela Hansford Johnson must have been reacting to the deification of motherhood that took place in the 1950s when she wrote *The Unspeakable Skipton*,[20] for the character of Dorothy Merlin is a glorious send-up of the sentimentalising of motherhood that took place at the time. Dorothy is not so much a mother as a Womb. She uses her motherhood as a weapon to subdue her husband and as material to ensure that her literary outpourings will be uncritically received because they affirm the sacredness of being a mother. Dorothy takes the ideology of motherhood and blows it up into a monstrous travesty, but as it is essentially a man-made travesty, created by men to limit and exclude women, the men themselves cannot challenge it. Even Dorothy's total lack of involvement in the upbringing of her seven sons – all sent away from home to be cared for by others – does not appear to undermine her authority to speak as the Universal Mother. She is a female version of Rousseau, whose callous handing-over of all his children to an orphanage appears to raise no doubts as to the validity of his theories on the education of children.[21] Pamela Hansford Johnson satirises the sociological and psychological construction of motherhood in the postwar period by inflating it to the point of ridicule. Dorothy's smatterings of Freudiana and her exploitation of her role as mother

remain unchallenged by the men around her, despite their private
reservations, and Dorothy uses this as the source of her power. The
men call her 'Dotty', but her apparently ridiculous behaviour is
fundamentally sane, ensuring her power and autonomy remain
intact.

Dorothy Merlin's children are notable for their absence; they do
not appear in the novel and in no way impinge on her life. The
reader never knows what happens to her children as a result of her
total lack of involvement in their upbringing. Pamela Hansford
Johnson is more concerned to attack the false ideas attaching to the
ideal of motherhood, rather than to suggest what effects emotional
deprivation may have on children. Elizabeth Taylor went further,
suggesting that too much emotion expended on children is more
dangerous than too little. There is a suggestion in her fiction that too
much absorption in motherhood, particularly when infancy has
passed, is potentially mutilating. In *Palladian*,[22] for example, Tinty
has been an emotional mother, quick to tears and flurries of alarm.
Her children, defending themselves from drowning in this flood of
emotions, ended up crippling themselves. For Tinty 'damned up'
her children's emotions, making them unable to deal with crises or
to cope with strong feelings. On the other hand, Beth's indifference
in *A View of the Harbour* and Isabella's detachment in *The Sleeping
Beauty* do not hamper their children's growth. Prudence emerges
from her unhappiness to fall in love and Laurence not only discovers
the difference between adolescent lust and love but, reaching
adulthood without bitterness, can approach his mother again, adult
to adult. The path is made easier for Laurence by his discovery that
his mother and he share a minor vice: a passion for betting on
horses. Isabella has hidden what she sees as a rather shameless but
exciting hobby from her family, but her son sees the evidence of a
shared humanity. At last he can enter into that bantering, teasing
mother-and-son relationship he has so much envied in his friends.

### The outside eye

Children's clear perception of their parents is frequently contrasted
with parents' bewilderment and incomprehension when faced with
their children's reactions. Often too blinded by their contradictory
emotions to be able to see the children clearly, it is sometimes the
outside eye, more detached and without guilt, that offers a surer

vision. Over and over again it is the stranger, the outsider to a family or the non-parent relative who seems to see the child more clearly and truly. Cassandra understands Sophy's need to lie about her mother, to talk about her, while neither her true nor her legal father can;[23] Tory is more perceptive about Robert's and Beth's elder daughter than about her own son;[24] in *The Sleeping Beauty*[25] Emily can communicate with Rose's maladjusted child who, to anyone else, including her mother, appears a 'mandrake-like horror', and when Emily leaves, her place is taken by another woman who also can understand and communicate with the violent and withdrawn Philly.

Inevitably these middle-class novelists wrote about the separate lives of mothers and children, the emotional distancing that takes place when a third person comes between mother and child. The result of this distancing on the children themselves is ambiguously portrayed. Generally it is the parents who seem the losers in the novels, rather than the children, for people paid to look after children often make a better job of it than the parents. Elizabeth Taylor suggests reasons for this in her portrayals of nannies. The nanny in *The Sleeping Beauty*, feeling no emotion for her charges, can use all her energy to look after them and control them. Emotion – and guilt – are not just tiring but they impede understanding. Nannies also revel in their adult power; they can turn the tables on their employers by using their 'expertise', or the children in their care, to create a power base from within their employers' homes, and it is a power base which is not lightly challenged. In *Palladian* Nanny has remained at Copthorne although there is now no need for her services, and has become a presence to be reckoned with. She views Marion's marriage to Cassandra with grim delight, for Cassandra as an ex-governess is a natural enemy twice over. Unlike governesses, who are hampered by their middle-class gentility and are therefore natural victims, nannies come from a class that has long practice in guerilla warfare against the bourgeoisie. Once inside that middle-class fortress, the home, they can strike at the soft underbelly of the family, using the children in their care as the shock-troops in a campaign without mercy.

## The 'good' mother

What is a 'good' mother according to these writers? Is there any such person? Certainly they reject, consciously or unconsciously, the ideology of the period and depict motherhood as a complex and changing state. Apart from Elizabeth Goudge – and I have already indicated the ambiguities in her fiction – the writers avoid coming to conclusions or laying down hard-and-fast moral precepts. Their fiction implies that flawed adults will make flawed parents and that immature and dependent women cannot be expected to help their children grow to independence. On the theme of motherhood generally, though, the fiction merely suggests, questions and points out anomalies, but reaches no conclusions.

# Women and work

'A man,' she thought, suddenly, 'would consider this a business outing. But, then, a man would not have to cook the meals for the day overnight, nor consign his child to a friend, nor leave half-done the ironing, nor forget the grocery order as I now discover I have forgotten it. The artfulness of men,' she thought. 'They implant in us, foster in us, instincts which it is to their advantage for us to have, and which, in the end, we feel shame at not possessing.' She opened her eyes and glared with scorn at a middle-aged man reading a newspaper.

'A man like *that*,' she thought, 'a worthless creature, obviously; yet so long has his kind lorded it that I (who, if only I could have been ruthless and single-minded about my work as men are, could have been a good writer) feel slightly guilty at not being back at the kitchen sink.'[1]

This passage appears in *A View of the Harbour*, its anger tearing the text apart to reveal an uncharacteristic show of temper by its author, Elizabeth Taylor. It is also uncharacteristic of Beth, whose immersion in her fictional world precludes such a sharp view of male manipulation. Apart from its anger, it effectively states the dilemma *any* work outside the family presents for a woman, and is still as true today as when it was written in 1947.

Patricia Stubbs, in *Women and Fiction*, makes the point that fiction in general rarely depicts women at work, preferring to focus interest on the private world of emotions. She talks about 'the novel's continuing indifference to the material, everyday part of women's lives' and points out that even among contemporary women writers this is the case, the only exceptions being those writers who use non-realist narrative forms.[2] Similarly Patricia Meyer Spacks also says, 'women have not created important fictional heroines who find gratification through doing something in the world'.[3] It is always dangerous to make generalisations and this generalisation is not strictly true. Certainly the women novelists of the postwar period did concentrate on the private world of emotion more than the public one of work, but there are working heroines in their novels and in some cases this work does provide gratification. Not surprisingly the jobs envisaged tended to be those open to middle-class women – governess, secretary, or some branch of the arts – and generally the work was of less importance in the novel than the personal relationships. The problem is that the use of nineteenth-century realist forms of fiction, in which women are depicted as the guardians of the world of private experience, with the home as their natural habitat, made it difficult for women writers, whose own experience of the public world of work may have been limited, to break this mould successfully. They could perhaps have used Charlotte Brontë's strategy of casting the heroine out of her home and placing her in an alien environment, making her parentless and homeless. Kate O'Brien did try this in *As Music and Splendour*,[4] one of the most determined attempts by a woman writer up to this time to give a woman's work the same, if not more, value than her emotional life. On the other hand, Elizabeth Taylor returned over and over again to the theme of the artist, though her women artists are confined to their homes. The world of work which, despite the back-to-the-home ideology of the period, was increasingly filled with women, remained shadowy and peripheral, and the problems women encountered when trying to combine their aspirations with their domestic 'duties' were explored by few writers.

**Handmaidens: the traditional 'servicing' jobs**

Generally, outside the arts, heroines had to be content with the helpmeet role in work. Some of Barbara Pym's heroines do work for their living and she drew from her own working experience to create the office workers and anthropologists who appear in some of her novels. However, office routine is repetitive and lacking in status, and Pym's women anthropologists are a rather depressing bunch, plain and sexless, who lead uncomfortable and monotonous lives. Only Helena escapes; she is both attractive, married and, we are assured, enthusiastic about her work.[5] However, there are only brief references to her actually working and her enthusiasm seems to have had as much to do with her romantic yearnings for Everard Bone as for the work itself. At the end of the novel she appears to have given up her work in favour of country life with Rocky, her husband. Barbara Pym certainly does not offer any hope of transcendence through work for women, banishment to the more menial areas of work being a recurrent theme in her novels.

Ellie, in Olivia Manning's *The Doves of Venus*,[6] has high hopes when she is transferred from the packing department of a furniture shop to the studio. But her job there is confined to varnishing and applying gold-leaf, and even this promotion has not been because she has been spotted as potentially artistic, but as a sort of payment by her lover, Quinton, for favours received. Ellie's enthusiasm and optimism are painted against a background of low expectations for women, with even the successful woman owner of the furniture shop suggesting that Ellie would be safer at home with her mother or contenting herself with her packing job – a job generally difficult to fill and therefore suitable for a skilless woman. Depressingly, she is right. Ellie, eventually jobless and moneyless, is only saved by marriage. She may continue her interest in painting, but the suggestion is that it will be pushed into second place, a tinkering with art rather than real immersion. Yet Ellie is far from being a passive victim; she has had the courage to fight the attitudes to art-teaching at the evening classes she attended at Eastsea Technical School and her escape from Eastsea itself demonstrates her enterprise. Sexually she is adventurous, embarking on her first affair with relish and celebrating the end of her virginity with a dance in her tiny room. Ellie's defeat is all the sadder for the imaginative boldness with which she had made a break from home, but her return there, even as a married woman, does not seem the victory that Ellie thinks it is. Ellie's problems highlight the real dilemma for ambitious women in this period: that the sort of work available for women tended to be repetitive and dull, with little chance of turning into a satisfying career. Inevitably, the private life of marriage offered more satisfactions.

Susan Ertz made an attempt to give some dignity to women working in jobs generally considered low-grade and repetitive. In *The Prodigal Heart*[7] she explores the contrasting attitudes of two generations of women to work, one pre-war and the other post-war. The pre-war generation – Medwin's employers, Miss Lyddon and Mrs Gresham – show the sort of administrative and organisational skills that would not have been out of place in running a large business, but as 'ladies' they can only use them in voluntary charitable work. Medwin also has these skills but she can use them to earn her living. One of the refreshing things about this novel is the description of the secretarial duties Medwin undertakes: not only the skills and tact necessary, but also the possibilities for innovation when the employer is able to delegate or ask for comments on decisions. The period difference is underlined by the contrast between the education of the older women and the younger. The older women have both received excellent educations (they were at Girton together), while Medwin, a pre-1944 Education Act girl, has barely been educated at all, her middle-class father preferring to leave her unschooled rather than send her to a 'council school'. The difference between the opportunities for moneyed middle-class girls and impoverished ones is noticeable; class here does not act in favour of the girls, since if Medwin had gone to the council school, she would most likely have received a reasonable education. Yet despite her disadvantages, Medwin seems to have made more of her life than the older women, escaping from the constrictions of class into autonomy. The difference, Susan Ertz suggests, is due to social change. In the aftermath of the Second World War, ideas about 'ladies' work' had virtually disappeared and Medwin became one of the many women who saw work as a solution to being single or widowed.

Susan Ertz's support for working women is also apparent in *Charmed Circle*.[8] Selma works to earn her living, and her sanity and sense of purpose are contrasted with the rich and idle Clarissa's bored and finally disastrous life. Education is not seen as the key factor in freeing women: work is. The 'sane' working heroines, Medwin and Selma, have values which will carry them through any vicissitudes; the neurotic women, Miss Lyddon and Mrs Gresham in *The Prodigal Heart*, and Clarissa in *Charmed Circle*, fail to lead rich lives. The frustrated energy of Miss Lyddon and Mrs Gresham, both educated and intelligent women, only finds an outlet in the intensity they put into their deep, but narrow, emotional lives. Clarissa has an even worse fate; bouncing from man to man, despite her fundamental frigidity, she becomes a meaningless plaything.

## Unskilled work

Unfortunately, most women at this time found little satisfaction in the type of work available to them, those who lacked marketable skills being especially limited in what they could do. The retail trade offered one possibility and, despite its low pay and long hours, was a large employer of women. However, the divide between the management, mainly male, and the female working force, was determined as much by gender as by class or education. In Elizabeth Taylor's *A Game of Hide and Seek*,[9] the skilless Harriet is initiated into her job as shop assistant by three indeterminately aged spinsters, who have developed a successful campaign against their employer. Resentment against long hours and low pay is expressed covertly; the women use the firm's time for their own private activities, extend their breaks to the limit and commandeer the firm's property – stamps, soap, even the clothing stock – for their personal use. It is a working-class strategy, a defence against exploitation. It is also a female strategy against male power, for the three women form an alliance against men – particularly the Manager, technically in charge of them. If he attempts to voice a criticism of them he is quickly put in his place. The women:

> retreated nicely, excluded him from their feminine world, threw tissue paper over bust-bodices – their eyelids so leaden, their look at one another so sinister – that he went back exasperated to his office, or round to a coffee-shop to talk to other men.[10]

Harriet is welcomed into their midst, taught the skills of survival, her mistakes 'applauded as disloyalty to the firm' and her virginity wondered at and seen as a positive asset. Despite the differences in class and age that Harriet represents, the women never exclude her from their informal 'trade union' solidarity (though they would have considered themselves too ladylike ever to join one). Trapped in demeaning and low-status work, they do not expect pleasure from what they do for a living; instead the social cohesiveness they display against employer and customer alike gives them a certain sense of power and control. They have not sought work for something to *do*, as Harriet and the other middle-class heroines have: they have no choice but to work. Harriet can escape the dead end of such a job by marrying into her own class; such a solution was never available to them.

Elizabeth Taylor was very perceptive about the strategies used by women who find themselves powerless at work, especially in the 'service' industries. Her shop assistants, nannies and cleaning women turn the tables on their employers, transgress in ways that are impossible to punish, and betray their contempt for those technically 'over' them in such a way that, though their employers are aware of the contempt, they are helpless to do anything about it.

Class and period dimensions are also important in Elizabeth Jane Howard's *The Beautiful Visit*.[11] The narrative begins just before the First World War and ends just after it. Like the Second World War, the first too provided opportunities for unskilled middle-class women to work or to be involved in the public sphere. These opportunities were quickly snatched away when the war ended. Like many middle-class women of her time, the heroine had received no formal education and the possibility of her having to earn her living had never been envisaged. Lacking marketable skills, her ambition is merely to survive. She fails even in this modest ambition. Her first attempt to work in the local library horrifies her parents, who see this as a job which will de-class her. In the end she settles for looking after children, taking them for walks – suitable work for a genteel, if impoverished, young lady. The outbreak of war seems to offer hope of a more significant life, but she is quickly disabused by the attitude of her brothers, who see her role as staying at home and keeping herself 'fascinating' for the men's return. Despite her insistence that she must *do* something, that there is nothing at all for her to do at home, they remain blankly unconvinced:

> I looked at them in despair. Did they seriously consider me so different from themselves? Did they think that I could live without any of the support they deemed so necessary and admirable? That to prepare meals and clothes and beds in which to sleep was for a woman an end in itself. I stared from Tom's pale moustache to Hubert's shaven cheek and hated them. That was all they need do, trim their moustaches and shave. Their clothes were mended; they did not cook their food or pull back the sheets each morning. They were able to use the means of living as a means: for me they were assumed to be an end.[12]

## Women as creative artists

The heroine of *The Beautiful Visit* is like a trapped animal; whatever she does she will fail. Constricted by class and gender, without the education or training that would make a job feasible, she can only beat her wings against the transparent barriers of her prison. What miserable work she can get – copying musical scores – pays so badly that she cannot afford the minimum level of life. Her courage and determination are not enough to ensure her escape, and Elizabeth Jane Howard can see no realistic solution to her heroine's problems. She shrinks from a deterministic ending, however, and prefers to provide her heroine with an escape. When the heroine's final desperate attempt to lead a life of her own is a failure, she is offered the chance of a mysterious journey and a 'quest'. The hazy nature of the work she is offered, the fact that it involves a voyage in a ship, the unfeminine clothes she has to put on when she sets out, place the solution in the realm of fantasy. The realism of the main narrative is framed by this fantastical element: the novel beginning and ending with the heroine awakening and discovering herself alone in a cabin on a boat, dressed in masculine clothes, with two exercise books which contain the story of her life. The masculine clothing put on by the heroine for her journey suggests that her normal clothes, which identify her with the female role, have had to be given up. It is unclear, however, whether this is meant to be an escape into androgyny, transvestism or disguise.[13] Nor is it just dress which confines her, but the conflation of concepts of women and home. When Elspeth points out to the heroine that the home from which she thinks she has escaped is still with her, she is suggesting that 'home' as a sphere which women are supposed to inhabit is not so much a place as a state of mind. Therefore it is only by using her mind, her imagination, that the heroine can be freed. The quest offered by Elspeth is a journey of the imagination, an open-ended search to prove . . . what? That the earth isn't round at all, or even spherical?

It is a curious and ambiguous solution of the heroine's problem. Is the author suggesting that, given the world as it is, round or spherical, the heroine will forever be trapped and that she will only truly escape by proving that the world is *not* round, that the values considered to be self-evident, the beliefs about woman's role, are all based on false evidence? If so, it is a surprisingly feminist statement,[14] and one that is more complex than merely thinking that with certain changes women can take their place in the world. Nor is it suggested that the world itself should be changed: it is human perception of the nature of that world that has to be altered. The unreal nature of the journey, the fact that the heroine begins and ends the novel alone, the presence of the exercise books on the bed, suggest that this is either a journey of the spirit or a hallucination. If the first, then the heroine is to question ideas about the nature of her world by writing her story. Her freedom will come from challenging male fictions about women by using fictional modes to create another view. Accuracy and imagination are the necessary requirements, according to Elspeth. The novel ends with the heroine, her life story told, beginning a new one. She takes an unlined exercise book and writes her title across the first page: 'The Four Corners of the Earth'.

If Elizabeth Jane Howard is suggesting that the writing of fiction is not just a way of earning a living but also carries the possibility of creating a different perception of the nature of the world, then her heroine will be a more subtle writer than Elizabeth Taylor's two writer heroines, Angelica Deverell in *Angel*[15] and Beth in *A View of the Harbour*. In nearly all Elizabeth Taylor's early fiction there is a portrait of an artist: painter or writer, female or male. It is almost a signature in her work, like Frances's cacti which appeared in most of her paintings, their prickly hostility suggesting that the prettiness of the painting hid a harsher view of reality. However, neither Angel nor Beth are going to alter perceptions of women through their novel-writing, since both write romantic escapist fiction.

Elizabeth Taylor celebrates all those 'women scribblers' who wrote their way out of poverty in the character of Angel, whose extraordinary success as a writer of high-flown romances takes her from a mean home above a shop in Volunteer Street to Paradise House, the 'big house' where her aunt had worked as a lady's maid when Angel was a child. Angel writes the sort of escapist fiction that is full of exotic aristocrats, castles and dungeons. Knowing nothing of the life of aristocrats, she writes 'with ignorance and imagination', putting her own fantasies into her books and some-how tapping into the collective fantasies of thousands of readers. Her lack of self-criticism and humour only gives her a tremendous confidence in her work. Convinced she is a great writer, she is bitterly angry at the derision of the critics, interpreting it as spite and envy. Angel's strength as a writer is that she believes her own fantasies, and this belief transmits itself through her novels to the readers who, like her, wish to escape the drabness of their daily lives. The stories of the real Paradise House, embellished and enlarged by Angel, become the inspiration for her first novel. Her fantasies of living there herself become a reality when Angel, a successful and rich novelist, buys the house. Paradoxically, the move to Paradise House, the realisation of her early dream, leads to her decline as a best-selling writer. Cut off from the real world, she is unable to see the changes taking place in that world and continues to write for a public that has vanished. As the house crumbles and decays around her, her daily living degenerates into squalor and poverty.

Elizabeth Taylor could easily have made Angel something ridiculous, a butt for our laughter; instead she gradually gains our respect for Angel's courage and determination by emphasising that her success has been achieved as a result of sheer hard work. Angel transforms her life by her own efforts, expecting no help or support from anyone. She only wishes for love and, until near the end of her life, assumes she had it from Esmé. She can be monstrously egotistical, but she also has her tender side, especially for animals. Angel's determination to assert her individuality, her 'I', on the world only partially succeeds, but this victory has been achieved by her work, not by the use of feminine wiles, and she does have the right to assert triumphantly on her deathbed: 'I am Angelica Deverell'.[16]

Angel is swallowed up by her own fiction; Beth, also a writer of romantic fiction, cannot transform her life so easily. I feel that through the character of Beth in *A View of the Harbour* Elizabeth Taylor may have explored some aspects of her own experience as a novelist, for Beth is married and has two children. Her writing has to be fitted into her domestic routine in much the same way that Elizabeth Taylor's had to be. There are some similarities in the characters of Beth and Angel – Beth too can be blind to what is happening round her – but reality is too solid for Beth to escape easily. She has developed the capacity to think of several things at once, planning lunch for her family while devising a fictional scene where her imaginary family are listening to the reading of a will. She takes advantage of the time that her husband is on his rounds, and her children out or at school, to work out her plots, but even while writing, 'hoping to have an only child dead by lunch', time can run out and Stevie arrive back from school while the scene remains uncompleted. 'But with the dying child still on her mind, Beth could not bring herself to welcome the living one.'[17] The interruptions to her life can be charted through the defects in her fiction, which she can trace to specific events: her children's illnesses or domestic crises.

Beth's fictional world is often more real than the everyday one, but she never confuses the two. However, the complications of plotting and dialogue that engage her attention lead her to simplify real life. Her emotions are straightforward: her love and trust in Tory is unshakeable, as is her belief that her marriage is a happy one. Towards her children she is detached, since her creativity has not found its outlet in motherhood but in authorship. Her casualness about domestic routine and her oblivion to the disorderliness and ugliness of her surroundings is contrasted with her care in 'putting one word alongside another, like matching silks, a sort of game'.[18] Cheerfully she cannibalises her friends' lives for incidents in her novel-writing, at one point making Tory ask her with amusement if anything – husband, children, friends – mattered more to her than her work. Another time, filled with guilt and love, Tory attacks her and her writing, suggesting that all writers are 'ruined people', inhuman and unconnected with real life. When anything important happens to them, Tory suggests, they react by using the experience which, with a little 'shifting here and a little adding there' can be cobbled into a decent bit of prose.

The use of a 'sewing' metaphor, as in the 'matching silk' simile, is apt for a woman writer, especially if she also uses the minutiae of everyday life to flesh out her characters and give credibility to her plots. The capacity to make do and mend, to use what is given, is particularly useful if your life is bounded by the home. A woman writer often has to pick up and put down her work just as a needlewoman has to, using the acceptable gaps in a wife and mother's life – a confinement, breast-feeding a child, darning socks – as an opportunity to plan details of her current novel, while lulling everyone into supposing she is merely carrying out her womanly duties. But Beth, unlike Angel, cannot so easily escape the ideology of womanhood. She *is* a wife and mother, and the expectations laid on her as a result of that are inescapable, making her feel guilt at her failure to be a 'good' mother and an attentive wife.

Patricia Meyer Spacks[19] suggests that women who wish to avoid adulthood remain adolescent by the use of fantasy, but this is a simplistic explanation of the role of fantasy. Beth's blindness to what is happening may be caused by her immersion in a fictional world, but she is a real, and successful, novel-writer, as is Angel in her heyday. It is true that the refusal to see the uglier truths in life has a Peter Pan element to it, but at the same time both Beth's and Angel's blindness to the truths about their husbands actually protects them. Subtly, Elizabeth Taylor suggests that those who see clearly are unhappy, while those who do not, retain their happiness. It is also perhaps unfair to suggest that only female fantasy is a form of adolescent escapism.

Both Beth and Angel use their imaginations to create worlds that have more to do with literary models than with real life, and their imaginary worlds are purely escapist. But Elizabeth Taylor knew that the ability to imagine can be used by anyone to escape reality. She frequently explored the differences between women and men as creative artists, suggesting that men too can be as escapist as women. Vinny, in *The Sleeping Beauty*,[20] does not paint or write, but has all the instincts of one who does. He is a man who cannot bear too much reality, falling in love with a woman whom he first sees in the distance, framed by a window. Vinny's preference for making love in the dark so that he cannot see the woman's body, and his seizing on the half-dead Emily to fall in love with, suggest one type of male fiction-making: the capacity to project on to a passive woman all that the man wishes to find in a lover. Emily becomes Vinny's creation, helplessly watching him 'inventing' her. Vinny is a Pygmalion, turning the emotionally dead Emily into a living woman, this being the only way of possessing his ideal. Vinny's is a rose-coloured dream which enables him to avoid confronting reality. Tom's imagination, on the other hand, draws its inspiration from a black vision, but it is still, in its way, as escapist as Vinny's. In *Palladian*,[21] Tom's drawings, apparently simple, objective, anatomical charts, are not as realistic as they first appear, as Tom himself admits. Tom uses them to express his savage hatred and contempt for people, reducing them to delicate black and white diagrams of bone, sinew and nerve. Tom and Vinny represent extremes of the male imagination: the dissecting, ruthless view of humanity and the romantic glossing of the nature of women.

Women artists from early times have suffered from the denigration of themselves as secondary to male artists.[22] Even women novelists have not been exempt. The librarian in *A View of the Harbour* expressed a not uncommon view of what he chose to call 'lady novelists': ' "No need to be prejudiced against lady novelists . . . Ladies – and you notice I say 'ladies' – have their own contribution to make. A nice domestic romance. Why ape men?"'[23] This view of women novelists as marginal footnotes in literary history has not changed a great deal: a recent BBC radio series about writers in the 1950s failed to mention that there were also women novelists around – though they found time to deal at length with Ian Fleming, rather than discuss what women writers of the period were making of their – the woman's – world.[24]

When women tried to express a harsher, more realistic view of life, the limitations of their own lives confined them and made it almost impossible to break through. Frances is a woman painter, and when *A Wreath of Roses*[25] opens, she is going through an artistic crisis. The subjects of her paintings have been drawn from real life, but it has been real life with a glow, a rosy light thrown over it, a 'gauziness': flowers, lemons on a dish, lovely women sitting or reclining. But Frances in her old age has become disillusioned about her painting, seeing herself as 'guilty of making ugliness charming'. Her new paintings try to express her new vision of the world, which she now sees as darkened by the terrible things people do to each other. Rejecting the 'prettiness' and English charm of her earlier paintings, she tries to go beyond her artistic range, struggling to express her new vision in paintings that have dark tormented skies and violent scenery. Morland Beddoes, her patron and admirer, is horrified by the change in her and tempts her back to her old style. But Frances is incapable of regaining her old view of life and her last painting for him remains uncompleted, its failure symbolised by the real wreath of faded roses she has been using as a model: for a wreath is ambiguous, its purpose bridal or funereal. Morland Beddoes has done what many male critics have done to women artists: tried to restrict them to their femininity. He dislikes women who make a loud noise, who cry out their pain or anger, and his attraction to Frances's painting has been because of her 'feminine' quietness and understatement. He is therefore distressed that 'his' painter is trying to change the very qualities he admires in her. Under his influence, Frances falters, and, to please him, attempts one last painting in her original style. Earlier she has accused him of being the devil sent to tempt her; viewing the unfinished result of her effort to please him, she realises she has been untrue to herself, a cardinal sin for an artist.

Elizabeth Taylor uses the character of Frances to explore her own problems as a woman writer. Frequently placed in the class of 'genteel' writers, her irony overlooked and her subtle suggestion of violence hidden below a calm surface ignored, perhaps she too struggled to find ways of expressing her horror at cruelty and violence in more covert ways, without losing her individual voice. She was never the conforming accepter of middle-class life she has been accused of being.[26] Several of her novels convey the surface prettiness and calmness of life, which can rupture to reveal ugliness and cruelty, like a toad hidden in the leaves – a favourite recurring image in her fiction. Elizabeth Taylor appears to be debating the attitude the dedicated artist should take to reality. The Second World War, with its horrific revelations of human bestiality and indifference, was a subject 'outside her range as an artist', but she attempted to convey the horror obliquely, through the violent but private deaths that occur in her novels and the sudden revelations of ugliness masked as beauty. The woman artist, she suggests, is wrong to allow herself to be confined by her femininity, her banishment to the private sphere and her exclusion from public events. Both Beth and Frances have limitations set on their art by being women. Frances's need to earn her living has meant she has spent too long being a governess teaching others, instead of developing her own art. Beth's involvement in domestic detail has led to failures in her fiction, which she describes as 'little jarring reverberations'. But Frances at least struggles to leave the confining limits set on women artists to express the vision that has come with maturity and experience. Her failure is interesting because it suggests a dilemma facing many women artists: how to represent conflict, even violence. As women they may tend to identify with the victim of aggression rather than with the aggressor, and they therefore write about conflict in ways that are different to men's; their emphasis is, necessarily, on survival, rather than on winning outright. At the same time they are confined within images of women as either passive victims or gallant survivors, a view which pressurises them into suppressing the expression of their own anger or passion for fear of being criticised as unfeminine.

There is a real-life contemporary echo of Frances's struggle to avoid 'niceness' and charm in Sylvia Plath's experience. In 1957 her patron and friend Olive Prouty, playing the Morland Beddoes role, wrote to her: '"Someone remarked to me after reading your poem in the *Atlantic*, 'How intense'. Sometime write me a little poem that *isn't* intense. A lamp turned too high might shatter its chimney.

Please just *glow* sometimes." '[27] The chimney metaphor with its sense of confinement and its phallic undertones is revealing. Later her mother too complained to Sylvia about her tendency to write her stories about sad or depressing subjects, and urged her to write instead about 'decent courageous people'. Sylvia's response was explicit: ' "Now stop trying to get me to write about 'decent courageous people','' she wrote back, advising her mother to ' "read the *Ladies Home Journal* for those!" '.[28]

Elizabeth Taylor also used the characters of Frances and Beth to explore some of the dilemmas she must have met in her own life as a creative artist, dilemmas which she shared with writers such as Jane Austen, Mrs Gaskell, George Sand, who all had to fit their writing into the gaps left them – George Sand even using night-time to write, her days were so filled with her house, her children, her visitors and her lovers. Women artists also had to contend with a view that saw women artists as freaks, unnatural creatures who showed none of the usual feminine virtues. Often they disguised themselves as normal. Frances, for example, went to great pains to present a picture of a domestically correct woman, wishing to be known for her crab-apple jelly rather than her painting, and would have been confounded if she had known how little effect this had on the village's perception of her. In earlier times she would have been regarded as a witch; the twentieth century, more charitably bracketing her with the village idiot and the absent-minded vicar, saw her as harmlessly odd and in need of protection.

One way a woman artist can dedicate herself wholly to her art is by removing herself from her ordinary environment and entering another where total artistic dedication is demanded equally of men and women. Kate O'Brien's *As Music and Splendour* took two Irish girls, Clare Halvey and Rose Lennane, removed them from their Irish homes and set them down in Italy where, cut off from family, culture, language and the Irish version of Catholicism, they had to undertake rigorous training to be singers. What Kate O'Brien really wanted to express was the idea that women, as well as men, wanted self-satisfaction and the selfish pleasures of individual achievement. Like other women writers, she saw the arts as one chance of providing a rewarding area of work for women. However, the inequalities that often prevented women from fully participating in artistic creation made it difficult to explore freely women immersed in such work. In 1943 she had created a heroine who was a dedicated actress. *The Last of Summer*,[29] however, fails to bring to life the reality of her heroine's working life, and we have to take her dedication on trust, as there is no concrete evidence of it.

In her last novel, *As Music and Splendour*, Kate O'Brien found what she had been looking for. Aware of the lack of women in music generally, she chose to make her two heroines singers, for here indeed, in a singing career, there is equality between women and men. Women singers are subjected to the same rigorous training as men and the same demands of musicality and skill are made of them as of their male counterparts. Opera singing, particularly, provided careers for women and men, with both equally rewarded in terms of fame and appreciation. Kate O'Brien's two heroines, Clare and Rose, are spotted as talented singers and despatched to Italy to learn their craft. The unusual element in the novel is the emphasis on the girls' commitment to their exhausting learning programme and their professional dedication when they emerge as adult singers. The *centrality* of singing in their lives endures through all the problems and delights of their sexual lives; it is their core. Not just a means of earning a living, it becomes a way of expressing themselves as women, and at a time when women found it difficult to leave the private sphere of home for the public sphere of work, Clare's and Rose's success as singers enables them to make this move effortlessly. I cannot think of another novelist who has treated women's careers in quite this way. Kate O'Brien provides a detailed and painstaking account of an opera singer's training and professional life. Her own knowledge of this area is amazingly wide and she paints a realistic picture of Clare's and Rose's development from two peasant Irish girls, desperately homesick for their families and their beloved Ireland, to the assured and successful singers they become. The sheer hard work, the excitement and terrors of public appearances, the triumph of success and the struggle for each singer to find her true voice become the central themes of the novel.

Certainly Kate O'Brien succeeded in her main objective of demonstrating that, given the right context, women are as serious and dedicated as men in their commitment, and are equally able to undertake punishing workloads without pleading feminine differences, and that this commitment can bring them immense satisfaction. To do it, though, she has had to cheat. Clare and Rose are cut off from family and social pressures that might conflict with their ambitions and they have had to become virtual exiles to achieve their ends. Neither has resolved her particular sexual problem by the end of the novel, and Rose's brilliant career seems to have a temporary cloud over it as she leaves La Scala to go to the United States because of a failed love affair. Clare's love for Luisa, too, is problematic, as Luisa's nature does not easily adapt to faithfulness. Love is still seen as a stumbling-block, but at least in the novel it does not prevent the heroines from achieving gratification in their singing careers.

*As Music and Splendour* is at times difficult to read and the copious detail of the singers' lives is not as riveting as it might be. There is also a certain sentimentality in the portrayal of the heroines, which makes for uncomfortable reading. The main problem, however, is that Kate O'Brien was attempting too much in one novel. She wanted to portray two dedicated women artists working and succeeding in the way men do, but she also introduced another socially sensitive theme: lesbianism. To tackle two difficult themes in the same novel was bound to present very special problems, especially when there were few, if any, literary models. Despite Kate O'Brien's undoubted feminism, her literary education seems, from the references she gives in her novels, to have been based almost entirely on male texts. In addition, because she was writing in the nineteenth-century-novel tradition, a tradition which placed women squarely in the private sphere of home, she is hampered in what she wished to express: the commitment women can make to the development of their talents, and the sexual love between women. She tries to make the women's world the most important in the novel, with the men marginal, seen only in reference to the women characters, but the form of the novel defeats her: its ideological basis and its place in history conflict with Kate O'Brien's attempt to change the image it presented of women. Like her heroines, she too is an exile, cut off from her literary foremothers, who might have been able to provide more fruitful models or certainly lead her to question her own choice of form and language.

In these novels about women artists, their limitations are explored and related to the way women's lives are bounded by the conventions which govern their life styles and by the demands made on them to perform two roles simultaneously. These restrictions begin in childhood, with girls and boys being taught early what is expected of them. Elizabeth Goudge, in one of her 'lapses', has a revealing moment in *The White Witch*, when she describes the different 'rites of passage' for a son and a daughter in the seventeenth century. Will has his passage to manhood marked by being dressed in clothes that will not hamper his movement and is given a weapon to symbolise his male power. Jenny, on the other hand, has her entrance into the woman's world signalled by being put in clothes that will prohibit the tomboy rompings she has been used to. She understood fully its meaning: 'From the hampering abundance of petticoat round Jenny's thin legs there was no release to be looked for in this world, and judging by the pictures of angels in the family bible, not in the next either.'[30] This may be a seventeenth-century setting, but it is quite possible to substitute modern equivalents of the hampering petticoats. Even Kate O'Brien's two successful singers, Clare and Rose, are bounded by the singing roles available to them, for these have been created by men, and the female roles are frequently vapid and banal, limited to existing stereotypes.

## Teaching

One profession open to women in the postwar years was teaching, and with the state taking over public education, there was a demand for trained, professional teachers. The role of governess had been a lowly one, demanding respectability and docility rather than professional skills. However, women saw in the expanding educational area a chance to acquire these skills and, at the same time, find work which provided the answer to combining a career with bringing up children. Because it was a 'caring' profession, teaching was considered acceptable work for a woman and did not involve her in conflict with ideas about 'femininity' and appropriate work for women. It could also provide some degree of self-satisfaction. Unfortunately women teachers were often regarded by their male colleagues as dilettante, not serious 'career' teachers (an attitude still prevalent among some members of the National Association of Schoolmasters in the 1970s),[31] and also suffered from the negative image of a woman teacher as a dried-up spinster. This meant that women teachers did not provide attractive role models for young girls and women. Here, for example, is Florence Howe talking about her teachers at Hunter College in the United States in the 1940s:

While I admired them, I did not want to be like them. They were spinsters; even a Dean I loved at Hunter was a spinster. I could not connect them with the women I read of in fiction; or the women men wrote poems about. Nor could I connect them with my mother or other mothers I knew. They were some strange form of being: neither male nor female. Or so I thought in my ignorance.[32]

One of the few novels of the time written by a woman teacher, which gave the impression of teaching as an exciting and innovative occupation, was written by a New Zealander,[33] but it is an exception.

One writer who did paint a positive picture of teaching as a career was Kate O'Brien, this attitude to teaching being part of her deeply-felt beliefs about the liberating potential of education for women. The theme of work as an alternative to marriage emerges in much of Kate O'Brien's fiction, but she was always hampered in her attempts to portray a believable working heroine by the historical period in which she grew up and wrote. The right to education she saw as only a preliminary to a life dedicated to some sort of work, and she balanced the sexual and affectional needs of her heroines against their desire for an autonomous life. Throughout her fiction these two are seen as mutually incompatible and her heroines often have to choose between marriage and autonomy. Sometimes they are uncertain where they will eventually find themselves, but they fight the prejudices against girls' education, aware that learning will widen the choices available to them. In *The Land of Spices*[34] and *The Flower of May*[35] she does not actually take her heroines as far as work or a career, concentrating instead on their fight to learn, their intellectual curiosity and excitement, and their courage in accepting the price: alienation from family and culture. However, she does portray working women in these novels, exploring one of the few accepted professions open to women: teaching. She portrays it as a positive choice, one that, with dedication, can bring satisfaction. However, her teachers are nuns and the conflict between sexual desire and a life of dedicated work has been decided once and for all on taking the veil. Set apart from men, nuns are to a large extent self-regulating. Their dedication to their chosen task is total and the best of them provide a type of education that will liberate those girls who take advantage of it. Kate O'Brien was of course drawing on her own experience of being taught by nuns, and I assume that this must have been positive. Unfortunately not every girl's experience of convent eduation is quite so happy or positive, and Kate O'Brien seems unaware of the contradictions inherent in the situation of a nun, enclosed and separated from the world, yet preparing girls to go into that world. Academic skills could certainly be taught, but as a preparation for life, a convent education, particularly in Ireland, could hardly be considered perfect. However, convent life can be used in fiction to portray women gaining gratification through their work, while avoiding the dilemmas of women in family relationships, with all the expectations laid on them as wives, daughters or sisters.

Teaching itself, especially when carried out in the convent enclosure, does not really challenge perceptions of women as carers and as unselfish givers; if anything, it reinforces them. It was only regarded as one step away from women's traditional role and therefore offered few opportunities to women novelists who wished to portray heroines breaking traditional stereotypes.

## 'Women's work'

Although confinement to the home was regarded critically, women writers did not neglect what is often dismissively referred to as 'women's work'. As women themselves, with domestic commitments, they knew perfectly well that running a home requires a whole battery of skills which can in themselves provide occasion for celebration and a sense of achievement. Confined to the home, women can and do take pride in their ability to master these skills. It can be a trap of course, as Betty Friedan's *The Feminine Mystique* demonstrates. Certainly the picture painted by Marylin French in *The Women's Room* of a woman card-indexing her domestic tasks is of gross maladaption to standards set not by women themselves, but by 'experts', frequently male, as to what a good housewife or mother should be. British women in the postwar period were not as efficiently brain-washed as American suburbanites, but the United States represented a stronger version of what was happening in Britain. Rebellion against confinement to the domestic role had to be repressed, and guilt at not carrying it out successfully came to dominate.

Women who were not trying to be anything other than housewives and mothers could continue to take pleasure in their housekeeping skills and find in them a source of self-satisfaction. When they looked for approbation, however, they had to turn to women, for perhaps the most insidious of all male attitudes to women and their work has been the depreciation and denigration of female domestic and child-caring skills. Sadly too there is a misinformed belief among many women that it is the feminists who are responsible for this downgrading, whereas the reverse is the case. The present women's movement has been at pains to reassess these skills, giving them a positive image, even elevating some of them into arts.[36]

Women writers often depicted characters who took pride in skills based on a female oral tradition and which had been built up over a lifetime of experience. Angel's mother, translated from domestic control of her own home to hanging about doing nothing, sinks into depression, her old certainties gone, and eventually dies. The arts she has spent a lifetime acquiring now fall into disuse: 'her weather-eye for a good drying day; her careful ear for judging the gentle singing sound of meat roasting in the oven; her touch for the freshness of bacon and how, by smelling a cake she could tell if it were baked . . .'[37] There is an episode which evokes perfectly her feeling of loss. While passing the hung-out washing at Alderhurst one day, she automatically tests it for dryness and, without thinking, begins to gather it in. She is unprepared for Angel's curt command to leave it to the paid help. Her useless life hangs heavy, and her sense of loss is increased when the 'smell of ironing or the sound of eggs being beaten' makes her restless and anxious to be doing something.

Pride in achievement can as easily be provided by making the perfect omelette as in painting a picture. Belinda's cry of joy when the pasta she is making from an Italian recipe comes out exactly right;[38] Frances's satisfaction at a successful jelly;[39] Tory's care of her home;[40] all are aspects of the pleasure of *any* work well done which can provide satisfaction and an enhancement of the ego. There are standards too, and contempt shown towards those who fail to reach them. Angel is horrified on her first visit to Esmé's room when she sees the squalor in which he lives, remembering that in Volunteer Street, despite its poverty, its inhabitants would not have put up with the dirt to which this scion of the aristocracy seemed indifferent. Similarly, Isabella's help, Mrs Dickens, is contemptuous of her employer's attempt to make a cake, glancing away from it as if 'she had glimpsed something indecent'. She sees straight away it will be a failure, her experience and skill providing her with a ready diagnosis: 'Slack mixture. Hot oven.'[41] In fact it is often the fate of middle-class women to be despised by their staff for lacking the knowledge and experience necessary to the successful cleaning of a home or the provision of a good meal. And the women themselves can sense the lack: Imogen in *The Tortoise and the Hare*[42] feeling herself out of place in her own kitchen. Nannies, too, having looked after many children can use their wide experience to pull rank over a mother, who has only her own family. The pleasure women can take in creating harmonious homes and appetising meals, and their delight in displaying the results of their skills, are never denigrated in these novels: in fact, criticism of slovenliness is often given expression through the reactions of a character in the novel.

## Work and satisfaction

Work, any work, and a set of skills learnt and used is seen as a potent source of satisfaction for women. Economic independence is not enough (the examples of Petta in *The Doves of Venus* and Clarissa in *Charmed Circle* demonstrate this), but work which defines you as a *person* and not in relative terms, provides a means for positive self-evaluation which is not necessarily dependent on male approval. This emphasis is especially interesting in a period which displayed such ideological confusion over the whole idea of women and work, seeing women's work outside the home as hostile to family life. In all these novels, the goal-less life is portrayed as a disaster for women and there is covert criticism of men who, by enforcing idleness on middle-class women so as to demonstrate their own status, rob them of any means of self-definition. At a time when equal rights to education for girls had been achieved and feminist groups were still campaigning for increased political and economic equality for women, these women novelists expressed through their fiction the view that work – not education, nor political and economic rights – was *the* essential factor in women's lives, and this included so-called 'women's work'.

Given the social realities of the postwar period, women novelists writing in a realistic tradition had difficulty in exploring what the relationship between work and women could be. There was still a discrepancy between the need for women to work so as to earn a living or contribute to the family income, and the preparation for work given to girls. In painting or sculpture they found difficulties when they stepped out of the role of model, inspiration or muse; it was inconceivable that Galatea could step down from her pedestal and start to sculpt. In theatre, opera and films, the hard work and skill that went into the making of women performers was hidden by the two-dimensional roles they were often expected to play. In addition, women were largely unrepresented in the ranks of playwrights, composers and producers, so that the world of theatrical entertainment lacked a female perspective. In the one area where they were almost equally as successful as men, novel-writing, what they wrote was often regarded critically as secondary in importance, a 'minor' art form, often on the basis that their themes were private and domestic, rather than public and 'universal'.[43] Outside the arts, the jobs set aside for them were those that fitted the stereotype of woman as carer. The lack of real-life models made it difficult for women novelists to explore wider possibilities for women. Most confined themselves to diagnosing the ills, and although beginning to be aware that this was a male-inflicted problem, they did not yet see how women could escape.

# 8

# Fictions: subverting the stereotypes

'Oh I am nothing without you,' she said. 'I should not know what to be. I feel as if you had invented me. I watch you inventing me week after week.'[1]

Storytelling belongs to a very long human tradition and has served many purposes other than entertainment. Anyone who writes stories is influenced by what goes before, by their own culture, and women novelists cannot ignore the messages embedded in the stories they inherit. Despite the number of women writing novels, it is the male viewpoint which dominates narrative patterns. The strong hold of the heroic pattern and a long line of sleeping princesses, maidens in distress, enchantresses and witches make it difficult to introduce new narratives with heroic women. Despite the fact that such women exist, they are seen as exceptions and do not therefore figure in narrative patterns, which instead emphasise women's passivity and their role as 'prizes'. In the fairy-tale of Sleeping Beauty, for example, she is completely passive – existing in a death-in-life state – waiting to be rescued by love in the form of a handsome prince. Like Galatea, Pygmalion's statue, she has no existence other than that conferred on her by her lover. Both Sleeping Beauty and Galatea are typical of the tradition of heroines waiting to be rescued and have life breathed into them. The underlying message of the storytelling is that it is woman's fate to be chosen, not to choose; to have her personality created for her, rather than expressing her own. Woman is, in other words, a male invention. Child psychologists used to talk of a child's mind at birth as a *tabula rasa* on which could be written whatever one wanted to write, and there seems to have been a similar view of women's minds. Women writers cannot easily ignore this tradition, but they can subvert it by reinterpreting the stories, inverting them or showing the damaging effect they have on women's expectations of love and lovers.

### 'The Sleeping Beauty': passivity and confinement

Stories such as *The Red Shoes* and *Snow White* can be the vehicles for socially repressed feelings. Angela Carter is one modern writer who has made brilliant use of the sexual themes embedded in what appear to be harmless fairy-stories,[2] but she was by no means the first woman writer to see the possibilities in such stories.[3] Several writers during the postwar period also drew on folk-stories or myths, especially Elizabeth Taylor. Like many women writers, her attitude to these stories is paradoxical. While accepting their power and 'truth', she also sees their danger for women. For example, in her novel *The Sleeping Beauty* she made the connections with the fairy-story clear with her title and with several direct references in the text, and a superficial reading of the novel reveals simply an updated version of the story. Emily has been in a serious car accident which has not only injured her but left her so physically altered that she is unrecognisable to those who knew her before and who now avoid her. She has completely withdrawn from life to devote herself to caring for her sister's mentally handicapped child. The sister, whose name is Rose, protects Emily from the outside world, which Emily now fears. Vinny sees her from a window in the distance and immediately falls in love with her. Gradually his love penetrates her isolation and warms her into life. The novel ends with Vinny marrying her and taking her away. Nothing here to disturb: a perfectly blameless tale of 'happily-ever-after'. Cunningly, Elizabeth Taylor sets her traps and the apparently simple tale displays rents and tears through which we glimpse older and more disturbing themes.

The details of Emily's accident and withdrawal bear a close resemblance to menstruation taboos:[4] Emily has been injured (blood) and is now shunned by former friends. She remains virtually confined in the house, only emerging to take walks with the child Philly. Her sister Rose (briar and thorns) guards her from the world. Vinny, the 'Prince', first sees Emily framed in a window, through glass, much as the Prince sees Snow White framed in her glass coffin. Her beauty, lacking the 'living stir of loveliness', reflects not only her own lack of life, but her loss of identity, her feeling that she was perhaps dead. Despite her beauty, therefore, there is something uncanny about her and Vinny's first reaction to a close view of her is one of terror.

Vinny is an unsatisfactory prince, nearly fifty and only able to make love to women in the dark, preferring wooing to love's satisfaction. As a bringer of life he is ambiguous; his preference for darkness, for Emily's pale deathly beauty, and his role as consoler of widows cast doubt on his effectiveness as a bringer of life. The happy marriage itself is threatened by Vinny's bigamy, brought about by his haste to marry Emily. Vinny is aware of his casting as the Prince, and also aware of the dangers of waking princesses. The difficulties, he explains to Rose, begin with the Prince's awakening kiss, for he awakens the princess's sexuality. He has to marry her to ensure that this sexuality will be in his possession. Like all fairy-tale princes, he releases the princess from one confinement only to bind her in another. Vinny realises something else about Emily: that before her accident she had been 'amorous, perhaps promiscuous as well'.[5] She had been punished by having her body appallingly scarred, to such an extent that her fiancé had rejected her. Vinny fears that Emily's reawakened sexuality will take her away from him, so he marries her, despite the fact that he already has a wife. Vinny's transgression may be more serious: not only is he married but he is old enough to be Emily's father, hinting at an incest taboo. The ending of the novel suggests that he too might be punished: Emily and he talk over the possibility of his imprisonment as a bigamist – a curious reversal, since he will be the one confined and shut away while Emily will be free.

There are of course two other Sleeping Beauties in the novel: Rose and her daughter Philly. Rose is the personification of the thorny briars that enclose the original Sleeping Beauty; at the same time she is another Sleeping Beauty, but one who remains unawakened. Her fear of life – expressed in her fear of sexuality – continues to imprison her and she prefers her long sleep: 'Life stop here!' she prays. Vinny, the professional consoler, will not let things be, but the nature of Rose's awakening might be catastrophic. Philly too remains confined in the strange world of the mentally ill, almost a physical expression of her mother Rose's own trapped and deformed psyche.

Elizabeth Taylor frequently uses the metaphor of briars to

suggest the way femininity cuts off her heroines from life. The rose is also a symbol of women's sexuality and the interplay between the flower and the thorny briar implies that femaleness itself is the trap. In *A Wreath of Roses*, the linking of the rose imagery with Frances emphasises how her sex and gender have both inspired and limited her art: Frances peeps out 'from the briers of her imagination';[6] her room has been papered in layers of rose-covered wallpapers – one peels off only to reveal another beneath; and her last painting is of a woman holding a wreath of roses, representing both entry into womanhood as a bride, and death, while the faded wreath which she has used as a model reflects the withering of Frances and her imagination.[7]

The confining briars in the Sleeping Beauty story become a metaphor for protection too. The thorns may keep out intruding life, but they also protect. Women who try to break the taboo may only find evil. Elizabeth Taylor's heroines 'part leaves' to discover evil, a hidden toad. The use of the toad as metaphor suggests another fairy-story: the Frog Prince. Not all toads, Elizabeth Taylor suggests, turn into princes though; some retain their toad character-istics, and even apparently harmless intruders, such as Vinny and Morland Beddoes, might not provide the release expected. In *A Wreath of Roses* Frances suggests that Morland is sent to tempt her into going back to her old way of painting: in other words, she must stay behind her hedge of thorns and must not look out at what is happening in the outside world. In *The Sleeping Beauty* Vinny breaks down the thorns that surround Emily, but is not going to let her have her freedom. As he points out, the prince who awakened the original Sleeping Beauty married her the same day. The first confinement which marked the emergence from childhood into womanhood is followed by a second: marriage. The problem facing women is which to choose. If staying behind the briars is as restrictive as emerging only to settle behind the hedge of domes-ticity, it seems impossible to resolve. Elizabeth Taylor explores the dilemma, but has no solutions.

In *A Wreath of Roses* she examines three women, all of whom have tried to resolve it in different ways. Frances has stayed behind the briars, but found an inner freedom in her art; Camilla is like Rose, still confined by her fear of life; and Liz has married the Prince but is cut off from the world of friendship. Three unhappy women, as Morland Beddoes points out. By staying behind the briars Frances has diminished her art and has sacrificed sexual and personal fulfilment; Camilla attempts to break out of her castle but only finds evil, a false Prince who is really a Toad; and Liz is cut off from growth as a human being. Camilla sums up the problem for rescued princesses when she talks to Liz about her husband: ' "He won't let you grow or change, but will contort you into something he wishes you to be, a sort of child-wife. It's a kind of murder." '[8]

### 'Pygmalion': woman as man's creation

Elizabeth Jane Howard also has a Sleeping Beauty heroine. Antonia's dreamlike existence in her country home and her awakening by a very false prince indeed – a veritable unregenerated Toad – is described in *The Long View*.[9] The briars that should have protected her, her parents and especially her mother, turn their thorns on her and tear her apart. Antonia's rapturous sexual awakening to the kiss is followed by an attempt on the 'prince's' part to ravish and abandon her. She sinks back into a trancelike detached state until awoken for the second time, but again by a false prince. Elizabeth Jane Howard suggests that there are no briars to protect the innocent and that they can be despoiled by any casual passer-by. Antonia's second prince, like Pygmalion, has been attracted not to a living active woman, but to one who had become so indifferent to life that she was almost dead. Conrad sees the possibilities: a beautiful statue that, warmed into life, will testify to his greatness as a creative artist, one who works with the living flesh of a woman rather than the cold marble of a statue. The Pygmalion story is reversed, for Conrad finds not a statue, but a living woman, and it is he who turns her into a statue. All Antonia's struggles against this process are useless: her rages dissolve into tears, her rebellions fade into passive acceptance. Conrad explains his view of the part that Antonia – and all women – should play in marriage. Marriage for men, he explains to Antonia, is ' "living in two bodies instead of one" ', while women, incomplete as they are, need ' "someone else to teach them to live in their own body. Without that they are lost, because they are never discovered." '[10] When Antonia protests at the passive role assigned to her, asking, as the heroine in *The Beautiful Visit* had asked her brothers, what *she* can do, Conrad replies simply, ' "Be my wife." ' The statue cannot protest as the hands shape her, and she watches the changes made to her with helpless dismay. 'In so short a time he had so much altered her that she felt lost, panic-stricken, almost unrecognizable to herself.'[11]

The statue in Pygmalion also has another advantage for its creator: it has no past. Conrad ensures that Antonia, too, will have nothing that could give substance to her memories of her childhood. When she first enters their future marital home, so perfectly arranged by Conrad, she realizes that there is nothing that had belonged to her before her marriage and she feels suddenly bereft. Not only is she to be cut off from her childhood memories, but she is to learn that it is not just her childhood that will be denied, but also the chance for her to have children of her own. Conrad's fury at the idea that he should be 'a means to an end', that, according to his distorted view, she would use her ability to become a mother to 'order, and dominate and control', is an expression of such ferocity towards the womb and women's creativity and fecundity that Antonia feels almost physically battered. His rage expended, and Antonia comforted, the hollowness of their recon-ciliation and the damage it has done to Antonia is succinctly expressed in the last sentence of the chapter, one oddly placed preposition sounding the false cracked note: 'She knew now he was again protecting her, she was safe from him.'[12]

Inside or outside the briars, women are vulnerable. The rescue by the Prince is viewed ambiguously; the princess waits passively for her deliverance which, when it comes, is not what she expected. The awakening can be painful, even violent, and protected princesses who have been prepared for love have no defences against betrayal, grief or abandonment.

### 'The Red Shoes': punishment of rebellion

A feature of many traditional stories is the punishment, even mutilation, of women who do not conform or who attempt to step out of their role. The Andersen story, *The Red Shoes*, is a typical example. Interestingly, the 1948 film version of *The Red Shoes* changed the original story to reflect postwar preoccupations about women. The Hans Andersen story is about the punishment of female vanity, symbolised by the heroine's obsession with the red shoes, which eventually dooms her to dancing without rest. In this version, she escapes by having her feet cut off, repents and goes to heaven. The 1948 film version, in both the ballet created for the film and the 'real' story framing it, changes the punishment of vanity into a punishment of the heroine's desire to become a great dancer. The film also introduces a husband, not present in the original version, who provides a focus for the conflict between conformity to the stereotyped pattern of supportive wife to the great man, and the individual desire for a 'career'. The heroine's feet are not cut off, but she commits suicide and is not allowed the redemptive ending given her by Andersen. In both versions the heroine is savagely chastised, but for apparently strikingly different reasons, each version reflecting the preoccupations of the period, and the central message carries a warning that non-conformity brings punishment.

There is an echo of this story in Elizabeth Jane Howard's *The Beautiful Visit*. As the heroine prepares for her first formal dance, scratching the soles of her pink dance slippers with the points of her scissors, she pricks her finger and her blood drops on to the shoe. Though she rubs at the bloodstain with her flannel, she cannot remove the mark and finds the 'little moist circle' disquieting.[13] Sleeping Beauty pricking her finger, the bleeding feet of the little mermaid, and the doomed wearer of the red shoes are evoked to underline not just the pain womanhood will bring, but the penalties attendant on seeking an individual destiny, for wanting something that is outside the role prescribed for her. But the heroine of *The Beautiful Visit*, unlike her fairy-tale sisters, does not accept her destiny: rebelliously she refuses to be cowed into submission by the suffering that will be her punishment.

The message from traditional stories is clear: virgins must wait to be 'found' by the Prince, who will reward them for their patience by marrying them. It is not for them to choose, but to be chosen. This is woman's destiny: any deviation will lead to pain, isolation and rejection. By exploring these myths and stories, and particularly the 'happily ever after', women novelists can question or undermine this narrow view of women's potential. While they recognise the power of the images and their hidden messages, they portray their heroines struggling instinctively against them, often not really sure what they are fighting. Their lack of insight into the nature of their dilemma means that not only will they often fail, but victory itself may resemble defeat.

Yet even though myths work against the women, confining them within male dreams of passive, compliant women, they can be transformed. The Sleeping Beauty story, for instance, is sometimes reversed by women novelists, making it the man who is rescued. This was memorably done in Charlotte Brontë's *Jane Eyre*, where Rochester plays the distressed maiden and is first 'rescued' by Jane at the aptly named Thornfield and then at Ferndean, a house surrounded by dense woods and hidden away from the world, where Rochester, confined by his blindness and half dead, awaits Jane to bring him back to life. Elizabeth Taylor also uses this reversal in *Palladian*,[14] for it is Cassandra, a Jane Eyre heroine, who finds Marion in his crumbling house, passive, waiting, obsessed with his dead wife. She performs the role of the Prince, breathes life into him and marries him. However, as a woman she cannot take him away from the enchanted palace; she remains in it with him, as Jane Eyre remains at the insalubrious Ferndean, and this, Elizabeth Taylor suggests, is a fateful choice. The house crumbles, a decaying statue kills a child and the conservatory crashes to the ground. Eventually the whole house will fall and crush its inhabitants.

**The romantic appeal of the fictional 'happy ending'**

Perhaps the worst aspect of these traditional images is the way they colour expectations and lead to false diagnoses. In *The Tortoise and the Hare*,[15] Imogen is exasperated at Evelyn's 'thankfulness' for Blanche's services, feeling that someone as plain and middle-aged as Blanche should be the one to be thankful to have caught such a man as Evelyn. She sees it as a gross parody of the Cinderella story, where at least Cinderella was young and lovely and aware of her good luck. What Imogen fails to see is that Blanche is not Cinderella, but one of the Ugly Sisters, who has managed to persuade the Prince that the shoe *does* fit. Not only that, but she does not have to suffer being crippled to do so: marriage to Evelyn will be an enrichment of her life, not an impoverishment. Imogen's ideas about infidelity have also been drawn from fiction. Brought up in a household with 'advanced' liberal views of marriage, she thought she had accepted the idea of husbands having mistresses, but her ideas about such a situation were drawn from fiction: a mistress tucked away discreetly in a small flat or house somewhere, whose presence in her husband's life she would tolerate as it would never challenge the centrality of her position. The reality comes as a terrible shock. Blanche not only represents the complete opposite of the self-effacing mistress of Imogen's imagination, but is obviously set on replacing her. Imogen's novel-reading has certainly not prepared her for defeat at the hands of one of the Ugly Sisters. She has accepted the traditional male fictions about women; the novel emphasises that this has been a fatal error and has left her unprotected and unable to take effective action to save herself. Not only are such fictions untrue, they are also dangerous.

It is not just traditional stories that provide messages for writers. For women novelists, too, there is the added dimension of other women authors and how they have written about women. The gothic horror stories, especially the women's versions, are viewed ambiguously by serious writers. The combination of affection and rejection of their simplifications is clearly exemplified in Elizabeth Taylor's *Palladian*, whose heroine Cassandra is as affected by her reading as is Catherine Morland in Jane Austen's *Northanger Abbey*. When Mrs Turner attempts to introduce her to another tradition of storytelling by giving her a copy of *The Classical Tradition*, Cassandra finds its detached formality unattractive and returns to her copy of *The Woman in White* with its Gothic horrors. Elizabeth Taylor shows how books can influence our expectations about life itself, and even the way we behave. Would Cassandra ever have fallen for Marion Vanbrugh if she had not read *Jane Eyre* or been influenced by Gothic novels to see something romantic, rather than depressing, about a decaying crumbling house, surrounded by 'Radcliffean' woods, and an introverted and melancholic man? Even her memory of her father's book-lined room, its dim green light and the flowers surrounding his coffin, is echoed in her first sight of Marion in his room, bathed in a shadowy green light filtered through drawn blinds. There is no blazing fire to suggest passion and warmth, as in Jane Eyre's first sight of Rochester at Thornfield. The deadness suggested by the echo from her memory of her dead father lying in his coffin not only makes Marion a Sleeping Prince but also a substitute for her dead father. Similarly, in *The Tortoise and the Hare*, Imogen, immersed in her reading, particularly of Charlotte Yonge, her head filled with romantic notions of love, and failing to understand the true nature of sexual attraction, does not recognise that a plain, middle-aged woman such as Blanche could possibly be her rival.

Books, novels, not only colour their readers' expectations of life but help them to escape the dreariness of everyday life. They can also provide messages. Tom, in *Palladian*, hoping to persuade Sophia of the delights of boarding school, gives her a book called *The Pluckiest Girl in the School*, but is dismayed to find that Sophia is writing her own book and calling it *The Lost Girl*. The clash between the two titles suggests that Tom's genuine concern for Sophia's future and his attempts to save her will founder on his failure to understand her true needs. His image of an autonomous self-defining woman is at total variance with Sophia's view of herself. In *The Beautiful Visit* the heroine reads a book called *The Wide Wide World* and finds that on every page there is a little girl who cries. Rejecting the implicit message, the heroine sets out to discover the 'wide wide world' for herself, determined that, whatever else happens, she will not cry.

It seems that the writers' feelings about this literary tradition were ambivalent. Steeped in it, affectionate about the writers who had given them pleasure, they suggest that the guidelines they have been given are unsatisfactory, the expectation of a happy ending perhaps not allowing them to try an alternative. In *The Beautiful Visit*, for example, the heroine rejects the possibility of her own happy ending: marriage to a tamed and damaged hero. Elizabeth Jane Howard's novel is full of literary echoes. The heroine's name is left deliberately vague, suggesting that Elizabeth Jane Howard was writing about literary heroines in general, as well as real ones. On the first page the heroine wakes to find herself without any memory of her immediate past: 'the ridiculous thought occurred to me that I had just been born'.[16] As indeed she had, in a literary sense. On her bed, where she should have been sleeping, were two exercise books inside which her story is written. They have 'slept' on the bed where the real heroine should have been. This story of her life had been left unfinished, but Elspeth had reassured her that they could 'invent' an ending. Elspeth – a name so close to Elizabeth that it cannot be coincidental[17] – could be the author of the heroine's life. It is she who has caused the heroine to be born again. But she gives her the opportunity to 'write' her own life, to create her own fictional self. She has also given the heroine a chance to write a freer, more imaginative book the second time, one not confined by the limited possibilities open to a middle-class heroine in the first half of the twentieth century. The unnamed heroine of *The Beautiful Visit* is at the same time author and character in the novel.

As character she is manipulated, as author she controls. As author too she ensures that events will be seen from the woman's rather than the man's viewpoint.

Fiction, paradoxically, can release or trap women. The strongest myths with which women have to contend are the male myths about them, with their tendency to dichotomise and to see women two-dimensionally, sometimes solely in terms of virtue or vice, like characters in medieval literature. Yet fiction itself, or the telling of it, can be used to question the conventional image of the heroine. Because women are the objects of so much 'fiction' (in both senses), women authors can use imaginative storytelling to explore and correct the male fictions about them. Many of the women characters in the novels are themselves readers of novels and make things happen so as to fit the expected pattern. Since false images of womanhood not only affect the choices women make, but decide what choices will be available in the first place, any writing that throws doubt on the authenticity of such images is liberating.

# 9

# Conclusions

The advantage man enjoys . . . is that his vocation as a human being in no way runs counter to his destiny as a male . . . He is not divided. Whereas it is required of woman that in order to realise her femininity, she must make herself object and prey, which is to say that she must renounce her claim as sovereign subject. It is this conflict that especially marks the situation of the emancipated woman. She refuses to confine herself to her role as female, because she will not accept mutilation to repudiate her sex. Man is a human being with sexuality; woman is a complete individual, equal to the male, only if she is a human being with sexuality. To renounce her sexuality is to renounce part of her humanity.[1]

Contrary to what appeared to be the contemporary idea that marriage and motherhood were what brought happiness to women, the women characters in these postwar novels show a complex and varying attitude to marriage and spinsterhood. Love and the choice of a marriage partner were important themes, but many of the novels showed young women hesitating before committing themselves, seeing in marriage a threat to their autonomy. Some writers portrayed women tempted by offers of marriage but turning back from them to follow less secure, but potentially more enriching, destinies. Other women writers rarely saw marriage and freedom as anything but mutually exclusive. When they wrote about marriage it was from a critical, even disenchanted point of view. The marriages portrayed in the novels were often either emotional deserts or diminishing to the women involved in them. The general impression is that, of the two imperfect states, marriage is the least desirable and the most constricting; associated with passivity and dependence, it stunts mental and spiritual growth. On the other hand, the single state, though characterised by loneliness and a yearning for human warmth, is viewed with less pessimism. Marriage is disappointment: spinsterhood is hope.

It is difficult to avoid concluding that some at least of this questioning of contemporary assumptions owes its existence to the earlier feminist movement. Feminism is only referred to directly by two authors: Kate O'Brien in *The Land of Spices* and Elizabeth Taylor in *A Game of Hide and Seek*. In the latter novel it is treated almost negatively, and the emphasis is on the generation gap between the views of Harriet's mother and Caroline (both of whom had been militant feminists) and the problems Harriet encounters in her life, with Harriet representing the post-feminist generation that supposedly turned its back on early feminist ideals because these ideals did not solve their problems. During the 1950s the initial aims of feminism – access to education and greater economic autonomy – were being achieved, widening the choices women could make. At the same time, these postwar authors, through their exploration of individual, unstereotyped women characters, reflected a growing awareness that women were still not as free as had been hoped, that the balancing that Simone de Beauvoir mentions between being truly feminine and being 'sovereign subject' was now the key issue. I would like to suggest that this was perhaps where the seeds of the new feminism lay, that during the fifties there may not have been a united feminist movement with its aims clearly articulated, but that this was because it was a period of 'digestion' and reappraisal. For so long the feminist emphasis had been on legal and economic rights for women that the failure of women really to take their place in society must have caused doubt and self-questioning among many of them. It almost seemed as if women were failing to take the opportunities offered to them because of an innate passivity. By exploring the nature of choice for women and the effects of the pressure on them to conform to the images of femininity current in their society, these women writers may have kept alive (or reflected) the debate in their readers' minds. I don't think they consciously set out to do this. Their main aim would have been to present fictional women as near to real women as they could. But although the writers were not necessarily feminist, either consciously or unconsciously, they did question or refuse to accept narrow stereotypes of women, and their celebration of the richness and diversity of the female personality may have been influenced by feminist thinking. Certainly their popularity, despite their portrayal of women who ran counter to the current stereotypes, indicates a higher consciousness of the real conflicts for women than critics generally allow.

What I find most attractive about these authors is their creation of positive images of 'odd' women, their refusal to accept unquestioningly the prescribed roles. The consequences of acceptance or rejection are explored, sometimes painfully, sometimes humorously, but always honestly. The ability of women to make something out of limited opportunities is celebrated, their failure to transcend their roles sympathetically portrayed. The authors are not pessimistic or deterministic but see possibilities for triumph in the most unpromising situations. As Jessie says to Fabian in *Jane and Prudence*, ' "Women are very powerful – perhaps they are always triumphant in the end." '[2] The fiction of this period does not necessarily portray women as 'always triumphant in the end', but it does reflect the fact that even the defeated will question the way their nature as women has somehow become distorted so as to ensure that instead of freedom, they will often blindly choose subjection, for it is difficult for women who have been exposed to images of femininity from childhood to understand their real needs and choose wisely.

I did not set out to 'prove' anything, merely to ask questions. Whether those who read this book agree or disagree with my interpretations, I shall be happy if it stimulates them into looking more deeply into this period in women's history and makes them realise that the evidence of what women thought and felt is not necessarily contained in public debate. Censorship is a more subtle weapon than Orwell supposed, and democracies can, in some ways, be as effective in silencing protest as any authoritarian regime. The difference is that it is more difficult to find the evidence of censorship. So much was *not* said in public debate about women during the postwar period and it is therefore difficult to hear these silenced voices. I have suggested one way; there must be others.

# Notes and References

**Preface**

1. Rosalind Coward, 'Are Women's Novels Feminist Novels?', *The Feminist Review*, no. 5 (1980).
2. Andrea Zeman, *Presumptuous Girls. Women and Their World in the Serious Woman's Novel* (London: Weidenfeld & Nicolson, 1977) Intro., p. 2.
3. Elizabeth Wilson, *Only Halfway to Paradise. Women in Postwar Britain: 1945–1968* (London: Tavistock Pubications, 1980).


**Introduction: a myth of happiness**

1. Elizabeth Wilson, *Only Halfway to Paradise. Women in Postwar Britain: 1945–1968* (London: Tavistock Publications, 1980) p. 69.
2. The Labour government was elected in 1945 in the first postwar election. The Socialists had already declared their total support for the Beveridge Plan and for the establishment of a welfare state that would take care of the needs of its population from birth to old age. Despite Mrs Thatcher's claim that 'socialism is now dead', many institutions now taken for granted began at this time.
3. Alva Myrdal and Viola Klein, *Women's Two Roles. Home and Work* (London: Routledge & Kegan Paul, 1968. First published 1956).
4. Betty Friedan, *The Feminine Mystique* (London: Gollancz, 1965).
5. Marilyn French, *The Women's Room* (London: Deutsch, 1978).
6. There are two excellent surveys of British women's magazines which cover the postwar period: Cynthia L. White's *Women's Magazines 1693–1968* (London: Michael Joseph, 1970); and Marjorie Ferguson's *Forever Feminine. Women's Magazines and the Cult of Femininity* (London: Heinemann, 1983). In addition, I looked at the 1945, 1950 and 1955 issues of *Woman's Own, Good Housekeeping* and *Everywoman*, the 1950 and 1955 issues of *Vanity Fair* and the first year's issues of *She* in 1955.
7. Wilson, *Only Halfway to Paradise*, p. 2.
8. Elizabeth Wilson's book, *Only Halfway to Paradise*, is a key book to read about this period, though she has largely confined herself to the same parameters set in most discussions of the era, i.e. women as wives and mothers.

177

9. Shortages of many commodities continued for a long time after the war and rationing of food did not officially end until 1954. Bread rationing, in fact, was introduced *after* the war.

10. John Westergaard and Henrietta Resler, *Class in a Capitalist Society* (London: Heinemann, 1975). Quoted in Wilson, *Only Halfway to Paradise*, p. 41.

11. Myrdal and Klein, *Women's Two Roles*, p. 182.

12. There was a survey by the AEU in 1945 of the views of 2000 women working in factories, which showed that two-thirds of them expressed a wish to go on working. Myrdal and Klein, *Women's Two Roles*, p. 155.

13. White, *Women's Magazines*, p. 135.

14. Wilson, *Only Halfway to Paradise*, p.47.

15. Myrdal and Klein, *Women's Two Roles*, p. 154.

16. *Report of the Special Committee on Higher Technology Education*, Chairman, Lord Eustace Percy (London: HMSO, 1945).

17. *Report of the Committee Appointed by Lord President of the Council Entitled "Scientific Manpower"*, Chairman, Sir Alan Barlow, Bart, (London: HMSO, 1946).

18. *15–18. Report of the Advisory Council for Education in England*, Vol. 1 (Report), Chairman, Sir Geoffrey Crowther (London: HMSO, 1959). The Crowther Report uses only masculine nouns and pronouns when discussing the science curriculum: 'The boy embarks on a chain of discovery . . . he begins to assume responsibility for his own education . . . a boy can be introduced into one or two areas which throw light on the achievement of man and the nature of the world he lives in . . .' etc. (from chapter 25, pp. 257–75). Girls, on the other hand, show a 'passionate interest' in 'living things', therefore 'It is not for nothing that biology is the main science taught to girls, as physics and chemistry are to boys.' This particular application of the 'Equal but Different' theory has resulted in Biology becoming a devalued subject in schools. Even where girls were demonstrably stronger, in English and literature, a blatant attempt was made to devalue this superiority. The Crowther Report stated that 'analytical and introspective interest in the widest sense . . . is not found in most girls at the beginning of the secondary course' (p. 112). According to the Report, 'Too many girls' reading interests are needlessly left fixed for life within the covers of a hopelessly unreal romantic love novel. Often enough reading in any serious sense soon disappears' (p. 112). No evidence is given in the Report for such a statement.

19. *Report of the Departmental Committee on the Youth Service in England and Wales*, Chairman, Lady Albemarle (London: HMSO, 1960). See especially chapter 3.

20. John Lawson and Harold Silver, *A Social History of Education in England* (London: Methuen, 1973) p. 436.

21. Crowther Report, chapters 6 and 9; Jean Floud, 'Are the Robbins estimates conservative?' *Forum* (1946, pp. 79–82); Layard, King and Moser, *Impact of Robbins*, p. 23. Quoted in Lawson and Silver, *A Social History of Education in England*, p. 436.

'A' Level examinations are generally taken at the age of seventeen or eighteen in the United Kingdom. They follow the General Certificate of Secondary Education (GCSE), which most pupils sit at the end of their schooling, at the age of sixteen. Success with 'A' Levels provides access to universities, polytechnics and further education courses.

22. The 11+ test was not totally objective. Not all children sat the test, and many schools had special classes set aside for children 'cramming' for it. Frequently other marks were added to the test marks (e.g. by the Head of the primary school), and as grammar-school places were limited, the number of 'passes' had to match the number of places available. In addition the final results were separated into two categories, girls and boys, in order to 'equalise' the balance between the sexes. Since girls generally performed better than boys, this could result in girls being excluded even when their marks were higher than those of some boys who had 'passed'. This is still the practice in some areas where grammar schools remain, and a recent court case (1988) brought by the parents of girls resulted in a ruling that under Equal Opportunities legislation such 'equalising' was illegal.

23. Crowther, *15–18*, p. 34.

24. Ibid, p. 33.

25. John Newsom, *The Education of Girls* (London: Faber, 1948).

26. John Newsom, 'The Education Women Need', *The Observer*, 6 September 1964. Quoted in Wilson, *Only Halfway to Paradise*, p. 35.

27. Judith Bardwick, *Psychology of Women* (New York: Harper & Row, 1971) p. 178.

28. Ibid, pp. 180–1.

29. Susan Brownmiller, *Femininity* (London: Paladin Books, 1986) p. 29.

30. Viola Klein, *The Feminine Character* (London: Kegan Paul, Trench, Trubner & Co, 1946) pp. 33–4.

31. See p. 100 of Wilson, *Only Halfway to Paradise*, where she quotes from an article in *The Guardian* in 1978 which suggests the real reason for the change of policy was because of the influx of West Indian women, many of whom, though living with a man, had not gone through a formal marriage. This was against a background of increasing racial tension and fear of a population explosion among the ethnic minorities.

32. See below, Note 1, Chapter 4 for divorce figures.

33. Wilson, *Only Halfway to Paradise*, p. 69.

34. 'The Feminists Mop Up', leading article in *The Economist*, 21 April 1956 (vol. 179, no. 5878, pp. 242–3).

35. Ashley Montagu, *The Natural Superiority of Women* (London: Allen & Unwin, 1954) pp. 245–6.

36. Philip Wylie, *Generation of Vipers* (London: Frederick Muller, 1955). See chapter 11, 'Common Women', pp. 194–317, and his discussion of what he calls the 'Cinderella myth' in the chapter 'A Specimen American Attitude'. The whole book is well worth reading for a good laugh, though that laugh may become a little uneasy on learning of the book's popularity!

37. Marjorie Rosen, *Popcorn Venus. Women, Movies and the American Dream* (New York: Coward, McCann & Geoghan, 1973) p. 255. Quoted in Wini Breines, 'Domineering Mothers in the 1950s: Image and Reality',

*Women's Studies International Forum*, vol. 8, no. 6 (1985) p. 606, footnote 10.

38. Doris Day was a famous singing-and-dancing star who appeared in many American films of the period. She was the epitome of the 'girl-next-door'.

39. Elaine Showalter, *A Literature of Their Own. British Women Novelists from Brontë to Lessing* (London: Virago, 1978).

40. Elizabeth Goudge, *The Joy of the Snow* (London: Hodder & Stoughton, 1974) p. 147.

41. Kate O'Brien, *The Land of Spices* (Bath: Cedric Chivers, 1970. First published in 1953).

**Chapter 1   Something to love: heroines and their heroes**

1. Susan Ertz, *The Prodigal Heart* (London: Hodder & Stoughton, 1950. Book Club edition, 1951) p. 47.

2. Nancy Mitford, *Don't Tell Alfred* (London: Hamish Hamilton, 1960). (Included in *The Best Novels of Nancy Mitford* (Hamish Hamilton, 1974) p. 666.)

3. Nancy Mitford, *The Pursuit of Love* (London: Hamish Hamilton, 1945). (Included in *The Best Novels of Nancy Mitford*.)

4. *The Best Novels of Nancy Mitford*, p. 151.

5. Mitford, *Don't Tell Alfred*, p. 616.

6. Barbara Pym, *Jane and Prudence* (London: Grafton Books, 1981. First published in 1953).

7. Ibid, p. 245.

8. Barbara Pym, *Some Tame Gazelle* (London: Panther, 1981. First published in 1950), Epigraph.

9. There are many feminist texts which examine the way male critics have misinterpreted or denigrated female texts. Among these are: Mary Ellman, *Thinking About Women* (Virago, 1979); Tillie Olsen, *Silences* (Virago, 1980); Joanna Russ, *How to Suppress Women's Writing* (The Woman's Press, 1984). Also see some recent reviews of women's novels by male critics: for example, Anthony Burgess, 'Water, Water Everywhere' (*The Observer*, 23 August 1987); the Richard Ingrams column in *The Observer* (17 April 1988) and the subsequent letters from Bernard Levin and Jill Tweedie reacting to his remarks (*The Observer*, 24 April 1988); and the Godfrey Smith comment on Margaret Drabble's male characters mentioned at the end of this chapter (see below, Note 43).

10. Elizabeth Jane Howard, *The Long View* (Harmondsworth: Penguin, 1976. First published in 1956).

11. Mitford, *The Pursuit of Love*.

12. Nancy Mitford, *The Blessing* (London: Hamish Hamilton, 1951). (Included in *The Best Novels of Nancy Mitford*.)

13. Davey figures mainly in *The Pursuit of Love* and in *Don't Tell Alfred*.

14. Nancy Mitford, *Love in a Cold Climate* (London: Hamish Hamilton, 1949). (Included in *The Best Novels of Nancy Mitford*.)

15. Elizabeth Taylor, *A Wreath of Roses* (Harmondsworth: Penguin, 1967. First published in 1949).

16. Ibid, p. 7.

17. Ibid, p. 173.

18. Elizabeth Taylor, *The Sleeping Beauty* (London: Virago, 1982. First published in 1953).

19. Elizabeth Taylor, *Palladian* (London: Virago, 1985. First published in 1946).

20. Ibid, p. 38.

21. Taylor, *The Sleeping Beauty*, p. 22.

22. Elizabeth Taylor, *Angel* (London: Virago, 1984. First published in 1957).

23. Ibid, p. 15.

24. Elizabeth Jane Howard, *The Beautiful Visit* (Harmondsworth: Penguin, 1976. First published in 1950).

25. Pym, *Some Tame Gazelle*.

26. Ibid, p. 158.

27. A series of radio programmes on 1950s writers in May 1987 discussed these 'angry young men' as the most significant writers of their time. Paul Ferris, discussing Martin Barber's radio programme, *A Look Back to Anger*, rejected this view of their impact (*Observer*, 7 June 1987).

28. John Wain, *Hurry on Down* (London: Secker & Warburg, 1953. Reissued 1978).

29. Colin MacInnes, *Absolute Beginners* (London: Allison & Busby, 1980. First published in 1959).

30. Kingsley Amis, *Lucky Jim* (London: Gollancz, 1954. Reissued 1965).

31. Ibid, p. 39.

32. Kingsley Amis, *Take a Girl Like You* (London: Gollancz, 1960. Reissued 1968) p. 227.

33. Amis, *Lucky Jim*, p. 109.

34. Ibid, p. 212.

35. Ibid, p. 145.

36. Amis, *Take a Girl Like You*.

37. Elizabeth Jenkins, *The Tortoise and the Hare* (London: Virago, 1983. First published in 1954).

38. Barbara Pym, *A Glass of Blessings* (Harmondsworth: Penguin, 1980. First published in 1958).

39. Pym, *A Glass of Blessings*, p. 210.

40. Howard, *The Long View*.

41. Howard, *The Beautiful Visit*, p. 82.

42. The heroine and her sister are left unnamed in the novel, suggesting that their plight is universal rather than particular.

43. See article by Godfrey Smith, 'The Importance of Being Drabble', *The Observer*, May 1987.

## Chapter 2 Happily ever after? The consequences of acceptance

1. Elizabeth Jane Howard, *The Long View* (Harmondsworth: Penguin, 1976. First published in 1956) pp. 223–4.

2. Simone de Beauvoir, *The Second Sex* (Harmondsworth: Penguin, 1972. First published in UK in 1953) p. 496.

3. Olivia Manning, *The Doves of Venus* (London: Virago, 1984. First published in 1955).

4. Ibid, p. 306.

5. Ibid, p. 37.

6. Elizabeth Taylor, *Palladian* (London: Virago, 1985. First published in 1946).

7. Ibid, p. 190.

8. Elizabeth Taylor, *The Sleeping Beauty* (London: Virago, 1982. First published in 1953).

9. Elizabeth Taylor, *A View of the Harbour* (London: Chatto & Windus, 1947. Reissued 1969).

10. Elizabeth Jane Howard, *The Beautiful Visit* (Harmondsworth: Penguin, 1976. First published in 1950).

11. Ibid, p. 309.

12. Ibid, p. 310.

13. Barbara Pym, *Jane and Prudence* (London: Grafton Books, 1981. First published in 1953) p. 52.

14. Pym, *Jane and Prudence*, p. 29

15. Ibid, p. 219.

16. Howard, *The Long View*.

17. Ibid, p. 254.

18. Howard, *The Beautiful Visit*.

19. Barbara Comyns, *Our Spoons Came from Woolworths* (London: Virago, 1983. First published in 1950).

20. Ibid, p. 9.

21. Ibid, p. 213.

22. Ibid, pp. 217–18.

23. Barbara Comyns, *Mr Fox* (London: Methuen, 1987).

24. The term 'wide boy' was used during the war to describe men who profited from activities bordering on the illegal, especially in the black market. More guilty of sharp practice than of outright crime, they used cunning and shrewdness to survive in difficult circumstances.

25. Quoted on the book jackets of several novels and in Madonna Marsden, 'Gentle Truths for Gentle Readers. The Fiction of Elizabeth Goudge', in *Images of Women in Fiction. Feminist Perspectives*, ed. Susan Koppelman Cornillon (Bowling Green, Ohio, USA: Bowling Green University Popular Press, 1973) p. 68.

26. Lucilla and Sally appear in the Eliot trilogy and Stella in *Gentian Hill*.

27. The 'green world' is particularly important in *The White Witch* (1958) and represents the true power centre of the novel (see chapter 3 of present book). Note also the suggestive episode of the casting-out of the image of the Virgin Mary with its echoes from the cult of the goddess Artemis.

28. See Elizabeth Goudge's autobiography, *The Joy of the Snow* (London: Hodder & Stoughton, 1974).

29. Ibid, p. 156.

30. Elizabeth Goudge, *Gentian Hill* (London: Hodder & Stoughton, 1950).

31. Elizabeth Goudge, *The Eliots of Damerosehay* (London: Hodder & Stoughton, 1957).

32. Ibid, p. 57.

33. Ibid, p. 53.

34. Elizabeth Goudge, *The White Witch* (London: Hodder & Stoughton, 1958. Reissued 1979).

35. Elizabeth Goudge, *The Heart of the Family* (London: Hodder & Stoughton, 1951. Reissued in *The Eliots of Damerosehay*).

36. Goudge, *The Eliots of Damerosehay*, p. 58.

37. Ibid, pp. 235–6.

38. See particularly the portrayal of Margaret's marriage in *The White Witch*. It is only on her widowhood that Margaret has the opportunity to mature and it is Parson Hawthyn who tells her, apropos of marriage, that 'the propped never grow'.

39. Susan Ertz, *Charmed Circle* (London: The Companion Book Club, 1957. First published by Collins).

40. Ibid, p. 270.

41. Ibid, p. 22.

42. Ibid, p. 148.

43. Ibid, p. 319.

44. Susan Ertz's earlier novels were not critical of family ideology. See, for example, the less subtle picture of a family during the war in *Anger in the Sky* (London: Hodder & Stoughton, 1943). The social concerns she expresses in the novel are watered down by her portrayal of a middle-class family who are almost too good to be true.

45. Betty Friedan, *The Feminine Mystique* (London: Gollancz, 1965).

46. Mary McMinnies, *The Visitors* (Bath: Cedric Chivers, 1971. First published in 1958).

47. Ibid, p. 199.

48. Margery Sharp, *The Tigress on the Hearth* (London: Collins, 1955).

49. Ibid, p. 42.

50. Ibid, p. 123.

51. Pym, *Jane and Prudence*.

**Chapter 3   Odd Women**

1. Elizabeth Taylor, *A View of the Harbour* (London: Chatto & Windus, 1947. Reissued 1969) p. 101.

2. Barbara Pym, *A Very Private Eye. The Diaries, Letters and Notebooks of Barbara Pym*, eds Hazel Holt and Hilary Pym (London: Macmillan, 1984) p. 1.

3. Barbara Pym, *Quartet in Autumn* (London: Macmillan, 1977).

184 Notes and references

4. Barbara Pym, *The Sweet Dove Died* (London: Macmillan, 1978).

5. Barbara Pym, *Some Tame Gazelle* (London: Panther, 1981. First published in 1950).

6. Ibid, p. 136.

7. Barbara Pym, *An Unsuitable Attachment* (London: Panther, 1983. First published, posthumously, in 1982) p. 102.

8. Barbara Pym, *A Glass of Blessings* (Harmondsworth, Penguin, 1980. First published in 1958) pp. 216–17.

9. Mildred Lathbury is in *Excellent Women*, Ianthe Broome in *An Unsuitable Attachment* and Belinda in *Some Tame Gazelle*.

10. Barbara Pym, *Excellent Women* (Harmondsworth: Penguin, 1980. First published in 1958) pp. 120–1.

11. Ibid, p. 11.

12. Barbara Pym is frequently very pointed in her references to the difference not just in the sort of food available to men and women, but also the conditions in which it is eaten and who prepares it. See, for example, *Jane and Prudence*, especially pp. 44–5 and pp. 55–7, where she also satirises the conflation of masculinity and the consumption of meat.

13. Olivia Manning, *School for Love* (Harmondsworth: Penguin, 1982. First published in 1951).

14. Ibid, p. 192.

15. Even Simone de Beauvoir was wilfully negative about lesbianism. See *The Second Sex* (Harmondsworth: Penguin, 1972).

16. For the concept of 'other', see de Beauvoir, *The Second Sex*.

17. Kate O'Brien, *The Land of Spices* (Bath: Cedric Chivers, 1970. First published in 1941).

18. Kate O'Brien, *The Flower of May* (Bath: Cedric Chivers, 1971. First published in 1953).

19. Kate O'Brien, *Presentation Parlour* (London: Heinemann, 1963).

20. Antonia White, *Frost in May* (London: Virago, 1983. First published in 1933); Edna O'Brien, *The Country Girls* (Harmondsworth: Penguin, 1986. First published in 1960).

21. Kate O'Brien, *That Lady* (Bath: Cedric Chivers, 1971. First published in 1946).

22. Elizabeth Goudge, *The White Witch* (London: Hodder & Stoughton, 1958. Reissued 1979).

23. 'Gorgio' is a Romany word for those who are not Romanies.

24. Kate O'Brien, *Mary Lavelle* (London: Virago, 1984).

25. Kate O'Brien, *As Music and Splendour* (London: Heinemann, 1958. Reissued 1964).

26. Susan Ertz, *The Prodigal Heart* (London: Hodder & Stoughton, 1950. Book Club edition, 1951).

27. Colin MacInnes, *Absolute Beginners* (London: Allison & Busby, 1959. Reissued 1980).

28. Susie Orbach in *Bittersweet* suggests another interpretation of this type of relationship. See Susie Orbach and Luise Eichenbaum, *Bittersweet* (London: Century, 1987).

29. O'Brien, *Presentation Parlour*, and Elizabeth Goudge's autobiography, *The Joy of the Snow* (London: Hodder & Stoughton, 1974) p. 28.

30. Elizabeth Wilson, *Only Halfway to Paradise. Women In Postwar Britain: 1945–1968* (London: Tavistock, 1980).

31. See Janice Raymond, 'Varieties of Female Friendship: The Nun as Loose Woman', in *A Passion for Friends* (London: The Women's Press, 1986) pp. 71–114.

### Chapter 4 'Remember Madame Bovary': infidelity.

1. The divorce figures in the years before and after the Second World War are listed in A. H. Halsey, *Trends in British Society* (London: Macmillan, 1972). However, Halsey warns against reading too much into divorce rates, pointing out that the figures are affected by the ease or difficulty of obtaining a divorce. He prefers to use the figures for petitions for divorce, rather than the decrees absolute, since the latter are affected by changes in the law suddenly expediting settlements of outstanding cases. The majority of petitions, he claims, end in divorce and are therefore a more reliable *annual* figure than decrees absolute (p. 28). Accordingly, I give these:

Divorce petitions in England and Wales rose from 4784 in 1931–5 (when divorce procedures became easier) to 38 382 in 1951, with the introduction of the Legal Aid Scheme, which made divorce available to all classes. The drop in 1956 to 28 426 was only a temporary drop, the figures for 1961 and 1968 being 31 905 and 55 007 respectively (p. 47). In percentage terms, the rise in England and Wales was from 0.80 per cent per 1000 married women between the ages of 20 and 49 in 1931–5, to 5.23 per cent in 1951 and 7.4 per cent in 1968 (p. 48). The rise is even more startling if the rate of increase is calculated on marriages contracted five to fifteen years earlier: from 1.9 per cent in 1937 to 7.4 per cent in 1953 and rising to 15.9 per cent in 1968 (p. 49). This indicates an increasing social acceptance of divorce among younger married couples.

2. It was still higher than the pre-war level, of course. See Note 1 above.

3. See Elizabeth Wilson, *Only Halfway to Paradise* (London: Tavistock, 1980). See also, *Royal Commission on Marriage and Divorce* (the Morton Commission) Cmd 9678 (London: HMSO, 1956).

4. The penalties could affect a mother's right to custody of her children. See, for example, the awarding of custody of a two-year-old child to the husband in 1951 on the basis that, according to the judge: 'It could never be in the interests of the child to be entrusted to a woman who had committed adultery' (Julia Brophy and Carol Smart, 'From Disregard to Disrepute: The Position of Women in Family Law' in E. Whitelegg *et al.* (eds), *The Changing Experience of Women* (Oxford: The Open University, 1982) p. 213). The same article also cites Lord Denning's argument in favour of conflating moral behaviour and mothering ability. The whole section of this analysis throws an interesting light on assumptions about women and marriage during the period. See especially pp. 211–19 of this article for a discussion on the laws relating to divorce.

5. Alfred Kinsey, *Sexual Behaviour in the Human Male* (Philadelphia:

Saunders, 1948); Alfred Kinsey, *Sexual Behaviour in the Human Female* (Philadelphia: Saunders, 1953).

6. Wilson, *Only Halfway to Paradise*, p. 74.

7. Elizabeth Taylor, *A Game of Hide and Seek* (London: Virago, 1986. First published in 1951) p. 177.

8. For those unfamiliar with *Madame Bovary*, Charles was the cuckolded husband of Emma Bovary.

9. Taylor, *A Game of Hide and Seek*. See p. 126.

10. Ibid, p. 245.

11. Elizabeth Taylor, *Palladian* (London: Virago, 1985. First published in 1946).

12. Cassandra's father was, of course, quoting from John Keats' poem, 'Ode on a Grecian Urn'.

13. Mrs Veal appears in *Palladian*, Vesey's mother in *A Game of Hide and Seek*.

14. Mary McMinnies, *The Visitors* (Bath: Cedric Chivers, 1971. First published in 1958).

15. Barbara Pym, *A Glass of Blessings* (Harmondsworth: Penguin, 1980. First published in 1958).

16. Barbara Pym, *Excellent Women* (Harmondsworth: Penguin, 1980. First published in 1952).

17. Olivia Manning, *The Doves of Venus* (London: Virago, 1984. First published in 1955).

18. Barbara Comyns, *Our Spoons Came from Woolworths* (London: Virago, 1983. First published in 1950).

19. Elizabeth Jenkins, *The Tortoise and the Hare* (London: Virago, 1983. First published in 1954).

20. Ibid, p. 36.

21. Ibid, p. 69.

22. Ibid, p. 245.

23. Ibid, p. 86.

24. Elizabeth Jane Howard, *The Long View* (Harmondsworth: Penguin, 1976. First published in 1956).

25. Elizabeth Taylor, *A View of the Harbour* (London: Chatto & Windus, 1969. First published in 1947).

26. Ibid, p. 66.

27. Ibid, p. 164.

28. Ibid, p. 152.

29. Ibid, p. 63.

30. Ibid, p. 121.

31. Olivia Manning, *Artist Among the Missing* (London: Heinemann, 1945. Reissued 1975).

32. One exception, perhaps, is *The Doves of Venus*, where there is a confusion between the setting of the novel – after the Second World War – and Manning's memories of being a young woman in the inter-war years.

33. Manning, *Artist Among the Missing*, p. 248.

34. Comyns, *Our Spoons Came from Woolworths*.

35. Taylor, *A View of the Harbour*, p. 95.

36. This view of women as a marketable commodity has not vanished. See, for example, Jolyon Jenkins's article in *The Observer* on the advertising of Third World women as wives for white men ('Bride Market', 13 Sept 1987), followed by the ambiguous colour-supplement treatment of the same subject the following week.

## Chapter 5   Ugly sisters

1. Olivia Manning, *The Doves of Venus* (London: Virago, 1984. First published in 1955) p. 269.
2. Pamela Hansford Johnson, *Important To Me* (London: Macmillan, 1974).
3. Mary McMinnies, *The Visitors* (Bath: Cedric Chivers, 1971. First published in 1958).
4. Barbara Pym, *Excellent Women* (Harmondsworth: Penguin, 1980. First published in 1952).
5. Barbara Pym, *No Fond Return to Love* (London: Panther, 1981. First published in 1961) p. 282.
6. Pym, *Excellent Women*, p. 195.
7. Ibid, p. 203.
8. Barbara Pym, *Jane and Prudence* (London: Grafton, 1981. First published in 1953) p. 158.
9. Elizabeth Goudge, *The Eliots of Damerosehay* (London: Hodder & Stoughton, 1957).
10. Elizabeth Goudge, *The Heart of the Family* (included in *The Eliots of Damerosehay*) p. 493.
11. Pamela Hansford Johnson, *The Unspeakable Skipton* (London: Macmillan, 1959) p. 13.
12. Published in, respectively, 1963 and 1965.
13. Manning, *The Doves of Venus*, p. 157.
14. Ibid, p. 159.
15. Ibid, p. 269.
16. Elizabeth Jenkins, *The Tortoise and the Hare* (London: Virago, 1983. First published in 1954).
17. Ibid, p. 130.
18. Ibid, p. 221.
19. Pamela Hansford Johnson, *An Avenue of Stone* (London: Macmillan, 1947. Reissued 1973).
20. Ibid, p. 24.
21. Manning, *The Doves of Venus*, p. 294.
22. Kate O'Brien, *That Lady* (Bath: Cedric Chivers, 1972. First published in 1946) p. 129.
23. Ibid, p. 118.

## Chapter 6   Children: 'strange unexpected flowerings'

1. Elizabeth Taylor, *A View of the Harbour* (London: Chatto & Windus, 1947. Reissued 1969) p. 25.

2. See, for example: John Bowlby, *Childcare and the Growth of Love* (Harmondsworth: Penguin, 1953); D. W. Winnicott, *The Child and His Family* and *The Child and the Outside World* (both London: Tavistock, 1957). For a contemporary view of such theories, see Denise Riley, *War in the Nursery* (London: Virago, 1983).

3. Elizabeth Goudge, *The Eliots of Damerosehay* (London: Hodder & Stoughton, 1957). The twins appear in *The Heart of the Family* (1951).

4. Olivia Manning, *School for Love* (Harmondsworth: Penguin, 1982. First published in 1951).

5. Elizabeth Jenkins, *The Tortoise and the Hare* (London: Virago, 1983. First published in 1954).

6. Elizabeth Taylor, *The Sleeping Beauty* (London: Virago, 1982. First published in 1953) p. 197.

7. Nancy Mitford, *The Blessing* (1951). Included in *The Best Novels of Nancy Mitford* (London: Hamish Hamilton, 1974).

8. Taylor, *A View of the Harbour*.

9. Elizabeth Taylor, *Palladian* (London: Virago, 1985. First published in 1946).

10. Elizabeth Jane Howard, *The Long View* (Harmondsworth: Penguin, 1976. First published in 1956).

11. Ibid, p. 365.

12. Jenkins, *The Tortoise and the Hare*.

13. Howard, *The Long View*, p. 274.

14. Barbara Comyns, *Who Was Changed and Who Was Dead* (London: Virago, 1987. First published in 1954).

15. Barbara Comyns, *Sisters by the River* (London: Virago, 1985. First published in 1947).

16. Comyns, *Who Was Changed*, p. 86.

17. Maureen Duffy, *That's How It Was* (London: Virago, 1983. First published in 1962).

18. Mitford, *The Best Novels of Nancy Mitford*.

19. See Harold Acton's biography of Nancy Mitford in which he makes the connection between Nancy's own father and the fictional Uncle Matthew. Harold Acton, *Nancy Mitford: A Memoir* (London: Hamish Hamilton, 1975).

20. Pamela Hansford Johnson, *The Unspeakable Skipton* (London: Macmillan, 1959).

21. Rousseau lived with a woman for many years, but each time she gave birth to a child Rousseau immediately handed it over to an orphanage, refusing to allow her to keep it. See Jean-Jacques Rousseau, *The Confessions* (Harmondsworth: Penguin, 1953).

22. Taylor, *Palladian*.

23. Ibid.

24. Taylor, *A View of the Harbour*.

25. Taylor, *The Sleeping Beauty*.

**Chapter 7 Women and work**

1. Elizabeth Taylor, *A View of the Harbour* (London: Chatto & Windus, 1947. Reissued 1969) p. 176.
2. Patricia Stubbs, *Women and Fiction. Feminism and the Novel 1880–1920* (Sussex: The Harvester Press, 1979) pp. 226–7.
3. Patricia Meyer Spacks, *The Female Imagination* (London: Allen & Unwin, 1976) p. 318.
4. Kate O'Brien, *As Music and Splendour* (London: Heinemann, 1958. Reissued 1964).
5. Barbara Pym, *Excellent Women* (Harmondsworth: Penguin, 1980. First published in 1952).
6. Olivia Manning, *The Doves of Venus* (London: Virago, 1984. First published in 1955).
7. Susan Ertz, *The Prodigal Heart* (London: Hodder & Stoughton, 1950. Book Club edition, 1951).
8. Susan Ertz, *Charmed Circle* (London: The Companion Book Club, 1957. First published by Collins).
9. Elizabeth Taylor, *A Game of Hide and Seek* (London: Virago, 1986. First published in 1951).
10. Ibid, p. 60.
11. Elizabeth Jane Howard, *The Beautiful Visit* (Harmondsworth: Penguin, 1976. First published in 1950).
12. Ibid, pp. 146–7.
13. See Marina Warner, *Joan of Arc: The Image of Female Heroism* (London: Weidenfeld & Nicolson, 1981) for a discussion of the possible reasons for Joan's assumption of male clothing and her tenacity in refusing to give it up.
14. Surprising because Elizabeth Jane Howard stated categorically that she did not write about 'social issues or values'. Quoted in James Vinson, *Contemporary Novelists* (London and Chicago: St James Press, 1986, 4th edn) p. 440.
15. Elizabeth Taylor, *Angel* (London: Virago, 1984. First published in 1957).
16. Ibid, p. 249.
17. Taylor, *A View of the Harbour*, p. 36.
18. Ibid, p. 104.
19. Spacks, *The Female Imagination*. See especially the chapter on the woman as artist.
20. Elizabeth Taylor, *The Sleeping Beauty* (London: Virago, 1982. First published in 1953).
21. Elizabeth Taylor, *Palladian* (London: Virago, 1985. First published in 1946).
22. See Note 9, Chapter 1, above. Also see Germaine Greer, *The Obstacle Race* (London: Secker & Warburg, 1979) for a description of the problems facing women painters.
23. Taylor, *A View of the Harbour*, p. 34.
24. A series of radio programmes on Radio 4 in May 1987. See Note 27, Chapter 1, above.

25. Elizabeth Taylor, *A Wreath of Roses* (Harmondsworth: Penguin, 1967. First published in 1949).

26. Not just in her own time either. See, for example, a review of *A View of the Harbour* by 'N.G.' in *Women's Review*, April 1987.

27. Sylvia Plath, *Letters Home. Correspondence 1950–1963*, ed. Aurelia Schober Plath (London: Faber, 1975). Quoted from a letter to Plath from Olive Prouty, 19 March 1957, p. 306.

28. Ibid. Letter to Plath's mother, 25 November 1962, p. 477. Her mother's letter, incidentally, was written at the time Sylvia's marriage to Ted Hughes was breaking up.

29. Kate O'Brien, *The Last of Summer* (Dublin and London: Arlen & Martin Boyars, 1982. First published in 1943).

30. Elizabeth Goudge, *The White Witch* (London: Hodder & Stoughton, 1958. Reissued 1979) p. 18.

31. A view expressed to me by more than one male member of the NAS to explain why women teachers' promotion prospects were so much poorer than men's. The attitude to male and female promotion in even the primary sector (where women outnumber men) was summed up in a speech I remember being given by a representative of the local education authority to final-year students in the early 1970s at my teacher-training college. Ignoring the women students, he turned to the significantly less numerous male students and promised them a brilliant future in the primary-school sector.

32. Florence Howe, 'Feminism and Literature', in *Images of Women in Fiction. Feminist Perspectives*, ed. Susan Koppelman Cornillon (Bowling Green: Bowling Green University Popular Press, 1973) pp. 253–77, see especially p. 256.

33. Sylvia Ashton-Warner, *Spinster* (London: Virago, 1980. First published in 1958). Her autobiographical description of teaching is in *Teacher* (London: Secker & Warburg, 1963).

34. Kate O'Brien, *The Land of Spices* (Bath: Cedric Chivers, 1970. First published in 1941).

35. Kate O'Brien, *The Flower of May* (Bath: Cedric Chivers, 1971. First published in 1953).

36. For example, Judy Chicago's work and the re-evaluation of the art of quilting.

37. Taylor, *Angel*, p. 73.

38. Pym, *Excellent Women*.

39. Taylor, *A Wreath of Roses*.

40. Taylor, *A View of the Harbour*.

41. Taylor, *The Sleeping Beauty*, p. 37.

42. Elizabeth Jenkins, *The Tortoise and the Hare* (London: Virago, 1983. First published in 1954).

43. See Joanna Russ, *How to Suppress Women's Writing* (London: Penguin, 1983) ch. 5, 'The Double Standard of Content', pp. 39–48.

**Chapter 8   Fictions: subverting the stereotypes**

1. Elizabeth Taylor, *The Sleeping Beauty* (London: Virago, 1982. First published in 1953) p. 187.

2. See, for example, Angela Carter, *The Bloody Chamber, and other stories* (London: Gollancz, 1979). There are, of course, others.

3. One interesting example of the use of traditional stories to examine unacceptable areas of a woman's experience occurs in the 'dream' sequence in Charlotte Brontë's *Villette*.

4. In some earlier societies women menstruating for the first time were (and still are in some communities) frequently isolated from the community, kept in darkness and only seen or attended to by women. Menstrual blood was considered not just dirty but dangerous to humans, animals and crops. These early beliefs remain as trace elements in the language and prohibitions surrounding menstruation. In the 1950s, for example, menstruation was generally referred to as 'the curse'. This tabooing signals a terror of female sexuality and power.

5. Taylor, *The Sleeping Beauty*, p. 144.

6. Elizabeth Taylor, *A Wreath of Roses* (Harmondsworth: Penguin, 1967. First published in 1953) p. 81.

7. There is a curious similarity between Elizabeth Taylor's description of the wallpaper in Frances's room and the wallpaper in Charlotte Perkins Gilman's *The Yellow Wallpaper*. In the latter case, the heroine's attempts to write are frustrated, and the wallpaper, with its lurid pattern, becomes connected in the heroine's mind with her enforced silence.

8. Taylor, *A Wreath of Roses*, p. 125.

9. Elizabeth Jane Howard, *The Long View* (Harmondsworth: Penguin, 1976. First published in 1956).

10. Ibid, p. 249.

11. Ibid, p. 246.

12. Ibid, p. 254. See the whole of this scene between Antonia and Conrad (pp. 244–54) for an insight into their relationship and the elements in it that will destory Antonia.

13. Elizabeth Jane Howard, *The Beautiful Visit* (Harmondsworth: Penguin, 1976. First published in 1956) p. 84.

14. Elizabeth Taylor, *Palladian* (London: Virago, 1985. First published in 1946).

15. Elizabeth Jenkins, *The Tortoise and the Hare* (London: Virago, 1983. First published in 1954).

16. Howard, *The Beautiful Visit*, p. 7.

17. Many of Elizabeth Taylor's novels also have variations on her own first name, e.g. Beth, Liz, Isabella.

**Chapter 9   Conclusions**

1. Simone de Beauvoir, *The Second Sex* (Harmondsworth: Penguin, 1972. First published in 1953) pp. 691–2.

2. Barbara Pym, *Jane and Prudence* (London: Grafton Books, 1981. First published in 1953) p. 125.

# Bibliography

Abel, Elizabeth, '(E)Merging Identities: The Dynamics of Female Friendship in Contemporary Fiction by Women', *Signs*, vol. 6, no. 3 (Spring 1981) pp. 413–35.

Acton, Harold, *Nancy Mitford: a memoir* (London: Hamish Hamilton, 1975).

Amis, Kingsley, *Lucky Jim* (London: Gollancz, 1954. Reissued 1965); *Take a Girl Like You* (London: Gollancz, 1960. Reissued 1968).

Ashton-Warner, Sylvia, *Spinster* (London: Virago, 1980. First published in 1958).

Attenborough, John, *A Living Memory: Hodder & Stoughton, Publishers. 1868–1975* (London: Hodder & Stoughton, 1975).

Bardwick, Judith, *Psychology of Women* (New York: Harper & Row, 1971).

Beard, Mary, *Woman as Force in History* (London: Collier Macmillan, 1962. First published in 1946).

Beauman, Nicola, *A Very Great Profession. The Woman's Novel 1914–1939* (London: Virago, 1983).

Beauvoir, Simone de, *The Second Sex* (Harmondsworth: Penguin, 1972. First published in UK 1953).

Beveridge, Lord, *Voluntary Action* (London: Allen & Unwin, 1948).

Birmingham Feminist History Group, 'Feminism as Femininity in the Nineteen-Fifties', *Feminist Review*, no. 3 (1979) pp. 48–65.

Breines, Wini, 'Domineering Mothers in the 1950s: Image and Reality', *Women's Studies International Forum*, vol. 8, no. 6, (1985) pp. 601–8.

Brophy, Julia and Carol Smart, 'From Disregard to Disrepute: The Position of Women in Family Law', in *The Changing Experience of Women*, eds Elizabeth Whitelegg *et al.* (Oxford: Martin Robertson, 1982, in association with The Open University) pp. 207–25.

Brownmiller, Susan, *Femininity* (London: Paladin, 1986).

Byrne, Eileen M., *Women and Education* (London: Tavistock, 1978).

Carter, Angela, *The Bloody Chamber & other stories* (London: Gollancz, 1979).

Comyns, Barbara, *Sisters by a River* (London: Virago, 1985. First published by Eyre & Spottiswoode, 1947); *Our Spoons Came from Woolworths* (London: Virago, 1983. First published by Spottiswoode, 1950); *Who Was Changed and Who Was Dead* (London: Virago, 1987. First published by Bodley Head, 1954); *The Vet's Daughter* (London:

Virago, 1981. First published by Heinemann, 1959); *Mr Fox* (London: Methuen, 1987).

Cornillon, Susan Koppelman (ed.), *Images of Women in Fiction. Feminist Perspectives* (Bowling Green, Ohio: Bowling Green University Popular Press, 1973).

Coward, Rosalind, 'Are Women's Novels Feminist Novels?', *The Feminist Review*, no. 5 (1980).

Duffey, Martha, 'In Praise of Excellent Women', *Time*, vol. 1221 (26 September 1983) p. 62.

*Economist, The,* 'The Feminists Mop Up', vol. 179, no. 5878 (21 April 1956) pp. 242–3.

Ellman, Mary, *Thinking About Women* (London: Virago, 1979).

Ertz, Susan, *Anger in the Sky* (London: Hodder & Stoughton, 1943); *The Prodigal Heart* (London: Hodder & Stoughton, 1950. Book Club edition 1951); *Charmed Circle* (London: The Companion Book Club, 1957. First published by Collins).

Ezell, Margaret J. M.,'"What Shall We Do With Our Old Maids?": Barbara Pym and the "Woman Question"', *International Journal of Women's Studies*, vol. 7, no. 5 (1984) pp. 450–65.

Ferguson, Marjorie, *Forever Feminine. Women's Magazines and the Cult of Femininity* (London: Heinemann, 1983).

French, Marilyn, *The Woman's Room* (London: Deutsch, 1978).

Friedan, Betty, *The Feminine Mystique* (London: Gollancz, 1965).

Gavron, Hannah, *The Captive Wife* (Harmondsworth: Penguin, 1968).

Goudge, Elizabeth, *Gentian Hill* (London: Hodder & Stoughton, 1950; *The Eliots of Damerosehay* (London: Hodder & Stoughton, 1957. Includes *The Bird in the Tree* (1938), *The Herb of Grace* (1945), and *The Heart of the Family* (1951)); *The White Witch* (London: Hodder & Stoughton, 1958. Reissued 1979); *The Joy of the Snow* (autobiography) (London: Hodder & Stoughton, 1974).

Graham, Robert J., 'Cumbered with Much Serving: Barbara Pym's "Excellent Women"', *Mosaic*, vol. 17, no. 2 (Spring 1984) pp. 141–60.

Green, Arnold W. and Eleanor Melnick 'What Has Happened to the Feminist Movement', in *Studies in Leadership*, ed. Alvin W. Gouldner (New York: Harper & Bros, 1950) pp. 277–302.

Hall, Carolyn, *The Forties in Vogue* (London: Octopus, 1985).

Halsey, A. H., *Trends in British Society* (London: Macmillan, 1972).

Heron, Liz (ed.), *Truth, Dare or Promise. Girls Growing Up in the Fifties* (London: Virago, 1985).

H M Government, *Report of the Special Committee on Higher Technology Education*, Chairman, Lord Eustace Percy (London: HMSO, 1945).

H M Government, *Report of the Committee Appointed by Lord President of the Council entitled "Scientific Manpower"*, Chairman, Sir Alan Barlow Bart (London: HMSO, 1946).

H M Government, *15–18. Report of the Advisory Council for Education in England*, vol. 1 (Report), Chairman, Sir Geoffrey Crowther (London: HMSO, 1959).

H M Government, *Report of the Departmental Committee on the Youth*

Service in England and Wales, Chairman, Lady Albemarle (London: HMSO, 1960).

H M Government, *Half Our Future: A Report. Central Advisory Council for Education* (England), Chairman, John Newsom (London: HMSO, 1963).

Howard, Elizabeth Jane, *The Beautiful Visit* (Harmondsworth: Penguin, 1976. First published by Cape, 1950); *The Long View* (Harmondsworth: Penguin, 1976. First published by Cape, 1956).

Hubback, Judith, *Wives Who Went to College* (London: Heinemann, 1957).

Jenkins, Elizabeth, *The Tortoise and the Hare* (London: Virago, 1983. First published by Gollancz, 1954).

Johnson, Pamela Hansford, *An Avenue of Stone* (London: Macmillan, 1947. Reissued 1973); *The Unspeakable Skipton* (London: Macmillan, 1959); *Night and Silence. Who is Here?* (London: Macmillan, 1963); *Cork Street, Next to the Hatters* (London: Macmillan, 1965); *Important to Me* (London: Macmillan, 1974).

Kamm, Josephine, *Hope Deferred* (London: Methuen, 1965).

Klein, Viola, *The Feminine Character* (London: Kegan Paul, Trench, Trubner, 1946).

Kolodney, Annette, 'Some Notes on Defining a "Feminist Literary Criticism"', *Critical Inquiry*, vol. 2, no. 1, pp. 75–92.

Lawson, John and Harold Silver, *A Social History of Education in England* (London: Methuen, 1973).

MacInnes, Colin, *Absolute Beginners* (London: Allison & Busby, 1959. Reissued 1980).

Manning, Olivia, *Artist Among the Missing* (London: Heinemann, 1945. Reissued 1975); *School for Love* (Harmondsworth: Penguin, 1982. First published by Heinemann, 1951); *The Doves of Venus* (London: Virago, 1984. First published by Heinemann, 1955).

Marsden, Madonna, 'Gentle Truths for Gentle Readers. The Fiction of Elizabeth Goudge', in *Images of Women in Fiction. Feminist Perspectives*, ed. Susan Koppelman Cornillon (Bowling Green, Ohio: Bowling Green University Popular Press, 1972. Revised edn, 1973) pp. 68–78.

Marwick, Arthur, *British Society Since 1945* (Harmondsworth: Penguin, 1982).

McMinnies, Mary, *The Visitors* (Bath: Cedric Chivers, 1971. First published by Collins, 1958).

McWilliams-Tullberg, Rita, *Women at Cambridge* (London: Gollancz, 1975).

Mead, Margaret, *Male and Female* (Harmondsworth: Penguin, 1962. First published in USA, 1950).

Miller, Jane, *Women Writing About Men* (London: Virago, 1986).

Mitford, Nancy, *The Best Novels of Nancy Mitford* (London: Hamish Hamilton, 1974): contains *The Pursuit of Love* (1945); *Love in a Cold Climate* (1949); *The Blessing* (1951); *Don't Tell Alfred* (1960).

Moers, Ellen, *Literary Women* (London: W. H. Allen, 1977).

Moi, Toril, *Sexual/Textual Politics* (London: Methuen, 1985).

Montagu, Ashley, *The Natural Superiority of Women* (London: Allen & Unwin, 1954. First published in USA, 1952).

Mumby, F. A. and Ian Norrie, *Publishing and Bookselling* (London: Cape, 1930. 5th edn, revised and reset, 1974).

Myrdal, Alva and Viola Klein, *Women's Two Roles. Home and Work* (London: Routledge & Kegan Paul, 1968, 2nd edn. First published 1956).

Newsom, John, *The Education of Girls* (London: Faber, 1948).

O'Brien, Kate, *The Land of Spices* (Bath: Cedric Chivers, 1970. First published by Heinemann, 1941); *That Lady* (Bath: Cedric Chivers, 1972. First published by Heinemann, 1946); *The Flower of May* (Bath: Cedric Chivers, 1971. First published by Heinemann, 1953); *Teresa of Avila* (London: Max Parrish, 1951); *Presentation Parlour* (London: Heinemann, 1963); *As Music and Splendour* (London: Heinemann, 1958. Reissued 1964).

Okely, Judith, *Simone de Beauvoir* (London: Virago, 1968).

Plath, Sylvia, *Letters Home. Correspondence 1950–1963*, ed. Aurelia Schober Plath (London: Faber, 1975).

Pratt, Annis, *Archetypal Patterns in Women's Fiction* (Brighton: The Harvester Press, 1981).

Pym, Barbara, *Some Tame Gazelle* (London: Panther, 1981. First published by Cape, 1950); *Excellent Women* (Harmondsworth: Penguin, 1980. First published by Cape, 1952); *Jane and Prudence* (London: Grafton, 1981. First published by Cape, 1953); *Less Than Angels* (London: Panther, 1980. First published by Cape, 1955); *A Glass of Blessings* (Harmondsworth: Penguin, 1980. First published by Cape, 1958); *No Fond Return of Love* (London: Panther, 1981. First published by Cape, 1961); *An Unsuitable Attachment* (London: Panther, 1983. First published by Macmillan, 1982); *Quartet in Autumn* (London: Macmillan, 1977); *A Very Private Eye. The Diaries, Letters and Notebooks of Barbara Pym*, eds Hazel Holt and Hilary Pym (London: Macmillan, 1984).

Raymond, Janice, G., *A Passion for Friends* (London: The Women's Press, 1986).

Riley, Denise, ' "The Free Mothers": Pronatalism and Working Women in Industry at the End of the Last War in Britain', *History Workshop Journal*, Spring (1981), issue 11, pp. 59–114; *War in the Nursery* (London: Virago, 1983).

Rolph, C. H. (ed.), *The Trial of Lady Chatterley* (Harmondsworth: Penguin, 1961).

Sharp, Margery, *The Foolish Gentlewoman* (London: Collins, 1948. Reissued by the Reprint Society, 1950); *The Tigress on the Hearth* (London: Collins, 1955).

Showalter, Elaine, *A Literature of Their Own. British Women Novelists from Brontë to Lessing* (London: Virago, 1978); 'Towards a Feminist Poetics', in *Women Writing and Writing About Women*, ed. Mary Jacobus (London: Croom Helm, 1979) pp. 22–41; (ed.) *The New Feminist Criticism. Essays on Women, Literature and Theory* (London: Virago, 1986. First published in USA in 1985).

Smith, Robert, 'How Pleasant to Know Miss Pym', *Ariel* vol. 2, no. 4 (October 1971) pp. 63–8.

Spacks, Patricia Meyer, *Contemporary Women Novelists* (New Jersey: Prentice–Hall, 1977); *The Female Imagination* (London: Allen & Unwin, 1976).

Steedman, Carolyn, *Landscape for a Good Woman* (London: Virago, 1986).

Stubbs, Patricia, *Women and Fiction. Feminism and the Novel 1880–1920* (Sussex: The Harvester Press, 1979).

Taylor, Elizabeth, *At Mrs Lippincote's* (London: Virago, 1985. First published by Peter Davies, 1945); *Palladian* (London: Virago, 1985. First published by Peter Davies, 1946); *A View of the Harbour* (London: Chatto & Windus, 1947. Reissued 1969); *A Wreath of Roses* (Harmondsworth: Penguin, 1967. First published by Peter Davies, 1949); *A Game of Hide and Seek* (London: Virago, 1986. First published by Peter Davies, 1951); *The Sleeping Beauty* (London: Virago, 1982. First published by Peter Davies, 1953); *Angel* (London: Virago, 1984. First published by Peter Davies, 1957).

Tilley, Louise A. and Joan W. Scott, *Women, Work and Family* (New York: Holt, Rinehart & Winston, 1978).

Titmuss, Richard M., *Essays on the Welfare State* (London: Allen & Unwin, 1963. First published 1958).

Vicinus, Martha, 'Distance and Desire: English Boarding-School Friendships', *Signs* vol. 9, no. 4 (Summer 1984) pp. 600–22.

Vinson, James (ed.), *Contemporary Novelists* (London: St James Press, 1972).

Wain, John, *Hurry On Down* (London: Secker & Warburg, 1953. Reissued 1978).

Warner, Marina, *Joan of Arc: The Image of Female Heroism* (London: Weidenfeld & Nicolson, 1981).

White, Cynthia L., *Women's Magazines 1693–1968* (London: Michael Joseph, 1970).

Whitelegg, Elizabeth, *et al.* (eds), *The Changing Experience of Women* (Oxford: Martin Robertson, in association with The Open University, 1982).

Williamson, Marilyn L. 'Towards a Feminist Literary History', *Signs*, vol. 10, no. 1 (Autumn 1984) pp. 136–47.

Wilson, Elizabeth, *Only Halfway to Paradise. Women in Postwar Britain: 1945–1968* (London: Tavistock, 1980); *Mirror Writing. An Autobiography* (London: Virago, 1982).

Woodhall, Maureen, 'It Is Worth Educating Women', *New Society*, vol. 6, no. 151 (19 August 1965) pp. 21–2.

Wylie, Philip, *Generation of Vipers* (London: Muller, 1955. First published in USA, 1942).

Young, Michael & Peter Willmott, *Family and Kinship in East London* (Harmondsworth: Penguin, 1962. First published in USA, 1957).

Zeman, Anthea, *Presumptuous Girls. Women and Their World in the Serious Women's Novel* (London: Weidenfeld & Nicolson, 1977).

Ziegler, Philip, *Elizabeth's Britain 1926–86* (London: Hamlyn, 1986)

# Index of Women Novelists

*Angel* (Taylor) 33–4, 148–9, 150–1, 160

*Artist Among the Missing* (Manning) 102–4

*As Music and Splendour* (O'Brien) 79–81, 142, 154–6, 157

Ashton-Warner, Sylvia 158
  *Spinster* 158

*Avenue of Stone, An* (Johnson) 118–19, 123

*Beautiful Visit, The* (Howard) 34–5, 41–2, 48, 50, 146–8, 167, 169, 172–3

*Bird in the Tree, The* (Goudge) 56

*Blessing, The* (Mitford) 29, 130–1

*Charmed Circle* (Ertz) 59–61, 144, 161

Comyns, Barbara 50–3, 93, 105, 134–5, 136
  *Mr Fox* 53; *Our Spoons Came From Woolworths* 50–3, 93, 105; *Sisters by a River* 134; *Who Was Changed and Who Was Dead* 134–5

*Cork Street, Next to the Hatters* (Johnson) 114

*Don't Tell Alfred* (Mitford) 25, 27, 30, 135–7

*Doves of Venus, The* (Manning) 45–6, 47, 93, 94, 105, 109, 115–16, 119–21, 143, 161

Duffy, Maureen 135
  *That's How It Was,* 135

*Eliots of Damerosehay, The* (Goudge) 55–8, 61, 92, 113

Ertz, Susan 22, 25, 59–61, 78, 81–3, 84, 143–4, 161
  *Charmed Circle* 59–61, 144, 161; *The Prodigal Heart* 25, 78, 81–3, 143–4

*Excellent Woman* (Pym) 70, 92, 107, 111, 112–13, 160

*Flower of May, The* (O'Brien) 74, 75, 158

*Game of Hide and Seek, A* (Taylor) 88–9, 93, 101, 145, 175

*Gentian Hill* (Goudge) 55, 59

*Glass of Blessings, A* (Pym) 40, 69–70, 92, 111–12

Goudge Elizabeth 22, 23, 53–9, 61, 76–8, 83, 84, 92, 113, 126, 137, 140, 156–7
  *The Bird in the Tree* 56; *The Eliots of Demerosehay* 55–8, 61, 92, 113; *Gentian Hill* 55, 59; *The Heart of the Family* 56, 57; *The Herb of Grace* 56; *The Joy of the Snow* 23, 54, 83; *The White Witch* 56, 57, 76–7, 157

197

*Heart of the Family, The*
(Goudge) 56, 57
*Herb of Grace, The* (Goudge) 56
Howard, Elizabeth Jane 29, 34–5,
41–2, 44, 48, 49–50, 98–9, 105,
110, 131–2, 133, 146–8, 167–8,
172–3
  *The Beautiful Visit* 34–5, 41–2,
  48, 50, 146–8, 167, 169, 172–3;
  *The Long View*, 41, 44,
  49–50, 98–9, 105, 131–2, 133,
  167–8
*Important to Me* (Johnson) 109

*Jane & Prudence* (Pym) 27–8, 35,
40, 48–9, 64, 111, 113, 176
Jenkins, Elizabeth 34, 94–9, 102,
104, 107, 116–17, 121, 127–9,
132–3, 161, 170–1
  *The Tortoise and the Hare* 39,
  94–9, 102, 104, 107, 116–17,
  121, 127–9, 132–3, 161, 170–1
Johnson, Pamela Hansford 23,
109, 110–11, 114–15, 118–19, 123,
124, 137–8
  *An Avenue of Stone* 118–19,
  123; *Cork Street, Next to the
  Hatters* 114; *Important to
  Me* 109; *Night and Silence.
  Who is Here?* 114; *The
  Unspeakable Skipton*
  110–11, 114–15, 123, 137–8
*Joy of the Snow, The*
(Goudge) 23, 54, 83

*Land of Spices, The* (O'Brien) 23,
74–5, 79, 158, 175
*Long View, The* (Howard) 41, 44,
49–50, 98–9, 105, 131–2, 133,
167–8
*Love in a Cold Climate*
(Mitford) 30, 135–7

Manning, Olivia 22, 45–6, 47, 71–
2, 93, 94, 102–4, 105, 109, 115–16,
119–21, 124, 127, 143, 161
  *Artist Among the Missing* 102–4;
  *The Doves of Venus* 45–6, 47,

93, 94, 105, 109, 115–16,
119–21, 143, 161; *School for
Love* 71–2, 127
*Mary Lavelle* (O'Brien) 78, 79
McMinnies, Mary 61–2, 91, 93,
110
  *The Visitors* 61–2, 91, 93, 110
Mitford, Nancy 25, 26–7, 29–30,
130–1, 135–7
  *The Blessing* 29, 130–1; *Don't
  Tell Alfred* 25, 27, 30, 135–7;
  *Love in a Cold Climate* 30,
  135–7; *The Pursuit of
  Love* 26–7, 29–30, 135–7
*Mr Fox* (Comyns) 53
*Night and Silence. Who is Here?*
(Johnson) 114
*No Fond Return of Love*
(Pym) 111

O'Brien, Kate 23, 73–6, 78,
79–81, 83, 84–5, 110, 121–3, 126,
142, 154–6, 157, 158–9, 175
  *As Music and Splendour* 79–81,
  142, 154–6, 157; *The Flower of
  May* 74, 75, 158; *The Land of
  Spices* 23, 74–5, 79, 158, 175;
  *The Last of Summer* 155;
  *Mary Lavelle* 78, 79;
  *Presentation Parlour* 83; *That
  Lady* 75–6, 84–5, 121–3
*Our Spoons Came from
Woolworths* (Comyns) 50–3,
93, 105

*Palladian* (Taylor) 32–3, 46–7,
89–91, 93, 131, 138, 139, 151, 170,
171, 172
Plath, Sylvia 153–4
*Presentation Parlour* (O'Brien) 83
*Prodigal Heart, The* (Ertz) 25, 78,
81–3, 143–4
*Pursuit of Love, The*
(Mitford) 26–7, 29–30, 135–7
Pym, Barbara 23, 27–8, 35, 39–41,
48–9, 56, 64, 66, 67–71, 83–4, 92,
107, 111–13, 115, 123, 126, 142–3,
160, 176

*Excellent Women* 70, 92, 107,
111, 112–13, 160; *A Glass of
Blessings* 40 69–70, 92,
111–12; *Jane and Prudence*
27–8, 35, 40, 48–9, 64, 111, 113,
176; *No Fond Return of Love*
111; *Quartet in Autumn* 67,
72; *Some Tame Gazelle* 35,
67–8; *The Sweet Dove Died*
67; *An Unsuitable Attachment*
68–9; *A Very Private Eye* 66

*Quartet in Autumn* (Pym) 67, 72

*School for Love* (Manning) 71–2,
127
Sharp Margery 62–4
*The Tigress on the Hearth* 62–4
*Sisters by a River* (Comyns) 134
*Sleeping Beauty, The* (Taylor) 32,
33, 47, 130, 138, 139, 151, 160–1,
163, 164–5, 166
*Some Tame Gazelle* (Pym) 35,
67–8
*Spinster* (Ashton-Warner) 158
*Sweet Dove Died, The* (Pym) 67

Taylor, Elizabeth 22, 30–4, 46–7,
66, 88–91, 93–4, 99–102, 105–6,
107, 110, 125, 129–31, 138, 139,
141, 142, 145–6, 148–54, 160–1,
163, 164–7, 170, 171, 175
*Angel* 33–4, 148–9, 150–1, 160;
*A Game of Hide and Seek* 88–9,
93, 101, 145, 175;
*Palladian* 32–3, 46–7, 89–91,
93, 131, 138, 139, 151, 170, 171,
172; *The Sleeping Beauty* 32,

33, 47, 130, 138, 139, 151,
160–1, 163, 164–5; *A View of
the Harbour* 47, 66, 99–102,
105–6, 107, 125, 129–30, 131,
138, 139, 141, 148, 149–52, 153,
154, 160; *A Wreath of Roses*
31, 33, 152, 153, 154, 160,
166–7
*That Lady* (O'Brien) 75–6, 84–5,
121–3
*That's How It Was* (Duffy) 135
*Tigress on the Hearth, The*
(Sharp) 62–4
*Tortoise and the Hare, The*
(Jenkins) 39, 94–9, 102, 104,
107, 116–17, 121, 127–9, 132–3,
161, 170–1

*Unspeakable Skipton, The*
(Johnson) 110–11, 114–15, 123,
137–8
*Unsuitable Attachment, An*
(Pym) 68–9

*Very Private Eye, A* (Pym) 66
*View of the Harbour, A*
(Taylor) 47, 66, 99–102, 105–6,
107, 125, 129–30, 131, 138, 139,
141, 148, 149–52, 153, 154, 160
*Visitors, The* (McMinnies) 61–2,
91, 93, 110
*White Witch, The* (Goudge) 56,
57, 76–7, 157
*Who Was Changed and Who Was
Dead* (Comyns) 134–5
*Wreath of Roses, A* (Taylor) 31,
33, 152, 153, 154, 160, 166–7